KING OF THE
Jews

RESURRECTING
THE JEWISH JESUS

KING OF THE *Jews*

RESURRECTING
THE JEWISH JESUS

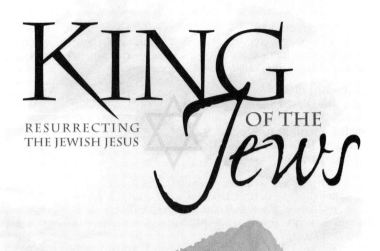

FIRST FRUITS OF
ZION

Proclaiming the Torah and its way
of life, fully centered on Messiah,
to today's People of God

First Edition, April 2006
Printed in the United States of America

Catalog Information: Theology
CBA Category Information: BST, DOT, OTT
ISBN: 1-892124-24-6

Unless otherwise noted, Scripture quotations taken from the New American Standard
Bible®, Copyright © 1960, 1962, 1963, 1968, 1971, 1972, 1973, 1975, 1977, 1995 by The
Lockman Foundation. (*www.Lockman.org*) Used by permission. Throughout this
publication the word Christ is rendered *Messiah*, Jesus is rendered *Yeshua* and Law is
rendered *Torah*.

Cover Illustration: Copyright © 2006, Andrew Paquette

ATTENTION CHURCHES, SYNAGOGUES, STUDY GROUPS, TEACHERS AND OTHER
ORGANIZATIONS: Quantity discounts are available on bulk purchases of this book
for educational, fundraising or gift purposes, or as premiums for increasing magazine
subscriptions or renewals. Special books or book excerpts can also be created to fit
specific needs. Additionally, D. Thomas Lancaster and other First Fruits of Zion team
members are available for speaking engagements, seminars and conferences. For more
information or to arrange a speaking engagement, please contact First Fruits of Zion.

First Fruits of Zion

PO Box 620099
Littleton, Colorado 80162–0099 USA
Phone (303) 933–2119 or (800) 775–4807
Fax (303) 933–0997
www.ffoz.org | Email: *feedback@ffoz.org*

Daniel Thomas Lancaster is the educational director of First Fruits of Zion and author
of several other works on the Hebrew Roots of our faith. He teaches at congregation
Beth Immanuel in Saint Paul, Minnesota where he lives with his wife, Maria, and his
four children: Isaac, Gabriel, Simon and Miriam. He studied rabbinic literature in the
U.S. and Biblical Geography at Jerusalem University College in Jerusalem. He has a BA
in Literature with a focus on biblical literature.

Other works by D. Thomas Lancaster
The Mystery of the Gospel: Jew and Gentile and the Eternal Purpose of God
Restoration: Returning the Torah of God to the Disciples of Jesus
Torah Club Volume Two: Shadows of the Messiah
Torah Club Volume Four: The Good News of Messiah
Torah Club Volume Five: Rejoicing in the Torah

TO MARIA ANNE AND TO THE
BEAUTIFUL CHILDREN SHE HAS GIVEN US:
ISAAC, GABRIEL, SIMON AND MIRIAM.

CONTENTS

Introduction

THE JEWISH JESUS

The average churchman is finally figuring out what New Testament scholars have always known: Jesus was Jewish. He wasn't Jewish like a famous actor might be Jewish. For example, you might have watched a lot of Star Trek episodes and never known that both Leonard Nimoy and William Shatner were Jewish. Shatner doesn't look particularly Jewish, and Nimoy looks Vulcan. On the show, neither of them do anything very Jewish. Their Jewishness is just their ethnicity.

Jesus wasn't like that. Jesus was really Jewish. If you saw Him, you could not possibly mistake it. The man was Jewish. Everything He did and said was patently Jewish. That's what this book is about.

Now you might think, "Why does the world need another book about Jesus?" Well, consider the recent success of *The Da Vinci Code*, a fictional book purporting to reveal the historical Jesus. The only thing that the five million copies of *The Da Vinci Code* actually prove is that people are still interested in reading about Jesus—five million books and a major motion picture, all about Jesus. Those of us who still regard ourselves as disciples of the man from Nazareth should be flattered.

Then again, Jesus has always been popular. In March of 1964, the *London Evening Standard* published an interview with John Lennon in which he claimed that his rock and roll band, *The Beatles*, was more popular than Jesus. He was wrong about that. Nearly four decades later, Jesus is still regularly making the cover of *Time Magazine*. Not so with John Lennon.

Still, the media attention that Jesus gets now-a-days is not what it used to be. Lately critics and scholars have been asking a lot of disturbing questions about the person they call "the historical Jesus." Even the implication of a "historical Jesus" as someone different from the iconic church Jesus is a little disquieting. The idea is that the Jesus venerated through the centuries is not exactly the same as the real Jesus of Nazareth who lived and taught in early first-century Galilee and Judea. It's like the difference between Leonard Nimoy and Mr. Spock. Nobody really believes in Mr. Spock. Leonard Nimoy is the historical Spock—the Jewish one.

Even the Gospels themselves are under scrutiny today. Textual criticism—the science of comparing documents and manuscripts and searching for their most original form—has been around for centuries, but in the last few decades it has begun to leak into the mainstream consciousness. As a result, people are asking questions about the veracity of the gospel stories. That's probably a good thing. Questions are always good, and truth, if it is truth, should be able to withstand inquiry. But some scholars and fiction writers have begun to suggest that our Bibles possess the wrong gospels altogether. Bart Ehrman, author of *Lost Scriptures, Books that Did Not Make It into The New Testament,* rightly points out that many early Christian writings and pseudonymous and apocryphal works never made canonization.[1] Several liberal scholars think that they should have. They regard these other works as extra books of the Bible, akin to the deleted scenes at the end of a DVD, and they are hoping they will be restored in an extended director's cut edition.

How do we know that the church canonized the right gospels? What makes the gospel of Mark a New Testament scripture, whereas the gospel of Mary Magdalene is neglected and forgotten? How do we know that the recently discovered gospel of Judas shouldn't be considered part of the Bible?

In his best seller *The Da Vinci Code,* fiction writer Dan Brown posits that the Roman Church purposely destroyed the authentic gospels because they wanted to suppress the truth about the humanity of Jesus. He purports that the second-century, apocryphal Gnostic gospels are more authentic and reliable than the canonized gospels. Thus the truth about Jesus is veiled behind a church conspiracy.

Dan Brown is right about one thing: Throughout the ages, the church has endeavored to conceal certain truths about Jesus. But it would be unfair to characterize this effort as a conspiracy. The real Christian conspiracy is more a collusion of prejudice, anti-Semitism and theological confusion than it is a sinister, secret plot.

The embarrassing secret about Jesus that the historical Christian church would have preferred to leave behind long ago is the Jewishness of Jesus.

Ironically, Leonardo Da Vinci's painting, *The Last Supper*, illustrates this point well. If you look carefully at the painting, you will notice several curiosities. Aside from the obvious absurdity of everyone sitting on the same side of the table, notice the dinner rolls in front of each disciple. *The Last Supper* is supposed to be a Passover *seder* meal, part of the Feast of Unleavened Bread. The only bread served at that meal was flat, unleavened bread (*matzah*), but Da Vinci's painting offers no suggestion of Passover. Stranger yet, notice that the only Jewish-looking person at the table is Judas; everyone else looks distinctly European. Da Vinci's painting gives us clues about the real agenda regarding Jesus: a reflexive denial of His Jewishness.

From the earliest church fathers, to the popes and reformers, to the great artists of Christian history, to the very architecture and iconography of the cathedrals, the clues are everywhere. The church wants to deny the Jewishness of Jesus. If it were possible to erase it, Christianity would have done so centuries ago. The historical Jesus was a Jew.

The first Christians were actually Jews who believed that their rabbi, Jesus of Nazareth, was the long-anticipated heir to David's throne. They believed He was the Jewish Messiah; that is to say, the King of the Jews. They pointed to His resurrection from the dead as evidence of their convictions. Those first Christians, however, did not consider themselves Christians. They did not even imagine a religion called Christianity. They were Jews practicing Judaism, just as their rabbi had taught them.

By the early second century, however, Christianity had come to identify herself as a religion distinct and separate from Judaism. The early believers were exiled from the synagogue. Systematic persecutions, two Jewish revolts against the Roman state and theological polemics with mainstream Judaism all shaped the emerging church. Churches became predominantly gentile and sects of the new faith divided on ethnic lines. The Jewish believers disappeared into obscurity, while a new gentile Christianity grew ever stronger and more dominant. The new Christianity defined herself against Judaism and Jewishness.

In order to suppress the Jewishness of Jesus, Christianity found it necessary to suppress the historical Jesus. His humanity—a thoroughly Jewish humanity—was diminished. Unfortunately, it is this suppression and diminishing of the historical Jesus that has left Christianity so vulnerable to attack from liberal theologians, critics and fiction writers.

However, the church's sacred writings—the Gospels and Epistles left behind by those earliest believers—testify to the absolute Jewishness of the man and the original faith. The evidence remains within the books of the New Testament, like an ancient, hidden code. Most Christians read over it without ever suspecting its existence.

The gospel writers did not intend to write in code. They intended to communicate forthrightly and clearly in their own language and cultural context. But when Christianity jettisoned Judaism, we quickly forgot that language and culture. We lost the interpretive tools to correctly understand the Gospels as the gospel writers had intended them to be understood. We began to read the words and deeds of Jesus without comprehension. We began to make up new meanings. The historical Jesus was lost.

The Jewish code language of the Gospels functions on several levels. At its most basic, the code could be described as the preponderance of semitisisms (Jewish ways of saying things) that constitute the text. Though the Gospels are written in Greek, the syntax, structure, idiom and semantic configurations often betray a Semitic origin. It seems evident that our Gospels were written by Jews who were far more accustomed to Hebrew and Aramaic than they were to Greek. They were working with Greek translations of Semitic documents, and translating the words of Jesus from Hebrew and Aramaic into Greek. The resulting Greek text is soaked in Semitic terminology and turns of phrase that can sometimes only be understood by first retro-translating a saying or phrase back to Hebrew or Aramaic.

On another level, the Jewish code language of the Gospels consists of innumerable allusions to the wider expanse of Jewish literature and rabbinic thought. These allusions are fraught with meaning. A reader unfamiliar with the works and concepts alluded to by the gospel writer inevitably misses the semantic point of the passage.

The code could also be described as a paradigm of thought and interpretation. The paradigm is late second-Temple Judaism. Therefore, our best resource for interpretation is Jewish literature that was written in the same paradigm. For example, it is hard to correctly interpret the parables of Jesus in isolation, but when the reader compares the parables of Jesus with the hundreds of similar rabbinic parables preserved in ancient Jewish literature, he suddenly has a contextual matrix from which to draw understanding. It's like flipping a light switch.

To decipher the code, we need to compare the New Testament (Apostolic Scriptures) with other ancient Jewish literature. For example, in the late second century, the sages of Judaism began compiling the oral teachings that had been transmitted to them from their teachers. Many of these oral teachings had been handed down from teacher to student for generations—even centuries. The first collection of those teachings is called the *Mishnah,* a book of legal codes redacted in the Galilee during the early third century. For the next several generations, Jewish rabbis and scholars poured their efforts into commenting and arguing over the Mishnah. Their commentary is called the *Gemara,* and along with the Mishnah, they form the voluminous works called the *Talmud.* In addition to these works of legislation, the rabbis recorded oral traditions, teachings and interpretations about the Bible called the *midrash.* The word *midrash* means "something searched out." The *Midrash* is a source of many parables similar to the ones Jesus used to tell.

By comparing these rabbinic works with the Gospels, we notice a great deal of crossover. Sometimes, the synonymy of the Gospels with the rabbinic literature is so great that it is difficult to tell if a certain teaching originated with Jesus or with the sages of His day. At other times, the sayings, maxims, parables and ordinances of the rabbis inform the language of the Gospels in a way that makes sense of what is otherwise obscure.

The gospel code is a real phenomenon, not some half-baked, flakey retelling of history. And what is more, the code can be broken. The original meanings can be recovered. Thanks to the wealth of early rabbinic literature preserved by the Jewish world, we are able to decipher the code. We are able to see Jesus from a Jewish perspective again.

The results of this kind of code breaking are very exciting. Dan Brown's *Da Vinci Code* suppositions, and the pseudo-scholarship from which he drew them, quickly evaporate when we begin to crack the real encoding around the historical Jesus. Thanks to the intrinsic Jewishness of our Gospels, their authenticity and antiquity are incontrovertible. No second-, third- or fourth-century church forgers could possibly have manufactured documents so genuinely Jewish. Nor would they have been motivated to do so. What is more, when tested for an authentic, first-century Jewish voice, the apocryphal Gnostic gospels and other non-canonical Christian writings perform very poorly. In the light of Judaism, they are exposed as the late counterfeits that they are.

The following chapters are examples of cracking the Jewish gospel code. They were all written originally as part of the research for *Torah Club Volume Four*, a year-long study program on the Gospels and Acts from a Jewish perspective, still available through First Fruits of Zion. Most of the chapters in this book previously appeared in print in First Fruits of Zion's *messiah magazine*. They all have a few things in common. They are all drawn from the actual text of the canonical Gospels. They all refute common church obfuscation and error regarding the historical Jesus and His message. They all rely heavily on ancient Jewish literature for corroboration. They are all historically rooted in the actual places, characters and events of the first century.

1. BIRTH OF A KING: THE KINGMAKER AND THE KINGDOM

The prologue and first chapter are mostly concerned with placing Jesus in His historical context. Drawing primarily on the Jewish historian Josephus, we are able to understand the birth of Jesus and the concept of Jewish messianism in the socio-political and religious world of His day. We realize that the term "messiah" is a Jewish idiom for "king." We also learn that the primary message of the gospel was not concerned with soteriology (salvation issues) as much as it was a proclamation of Jesus' kingship over Israel and the resulting urgent call to repentance. Understanding these issues brings the otherwise enigmatic role of John the Baptist into perspective.

2. NEW WINESKINS FOR NEW WINE

The second chapter addresses the double parable of Luke 5:33–39 and illustrates the problem with trying to interpret the Gospels outside of the matrix of classical Judaism. Traditional Christian exegesis of these parables—the parables of the new and old wineskins and the new and old coats—has consistently been interpreted as teaching the incompatibility between Judaism and Christianity. By comparing the parables with similar rabbinic sayings, however, we realize that the parables were never meant to contrast religions; they were meant to contrast types of disciples.

3. THE GREAT OMISSION

Chapter three explores the institution of discipleship as it existed in the rabbinic schools before and after the days of the apostles. By comparing Jesus and His disciples with the other sages and rabbis and their schools of students, we are in a far better position to understand the calling and vocation of Jesus' first followers. We can also see how historic Christianity has at times gone awry by placing her emphasis on conversion rather than discipleship.

4. CARPENTER AMONG THE NAZARENES

In chapter four, we look at the honest humanity of the historical Jesus by considering His family life in Nazareth, His relationship to His father's carpentry trade and the family conflict over His taking disciples and relocating to Capernaum. By investigating early rabbinic texts about domestic life, we are able to infer several things about Jesus and His apprenticeship under His father Joseph. In addition, by considering the Hebrew behind the word "Nazareth," we can speculate about His relationship with His family and the village of Nazareth. We also find a name for ourselves in the vernacular of the apostles: Nazarenes.

5. THE PHARISEES AND JEWISH TRADITION

Chapter five re-examines the old church stereotype of the "hypocritical Pharisee" by investigating Jesus' relationship with the Pharisaic teachers of His day. Jesus' conflicts with the Pharisees are so cliché in Christianity that His affinities with them are completely ignored. When Jesus is examined in the light of rabbinic literature, however, it becomes clear that He was a Jew practicing

Judaism according to the strict interpretations of Jewish traditional law. Contrary to the modern notion that Jesus rejected Jewish tradition, the Gospels demonstrate that He practiced both the written commandments and the oral traditions that defined Judaism of His day. In short, if He were in the flesh among us today, He would look like an Orthodox Jew.

6. NONE GREATER THAN JOHN

Matthew 11 and its parallel in Luke 7 are fraught with several obscure and difficult sayings. In these passages, the Master discourses regarding His older cousin John the Baptist (John the Immerser) and comments on His relationship with him. The passages raises several questions. Was John losing His faith in Messiah? Why did Jesus contrast John against a reed blown in the wind? How is the least in the kingdom greater than John? What does it mean that the kingdom suffers violence? Did the Torah end with John? What does flute playing have to do with anything? In the end, it turns out that the obscure and difficult sayings of Matthew 11 and Luke 7 regarding John and Jesus and their relationship with each other are far less obscure when read in light of their traditional and historical Jewish context.

7. THE VILLAIN WHO WOULD BE KING

Chapter seven relies heavily on the Jewish historian Josephus to fill in the missing details behind the untimely death of John the Baptist and the political problems facing any would-be king of the Jews in the days of Jesus. By comparing the John the Baptist narratives with relevant passages from Josephus, we discover that the Gospels stand on solid historical footing. The infamous dance of Salome can be connected with the characters and situations that shaped first-century Jewish politics.

8. LET THE DEAD BURY THE DEAD

Chapter eight brings clarity to two gospel passages by examining the protocol and procedure of first-century Jewish burial customs. The "let the dead bury the dead" saying in Matthew 8:21–22 makes better sense in light of these burial customs. Even more compelling, the resurrection of the young man at Nain in Luke 7 can be compared with Talmudic tradition to reveal a messianic declaration of Jesus' kingship.

9. The High Mountain

Chapter nine looks at the story of the transfiguration from the perspective of Jewish messianic expectations. The telling of the transfiguration of Jesus is familiar to Christians, but the details of the story suggest Jewish traditions and practices that symbolically tie it to the Feast of Tabernacles. Moreover, by invoking Moses and Elijah, the incident firmly ties the messiahship of Jesus to prophetic traditions of the Hebrew Scriptures. If the transfiguration event was meaningful in a plain reading of the Gospels, it is even more so in the light of Jewish messianic expectation.

10. Across the Great Divide

In chapter ten we read Luke 16's parable of the rich man and Lazarus to get a perspective on Jesus' views of the afterlife. Interpretive problems have arisen because of confusion with the Greco-pagan terminology employed by the Greek translation of the Gospels. However, by allowing rabbinic literature to inform the terminology in Jesus' parable, we can recover the original meaning of the parable and Jesus' own beliefs about heaven and hell.

11. House of the Water Drawing

Chapter eleven illustrates the color and detail rabbinic literature adds to a simple gospel narrative. By reading about the Temple water pouring ceremony during the Feast of Tabernacles, we discover the perfect *sitzen im leben* (setting in life) for John 7. Jesus' words, "If anyone is thirsty, let him come to Me and drink. He who believes in Me, as the Scripture said, 'From his innermost being will flow rivers of living water,'" (John 7:37–38) spring to life in the context of the festival as described in the Mishnah and Talmud. Herein we discover the public event that led up to the dramatic triumphal entry into Jerusalem.

12. Heir to the Vineyard

Jesus' parable of the vineyard is most often explained as an illustration of how Christianity replaces Judaism. The vineyard is understood to be the kingdom of heaven. The wicked tenants are the Jews. Thus the Jews are thrown out of the kingdom, and their place as God's elect is given to others—namely Christians. Chapter twelve demonstrates how this reading of the parable is heavily colored by the assumptions of replacement theology. By comparing the parable with other similar rabbinic parables, we discover that it is not the Jewish people who are being replaced in the story; it is the corrupt religious and political authorities of first-century Jerusalem. The vineyard in which they have been employed is Israel.

13. The Stone the Builders Rejected

Chapter thirteen investigates Jesus' application of Psalm 118:22 and its meaning in the broader context of Jewish interpretation: "The stone which the builders rejected has become the chief corner stone." By comparing Jesus' use of this text with the rabbinic midrash on the passage, we are able to get a glimpse of Rabbi Jesus at work in the world of Jewish hermeneutics. By calling Himself the "stone the builders rejected," Jesus claims to be the Davidic heir and rightful king of the Jews. Without the broader context of Jewish interpretation, however, this message would be lost.

14. The King in Disguise

In chapter fourteen, we turn once again to classical rabbinical literature to provide the contextual background for more of Jesus' parables. As we do, we note the thematic link between the parables of Matthew 25 and the biblical high holidays of the Feast of Trumpets and the Day of Atonement. Moreover, by comparing Matthew 25 with similar stories in Jewish literature, we are able to speculate that this passage may actually contain clues to two missing parables. When read from a Jewish perspective, the theological impact of the Matthew 25 parables shows Jesus as the Jewish king, rewarding those who have shown kindness to the Jewish people and punishing those who have not.

15. Yeshua the Nazirite

Chapter fifteen considers Jesus' words, "I will not drink of this fruit of the vine from now on until that day when I drink it new with you in My Father's kingdom" (Matthew 26:29). According to rabbinic law as reported by the Mishnah, Jesus' famous declaration is nothing short of a binding oath to become a Nazirite as outlined in Numbers 6. The chapter explores *nazarism* and its role in the apostolic community, pointing out that several New Testament notables undertook the Nazirite vow, even after the death and resurrection of Jesus.

16. ONE LONG DAY

The passion of Jesus is the most well-known episode from the Gospels, but when it is examined in the light of historical witnesses and rabbinical literature, a very non-traditional passion play emerges. The bad guys, it turns out, are not the Jewish people of Jerusalem but a few, corrupt, power-elite priests. Pontius Pilate, it turns out, was not a pathetic, unwilling participant in the crucifixion but a cruel and calculating political shark who took curious delight in mocking Jesus' claim to be the King of the Jews. Furthermore, by comparing the Temple rituals of Passover with the crucifixion narrative, a remarkable coincidence between the death of Jesus and the slaughter of the Passover lambs emerges.

17. THE KING OF ISRAEL LIVES

Critics of the Gospels often point to the discrepancies in the resurrection narratives as evidence that they are not historically reliable. To be certain, discrepancies do exist, but when considered in the context of Jewish practice, many of the disagreements can be reconciled. Chapter seventeen employs all four gospel resurrection narratives to create a harmony that incorporates all of the available information. In the process, we discover, to our surprise, that the resurrection may have occurred on a Saturday night rather than a Sunday morning.

18. HANDMAIDEN OF THE KING

Chapter eighteen looks at the character of Mary Magdalene from Jewish, Christian and Gnostic sources in an attempt to get to the bottom of the assertions made in Dan Brown's popular book *The Da Vinci Code*. In so doing, we also have the opportunity to consider the difficult question of Jesus' celibacy, an issue best explained in the light of Jewish traditions about Moses.

19. He Lifted His Hands

In chapter nineteen, we examine the Master's parting blessing over His disciples in the light of early rabbinic literature and discover an amazing correlation to the practice of the Aaronic priesthood. The evidence suggests that Jesus' last words to His disciples were the words of the Aaronic benediction found in Numbers 6:24–26.

Most of this book's nineteen chapters were published independently over a period of several years. They do not necessarily work together to create a cohesive whole. Nevertheless, they do work together to paint an increasingly clearer picture of the historical Jesus. It is a very Jewish picture.

It turns out that the historical Jesus is not a one-size-fits-all mystic. He wasn't a Christian either. Jesus was a Jew. Make that "is a Jew." He was born of a Jewish mother. His Jewish father circumcised him on the eighth day, according to Jewish law. His Jewish parents gave Him the Hebrew name *Yeshua*.

He ate *kosher*. He learned Hebrew. He learned the blessings. He learned the Torah. He wore fringes on the corners of His garments. He ate *matzah* on Passover; He fasted on the Day of Atonement. He wore phylacteries. He went to synagogue on Sabbath. He taught the Torah. His disciples were all Jews. They called him "Rabbi," and in the Gospels, He was very much a part of the Judaism of His day.

The movement Jesus began has grown to include every tribe and nation on earth. Jesus is bigger than John Lennon, the Beatles, Dan Brown and Mr. Spock combined. The Christian faith has crossed over every cultural line and social barrier. Within the Christian faith, there are to be no ethnic divisions or racial walls. Nevertheless, the center of Christianity is Jesus, and Jesus is a Jew. He lived as Jew, He taught as a Jew, He prayed as a Jew and He died as a Jew. His blood was Jewish blood. The sign above His head on the cross said, "Jesus of Nazareth, King of the Jews."

He is the King of the Jews.

Prologue

BIRTH OF THE KING

> The moon begins to shine on the first day of the
> month and goes on shining until the fifteenth
> day, when she is full. After the fifteenth day
> her light wanes until on the thirtieth day it
> is not seen at all. With Israel too, there were
> fifteen generations from Abraham to Solomon.
> …[After Solomon] the kings began to wane
> … [until] Zedekiah when the light of the moon
> vanished completely. (*Exodus Rabbah* 15:26)

His mother was named after a prophetess: *Miriam*, the sister of Moses. In English, she is known as Mary. She was betrothed to a man named *Yosef ben Yaakov*, a descendant from the noble lineage of David. In English, he is known as Joseph. Although their marriage was not yet consummated, Miriam was, for all practical purposes, a married woman. In the world of first-century Judaism, a betrothal was as binding as marriage. A courting couple sealed their betrothal with a written contract. The betrothal could last a year or longer,[2] but while betrothed both parties were regarded as legally wed. Only a formal writ of divorce delivered before witnesses could end the betrothal.

THE NAME OF THE KING

Not wanting to bring the weight of law upon his seemingly unfaithful bride-to-be, nor wanting to publicly humiliate her, Yosef intended to divorce her quietly. This could be done by giving Miriam written notice of the divorce in the presence of legal witnesses. Before Yosef had time to hire a scribe to write out the certificate of divorce, an angel of the Lord appeared to him in a dream and warned him:

> Joseph, son of David, do not be afraid to take Mary as your wife; for that which has been conceived in her is of the Holy Spirit. And she will bear a Son; and you shall call His name Jesus, for it is He who will save His people from their sins. (Matthew 1:20–21)

The angel told Yosef that the child was to be named Jesus. Well, sort of.

HIS REAL NAME WAS NOT JESUS.[3]

"Jesus" is an English transliteration of a Greek transliteration of His Hebrew name, *Yeshua* (ישוע). Yeshua is a short form of the common Hebrew name *Yehoshua* (יהושע), which we pronounce in English as Joshua. So why do we call him Jesus?

When the name *Yeshua* is translated into the Greek language, the closest phonetic approximation is *Iesous,* pronounced "YAY-soos." Two hundred years or more before His birth, the translators of the *Septuagint* (a Greek version of the Hebrew Bible) were translating the names Yehoshua and Yeshua as *Iesous*. The "oos" ending on the name indicates a masculine subject. Without that ending, the name Yeshua would sound like a girl's name in Greek. Further phonetic changes occurred as the church translated the Greek to Latin and the Latin to English. The name finally ended up as Jesus. But His real name was Yeshua. Yeshua is the Hebrew word for "salvation."

When the angel announced the child's name to Yosef, he made a play on the word, saying, "You shall call His name Yeshua, for He will save (*yoshia*) His people from their sins."

THE DAVID CODE

In the dream, the angel addressed Yosef as "Yosef ben David"; that is, "Joseph son of David." Son of David is a biblical title for the king of the Jews. Rabbinic sources frequently refer to the coming Messiah as the Son of David.

Matthew begins his gospel with a genealogy that traces the lineage of Joseph back to David and through David back to Abraham. Many scholars have puzzled over Matthew's genealogy. Although it ostensibly attempts to produce the same result as Luke's genealogy of Yeshua, it in fact contradicts it. Furthermore, Matthew's genealogy seems artificially manipulated. It appears that generations are left out and passed over in silence in order to achieve the symmetrical triad of fourteen generations:[4]

> Therefore all the generations from Abraham to David are fourteen generations; from David to the deportation to Babylon fourteen generations; and from the deportation to Babylon to the time of Messiah fourteen generations. (Matthew 1:17)

What is the significance of the fourteen generations? Matthew was under no compulsion to record every generation. He was, perhaps, less concerned with the absolute accuracy of Yeshua's genealogy than with the message of the genealogy. The message is simply this: Yeshua is descended directly from David. He is the Son of David, the promised Messiah.

The fourteen generations does hold special significance, however. One ancient method of rabbinic interpretation is a mathematical reading of the Hebrew text called *gematria*. In *gematria*, each Hebrew letter is assigned a mathematical value. The reader can then add up the letters of a word to produce a numerical value for that word, which can, in turn, be compared to other words with the same numeric value. It may be a far-fetched and spurious way to approach the biblical text, but it is, nonetheless, an ancient and time-honored method.

King David's *gematria* works out as follows. The word *David* consists of three Hebrew letters: a *dalet* (ד) with a numeric value of 4, a *vav* (ו) with a numeric value of 6, and another *dalet* (ד) with a numeric value of 4. The sum of the letters equals fourteen: David's numeric value is fourteen. When Matthew tells us that there are fourteen generations, fourteen generations and fourteen generations, what he means for us to hear is *David! David! David!* Yeshua is descended from David; He is the new David.

THE RIGHTFUL KING

If Yeshua was not a descendant of David, He would not be the Messiah. God entered into an eternal covenant with King David, promising him that his house and his throne would endure forever.[5]

Therefore, all the true and rightful kings over the Jews must be descended from the house of David.

In the days of Yeshua, no Davidic king had sat on the throne of Israel for hundreds of years. The Judean monarchy ended with the Babylonian siege of Jerusalem in 586 BCE. The line of David continued, but his descendants no longer possessed the throne of Israel.

The prophet Isaiah compared the royal dynasty of David to a tree stump. Though the house of David was once like a mighty tree possessing the throne and crown of Israel, Isaiah predicted that it would be shorn down to nothing but a stump, a sad memorial to its former glory. Yet the prophet promised that one day a new branch would grow up from the old stump of the Davidic dynasty. A new king over the Jews from the house of David would arise. "Then a shoot will spring from the stem of Jesse, and a branch from his roots will bear fruit" (Isaiah 11:1).

At the time the first Judeans returned from exile,[6] Zerubbabel was the heir to the throne. The community of the returnees anticipated that he might be the promised king, the shoot from the stump of David's house. He was not. Israel's political subjugation to Persia precluded the possibility of restoring the crown. Generations passed. The heirs to the throne of David continued to wait. Empires rose and fell. Still there was no king. No branch grew from the stump.

THE WRONG KINGS

Hundreds of years later, during the great Hanukkah revolt, the Maccabees arose to lead a rebellion against the tyrant Antiochus Epiphanes.[7] The Maccabees were from the priestly family of the Hasmoneans. After leading the Jews to victory, they presumptuously took the throne of Israel for themselves, assuming the crown and the high priesthood. Their right to the crown was illegitimate; they were not descendants of David.

The Hasmonean kings proved to be wicked. They often persecuted men and women of Torah. Their short dynasty collapsed into a civil war between two brothers, both fighting for the throne in Jerusalem.

About sixty years before the birth of Yeshua, while the heated civil war between the two Hasmonean brothers waged, a certain

Edomite noble by the name of Antipater called upon Rome to intervene and settle the conflict. The Roman general Pompey marched on the land of Israel, seized Jerusalem and the Temple, and settled the civil war by force. As a result, Israel became a subject of Rome. Rome promoted Antipater to govern it.

When Antipater died, the Roman Caesar Augustus promoted Antipater's son Herod to the position of king over Israel. As a military general, politician, and builder, Herod was truly great; hence, the name Herod the Great. But as a king he was a tyrant. The stories of Herod's paranoia and butchery are infamous.

Herod was an illegitimate king over Israel. He was not born from the house of David; he was not even Jewish by birth. He was an Edomite. Desperate to validate his claim to the throne of Israel, Herod inquired of the Sanhedrin and asked them to explain the verse from Deuteronomy that says, "One from among your countrymen you shall set as king over yourselves; you may not put a foreigner over yourselves who is not your countryman."[8] The Sanhedrin explained the verse, but not to Herod's satisfaction. According to the Talmud, Herod rose up and had the men of the Sanhedrin slain.

Herod knew his right to the throne of Israel was artificial, and this knowledge drove him to guard his crown from every real or imagined usurper. To protect his throne, he murdered his wife (a daughter of the Hasmonean dynasty) and had his sons strangled. Friends and family were routinely poisoned, tortured and murdered to keep the throne safe. Augustus Caesar commented on Herod's bloody reign of terror by saying, "I'd rather be Herod's pig than Herod's son."[9] Herod may have eaten kosher food, but he wasn't a kosher king.

The Jewish historian Flavius Josephus, though clearly an admirer of Herod, was compelled to write, "Even if a raging beast had reigned over us, the calamity would not have been as enormous as the disasters that were inflicted upon us during the period of Herod's rule. ...What happened to the Judeans in the days of Herod has no likeness and no counterpart ... nor does the history of other peoples know anything like it."[10]

One day astrologers from the east came to Herod, asking, "Where is He who has been born King of the Jews? For we saw His star in the east, and have come to worship Him" (Matthew 2:2). The gospel of Matthew says that "when Herod the king heard it, he was troubled, and all Jerusalem with him" (2:3). Everyone in Jerusalem knew the potential violence of his paranoid temper. Herod assembled the new Sanhedrin to consult them on the question. The sages of the Sanhedrin well remembered what had happened to the last Sanhedrin that answered Herod's messianic question wrong. And yet, what could they do but answer honestly? When Herod asked them where the Messiah was to be born, they answered in unanimity, "Bethlehem in Judea" (Matthew 2:5).

To escape Herod's arm, Miriam, Yosef, and the child Yeshua fled into hiding in Egypt. The infant sons of Bethlehem were not so fortunate. Matthew tells the story of the slaughter of the innocents to allude to the birth of Moses, the first redeemer of Israel. Moses was born under Pharaoh's decree to cast the male children into the Nile. Pharaoh was paranoid that the growing Hebrew population would rise up in revolt against Egypt and overthrow his dynasty.

According to an ancient rabbinic legend, Pharaoh's astrologers foresaw the birth of Moses. Like the astrologers of Matthew 2, the astrologers of Egypt read in the stars that the redeemer of Israel was about to be born. "The astrologers told Pharaoh, 'The mother of Israel's savior is already pregnant with him!'" [11] When the astrologers told Pharaoh that Israel's redeemer was about to be born, Pharaoh issued the decree to have all the male babies cast into the river. After Moses was born, his mother complied with Pharaoh's order by putting the baby in a basket and floating him in the Nile.

Matthew's Jewish readers certainly knew this tradition well. As Matthew told the story of Yeshua and Herod and the astrologers from the East, his readers quickly connected those events with the birth of Moses. They saw that the birth of Yeshua followed the pattern set by Moses. They would have seen that Israel's ultimate Redeemer was like her first redeemer. Matthew's birth narrative is a direct allusion to Moses.

THE GOLDEN EAGLE

While Miriam, Yosef and the child born King of the Jews were hidden away in Egypt, Jerusalem fell into a state of turmoil and political crisis. Rome requested that her standard be affixed above the Temple gates. Herod complied and had a great golden eagle set over the gates to the Temple of the Lord in Jerusalem. The people were incensed that the Temple should be so blasphemed as to have a forbidden image upon it, not to mention an image representing the pagan power of Rome.

Surely this happened in order to fulfill what was spoken by the prophet Hosea when he declared, "The eagle is upon the house of the LORD because they have transgressed My covenant and rebelled against My Torah" (Hosea 8:1, my translation). A sign such as this could not bode well for Jerusalem. Several disciples of the sages scaled the Temple walls and threw down the golden eagle. Herod reacted to the vandalism with mass arrests, persecutions and executions.

But Herod was not faring well physically. He became sicker and sicker. When he knew he was about to die, he again summoned the prominent sages of the land. This time he had them brought to his winter palace at Jericho, where he had them imprisoned in the hippodrome. Determined to keep the Jews from rejoicing over his death, he gave orders to have the sages slain as soon as he died. That way, he would be guaranteed that Israel would mourn on the day of his death.

His plan failed. He died, but his sister Salome (who would be left behind to face the political repercussions of such an atrocity) reached the guards in Jericho before news of Herod's death, and she released the sages. Israel rejoiced. The king was dead.

Chapter 1

THE KINGMAKER AND THE KINGDOM

Rav Yehudah said, "If Israel does not repent,
they will not be redeemed … And there will
be no great repentance in Israel until Elijah of
blessed memory comes, as it is said [in Malachi
4:5–6], 'Behold, I am going to send you Elijah
the prophet before the coming of the great
and terrible day of the Lord. He will restore the
hearts of the fathers to their children and the
hearts of the children to their fathers, so that I
will not come and smite the land with a curse.'"
(*Pirke De Rabbi Eliezer*, Chapter 43 [60])[12]

When Herod the Great, the king of the Jews, died, he left his
kingdom divided among three sons: Archelaus, Antipas and
Philip.

Israel rejoiced over Herod's death, and a new spirit of opti-
mism arose in the land. The Jews assumed that Herod's son and
heir apparent, Archelaus, could not be as bad as Herod had been.
That Passover, pilgrims crowded into Jerusalem for the feast. They
staged demonstrations in the Temple and petitioned Archelaus
to release political prisoners arrested during Herod's tyrannical
reign.

Archelaus waited until the Passover sacrifices had begun before
responding to their entreaties. When the crowds of pilgrims filled
the Temple, he sent armed troops in among the worshippers. The
soldiers slaughtered the Jews indiscriminately. Three thousand
died that day. The soldiers stacked their bodies in heaps in the

Temple courts. Any hope that Archelaus might provide a reprieve from his father's tyranny vanished. Clearly, this son of Herod was cut from the same cloth.

Meanwhile, a Jew named Yosef ben Yaakov was hiding in Egypt with his young family. He had fled there with his wife and infant son to escape from King Herod. News of Herod's death came to Egypt, and Yosef ben Yaakov supposed he might return to Judea. But when he heard about Archelaus, he was afraid to go there. Instead, "he departed for the regions of Galilee, and came and resided in a city called Nazareth, that what was spoken through the prophets might be fulfilled, 'He shall be called a Nazarene'" (Matthew 2:22–23).

After Archelaus' bloody Passover slaughter, Rome deposed him and appointed regional governors over Judah and Jerusalem. The throne of Jerusalem was left empty. During all the years of Yeshua's life in Nazareth and His ministry among His disciples, there was no king in Jerusalem. There was no king of the Jews.

Prophet from the Wilderness

Some thirty years later, a priest named Yochanon ben Zecharyah (better known as John the Baptist) came, declaring a Jewish king and kingdom. As a *cohen* (the son of a priest) over the age of thirty, John should have been serving in the Temple. Instead, he was out in the wilderness of Judea, preaching repentance, baptizing people in water and declaring the advent of the long-promised king of the Jews.

John was not the only priest in those days to shirk his Temple responsibilities. A whole sect of disenfranchised priests had separated themselves from the ranks of the Jerusalem priesthood. As a measure of protest against the sold-out, corrupted, Rome-loving, Hasmonean and Herodian priesthood of Jerusalem, these separatists took refuge together in the wilderness of Judah near the Dead Sea. They were the Essenes of Qumran. They were the community that left us the Dead Sea scrolls.

We cannot be certain that John the Baptist had any contact with the Essene community, but there are several amazing parallels between them. Both John and the Essenes were separatists from the priesthood. Both John and the Essenes believed in an imminent eschaton. Both John and the Essenes believed they were preparing for a messianic redeemer-king. Both John and the Essenes placed a high priority on ritual immersion (baptism) for purification. Both John and the Essenes taught a theology of repentance. It seems improbable that John was not in some way influenced by the thinking of the Qumran community.

John came in the tradition of several great prophet-priests. Moses, Samuel, Jeremiah, Ezekiel and Zechariah were all similar to John in that they were prophets who served in the priesthood. But more than any of these, John came in the spirit and tradition of the prophet Elijah. John's camel-hair coat and leather belt allude to Elijah, who wore the same. Yeshua even said, "If you care to accept it, he himself is Elijah, who was to come" (Matthew 11:14).

In Jewish messianic expectation, Elijah is the forerunner of Messiah. Traditional Judaism expects Elijah to come heralding the messianic king. He is to anoint him with oil, just as Samuel anointed King David with oil. According to the prophet Malachi, Elijah is supposed to show up and convince Israel to repent before the day of the Lord:

> Behold, I am going to send you Elijah the prophet before the coming of the great and terrible day of the Lord. And he will restore the hearts of the fathers to their children, and the hearts of the children to their fathers, lest I come and smite the land with a curse. (Malachi 4:5–6)

THE KINGMAKER

Like the prophet Samuel, John was a kingmaker.

The ancient prophets—the kingmakers of long ago—invested men with the office of king through means of a ritual anointing with oil. Samuel anointed Saul as king of Israel by pouring out a horn of oil over his head. Subsequently, he anointed David in the same manner. A common biblical title for the king is "anointed one." In Hebrew, the word for "anointed one" is *mashiach* (משיח). The Aramaic version of the same word finds its way into English as *messiah*. The Greek equivalent of "anointed one" is *christos,* a word from which we derive the English title Christ.

Christ was not the Master's last name. Christ is a title, not a surname. It means "anointed one," which by extension means "king." In that sense, all the duly anointed kings of Israel were "christs." Translators would do better to render the Master's name in English as "Jesus the Anointed One," or better yet, for maximum communication and comprehension, "Jesus the King."

- ◊ *Mashiach* = Anointed One
- ◊ Messiah = Anointed One
- ◊ Christos = Anointed One
- ◊ Christ = Anointed One
- ◊ Anointed One = King

But if Yeshua is really the Anointed One, when did His anointing occur? At what point in His ministry was He anointed with oil? Strangely enough, as much as we might search, we will not find that He was ever anointed with oil. Rather, His anointing seems to occur with John at the Jordan.

The ancient anointing ritual symbolized an investment of the Spirit of God. In the Bible, anointing is "accompanied by a coming of the Spirit." [13] Thus the Spirit of God advanced upon Saul just after his anointing.[14] Regarding David we read, "Then Samuel took the horn of oil and anointed him in the midst of his brothers; and the Spirit of the LORD came mightily upon David from that day forward" (1 Samuel 16:13). After being anointed, the king is called "the Lord's anointed." All of this implies that the pouring out of olive oil over the king's head was a ritual that symbolized the greater, mystical reality of the pouring out of God's Spirit onto the king.

When Yeshua came up out of the water of John's baptism and the Holy Spirit descended upon Him, a spiritual anointing took place. He became the Anointed One, the *Mashiach*, Messiah, *Christos*, Christ and King.

PREPARING THE WAY FOR THE KING

John the Baptist is the Elijah figure of the Gospels. His job was to prepare the way for the king.[15] He busied himself with bringing Israel to repentance in preparation for the coming of the king. "Repent," he shouted to the crowds, "for the kingdom of heaven is at hand" (Matthew 3:2).

As he called people to repentance, he urged them to step down into the water of the Jordan River and immerse themselves as a ritual expression of their repentance. Such immersions were a common part of Jewish practice and still are today. Therefore, it may be more historically accurate to refer to him as John the Immerser. In his description of John's ministry, the first-century Jewish historian Flavius Josephus makes it clear that John's baptism was an outward sign of inward conviction:

> John was a good man and had exhorted the Jews to lead righteous lives, to practice justice toward their fellows and piety towards God, and so doing to join him in baptism. In his view this was a necessary preliminary if baptism was to be acceptable to God. They must not employ it (baptism) to gain pardon for whatever sins they committed, but as a consecration of the body, implying that the soul was already thoroughly cleansed by right behavior. (Josephus *Antiquities* 18.5.2)

John's call to repentance was a call to right behavior. Examples and extracts of John's preaching are preserved in the third chapter of Luke, where he urges people to share with the needy, to conduct business fairly, to treat others equitably and to avoid the misuse of authority. To John, repentance was not an intellectual assent to a creed or belief, it was right behavior. He said to the religious leaders of his day, "Bear fruit in keeping with repentance" (Matthew 3:8). That is, "Practice what you preach!" The fruit of repentance is a life of good deeds, a righteous life of Torah and obeying the commandments, a faith expressed in justice toward man and piety toward God.

In the world of first-century Judaism, the call to repent was a call to return to Torah. John's call for repentance was in keeping with his mission, as expressed by Malachi:

> Remember the Torah of Moses My servant, even the statutes and ordinances which I commanded him in Horeb for all Israel. Behold, I am going to send you Elijah the prophet before the coming of the great and terrible day of the LORD. (Malachi 4:4–5)

Consider John the Immerser and his mission while reading the following stanza from a popular Jewish folk song about Elijah the prophet:

The man prepared to be sent from the heavens
The man appointed over gospel (good news)
The man, the true ambassador to turn the heart of the
children to the fathers...
May he proclaim to us gospel (good news).
Elijah the prophet, Elijah the Tishbite, Elijah the Gileadite
May he come to us quickly with Messiah son of David.

(*Eliyahu HaNavi*, Jewish Folk Song)

REPENT, FOR THE KINGDOM OF HEAVEN IS AT HAND

John only had one sermon. He probably had many different versions of it, but the message was always the same: "Repent, for the kingdom of heaven is at hand" (Matthew 3:2). Those nine words are the gospel message in a nutshell.

When He was teaching the crowds, Yeshua never preached a sermon presenting the plan of salvation. Nor did He ever bother to share a tract. We never hear Yeshua ask anyone, "If you died today, do you know for sure that you would go to heaven?" We never hear Him ask, "Do you have Me in your heart?" or "Are you saved?" But if those clichés were not the gospel message taught by Yeshua and His disciples, what was the message? What was He preaching? He was preaching John's nine-word sermon.[16] When He sent out His disciples, He told them to preach the same thing.[17]

John's sermon was "Repent, for the kingdom of heaven is at hand." Yeshua's sermon was "Repent, for the kingdom of heaven is at hand." The apostles' sermon was "Repent, for the kingdom of heaven is at hand." The message of the gospel is "Repent, for the kingdom of heaven is at hand." But what do those words really mean?

REPENT

In Hebrew, the word for "repent" is *shuv* (שוב). It means "to turn around." Repentance (*teshuvah* תשובה in the noun form) is a foundational concept in Judaism. It means "to return." Unlike the Greek equivalent, that implies a change of mind, *teshuvah* means "to turn around and go back the other direction." The call to repent is an imperative to turn one's life in the opposite direction. In the mouths of the prophets, it meant "quit sinning, turn around and start doing good." It is more than just a change of mind; *teshuvah* demands of change of behavior. In Judaism, "to return" means "to return to the covenant norms of Torah." Sin is defined as a transgression of Torah.[18] Therefore, the call to repent is the call to quit sinning, turn around and return to obedience to God's commandments.

THE KINGDOM

When we think of a kingdom, we tend to think of a geographic territory with political borders under the domain of a sovereign. When we think of the kingdom of heaven, we tend to think of the same thing, but somewhere beyond the sky (perhaps with pearly gates and streets of gold), or in the future when heaven is on earth.

The Hebrew word *malchut* (מלכות) is the word John and Yeshua would have used for "kingdom." While it might be understood to refer to a territorial domain, it is better understood as the active rule and reign of a sovereign. To be in the *malchut*, one must be under the reign of the *melech* (מלך). To be in the kingdom, one must be under the reign of the king.

The sages of second-Temple Judaism understood the kingdom of heaven to be lives lived in obedience to God. They spoke of the recitation of the *Shema* (Deuteronomy 6:4–9) as "taking on the yoke of the kingdom." Yeshua described the kingdom in these terms when He said, "The kingdom of God is not coming with signs to be observed; nor will they say, 'Look, here it is!' or, 'There it is!' For behold, the kingdom of God is in your midst" (Luke 17:20–21).

In this perspective, the kingdom of heaven is not a place; it is a status. Those who choose to obey the king are under the reign of the king; that is to say, in the kingdom.

But there is a visible aspect to the kingdom of heaven as well, and that is the literal presence of a reigning king on earth. The ancient prophets of Israel promised that one day God's anointed king, a descendant of the house of David, would reign over Israel and the entire world. To make a kingdom, you need a king. Yeshua came as that promised King, and John the Immerser fully expected Him to establish His kingdom in short order.

KINGDOM OF HEAVEN

John and Yeshua referred to the coming kingdom as the kingdom of heaven (*shamayim*, שמים). We are a long way from their intended meaning if we think of pearly gates and streets of gold. In the days of the Master, the Jewish people had ceased using the name of God for fear of breaking the third commandment. Instead of pronouncing God's name as it is spelled, they employed circumlocutions. These evasive synonyms were understood to be just that, even as they are to this day. For example, our English translations of the Bible employ such circumlocutions by translating the holy and unspeakable name of God (Y/H/V/H) as Lord. Yeshua Himself used evasive synonyms like this to speak of God. In all the Scriptures, neither He nor His disciples ever pronounced the name of God. Instead, by all appearances, they reverenced and sanctified His name, setting it apart from common use. When speaking of God, Yeshua referred to Him as the Father, my Father, the Spirit, the Mighty One, God, Lord and Heaven. The word *heaven*, as used in the term "Kingdom of Heaven," functions as such a circumlocution, just as it does in the common English term of exasperation, "Oh, for heaven's sake!"

The gospel writers Luke and Mark understood that the subtlety of this idiom would be lost on readers unfamiliar with the Jewish context, so in their gospels they translated the term as "kingdom of God." The terms *Kingdom of Heaven* and *Kingdom of God* are actually synonymous.

IS AT HAND

The gospel message of "the kingdom of heaven is at hand" seems to imply that the kingdom of heaven is very close but has not yet arrived or that it is about to begin but has not yet begun. Bivin and Blizzard point out that in Hebrew the connotation of the phrase has the opposite meaning:

> The Hebrew word for near (*karav*, קרב) "does not imply that there necessarily has to be any distance at all between that which is coming near and that which is being approached. ... We can see how the Greek or English leaves the wrong concept of Kingdom of God: futuristic. The Hebrew leaves the correct concept: present tense— NOW! The Kingdom of Heaven ... is always present tense,

"right now," according to Jesus' understanding, and in rabbinic usage as well."[19]

It follows that where there is a king, there is a kingdom. The message of John, Yeshua and the disciples was consistent. The king is here! The kingdom is now because the king is here! If we translate the terminology back to Hebrew, we can see the heightened sense of urgency with which John, Yeshua and the disciples all delivered the gospel message. Repent quickly because the Kingdom of Heaven is already here!

If we put it all together, the meaning of this central message of the gospel comes through loud and clear: "Quit sinning, turn around and start obeying God because the King is already here and the reign of God is starting right now!" The good news of the gospel is that the King has arrived. The demand of the gospel is repentance.

PREPARING THE WAY

The prophets spoke of John the Immerser as one who comes preparing "the way" for the king. The gospel of Luke applies Isaiah 40:3 to John the Immerser:

> And he came into all the district around the Jordan, preaching a baptism of repentance for the forgiveness of sins; as it is written in the book of the words of Isaiah the prophet, "The voice of one crying in the wilderness, 'Make ready the way of the LORD, make his paths straight.'" (Luke 3:3–4)

At the time Luke's gospel was being written, that passage from Isaiah regarding a messenger who prepares "the way" for the Lord was much more meaningful to believers than it is today. In Luke's day, "The Way" was one of the names for the sect of Judaism that had identified Yeshua as Messiah.[20] John's role was to make ready "The Way" for King Messiah. In other words, he was to prepare those who would become the followers of Yeshua. One of the criteria for the twelve disciples was that they had each been present since John's ministry.[21] That means that each of the disciples had heard John proclaim the good news about Yeshua. John had prepared them for Messiah by calling them to repent. He had prepared those men and women who would be called "The Way."

Chapter 2

NEW WINESKINS FOR NEW WINE

THE DOUBLE PARABLE OF LUKE 5:33–39 REEXAMINED

> Elisha ben Avuyah said: "He who studies as a
> child, unto what can he be compared? He can be
> compared to ink written upon a fresh [new] sheet
> of paper. But he who studies as an adult, unto
> what can he be compared? He can be compared
> to ink written on a smudged [previously used
> and erased] sheet of paper. (m.*Pirke Avot* 4:20)

Imagine, if you will, a banquet at the house of Levi, the tax collector. There is singing and drinking and eating and merriment,
and in the midst of it recline the Master and His disciples. On the
periphery of the scene are the Pharisees and several disciples of
John the Immerser.[22] They have been following Yeshua, learning
from Him and scrutinizing Him. They would not deign to eat with
the sinners and tax collectors who constitute Yeshua's friends and
followers, but they are intrigued enough to stay close and observe.
As the meal progresses, the Pharisees begin to ask Yeshua's disciples some questions, such as, "How often do you fast?" The disciples are unable to answer with their mouths full, so they shrug
and look to Yeshua for a response.

When these same critics turn to Yeshua, informing Him that
His disciples don't fast as the disciples of John and the disciples of
the Pharisees do, Yeshua disarms them with the double parable
of the old coat and the new wine.

> No one tears a piece of cloth from a new garment and puts
> it on an old garment; otherwise he will both tear the new,
> and the piece from the new will not match the old. And
> no one puts new wine into old wineskins; otherwise the

new wine will burst the skins, and it will be spilled out, and the skins will be ruined. But new wine must be put into fresh wineskins. And no one, after drinking old wine wishes for new; for he says, "The old is good enough." (Luke 5:36–39)

It seems that the Master's profound observations concerning old wineskins, torn coats and new patches leave them speechless. They don't ask Him any more questions, but perhaps that was only because, like the rest of us, they had no idea what Yeshua was talking about.

INCOMPATIBILITY

Expositors have explained the double parable of Luke 5:33–39.[23] The meaning of the parable seems obvious. The new garment is the gospel/grace/kingdom/church and the old garment is the old covenant/law/Judaism. No one tears a new garment to patch an old one. Grace and law do not mix. Similarly, the new wine is the gospel/grace/kingdom/church and the old wineskin is the old covenant/law/Judaism. Just as the new wine would burst the old skins and be spilled, so too the new covenant gospel of the church kingdom would be wasted if it were poured into the old covenant, Mosaic, legalistic religion of Judaism.

In almost unanimous consent, interpreters and commentators have agreed that the old wine, the old wineskins and the old coat are all symbols of Judaism and Law, whereas the new wine and the new coat are symbols of Christianity and grace.[24] As Kee aptly observes (1970), this "traditional interpretation of the double parable can be summed up in one word: incompatibility. It is supposed to teach that the Old and the New are incompatible, that Judaism is incompatible with Christianity." The old is worn and obsolete. The church must be a new and separate movement, not a patch attempting to prolong the institutions of the old covenant. The new covenant has erased and replaced the old. This meaning of the double parable seems obvious. Or perhaps not.

SERIOUS PROBLEMS

There are serious problems with the incompatibility interpretation. For example, it is anachronistic. Critical scholarship now acknowledges that Yeshua was not starting a new religion, nor intending to dismantle Judaism. When Yeshua gave the double parable, there was no Christianity, no church, no new religion for Judaism to be incompatible with. When the gospel writers recorded the double parable, the picture of Yeshua as an antagonist of the old covenant and Judaism had not yet been conceived. Instead, what has become worn and obsolete is the notion that Yeshua was opposed to the Torah and Judaism. Regarding this incompatibility interpretation, Kee says:

> There is no denying that Jesus radically transformed [and] revolutionized Judaism for his followers, but surely we need not labor the point that it was in fact Judaism which he transformed for them. ...To attribute the idea of incompatibility to Jesus, as a way of describing his relationship to Judaism, is bad theology and bad history.

His point is well taken. The incompatibility interpretation stems from a supersessionist theology of a later century. To place it into Yeshua's mouth is absurd.[25]

Another serious problem with the incompatibility interpretation is the last line of Luke 5:39: "And no one, after drinking old wine wishes for new; for he says, 'The old is good enough.'"[26] This troublesome verse is found only in Luke's version of the double parable, and the Western version of the text omits it. It creates a serious problem for the incompatibility interpretation because it seems to reverse the value of the new wine. If the gospel is really the new wine, the statement—and even the entire metaphor—is ridiculous in Yeshua's mouth. It is "as if Yeshua was comparing Judaism to good claret and the gospel to cheap plonk."[27]

Marcion the Heretic deemed the end of Luke 5:39 to be a Jewish interpolation,[28] it's no surprise that the Western text completely omits it. The omission, however, reveals an anti-Judaic bias in the scribal transmission.[29]

ATTEMPTS TO SALVAGE

Recognizing that the incompatibility interpretation is flawed, some scholars have made valiant attempts to reinterpret the double parable. R. S. Good and David Flusser, for example, both try to force an explanation of the words "the old is better" by reversing the direction of the double parable in Luke. According to Good, Luke intentionally reinterpreted the two parables to mean that the old is better because it is the old Israel that Yeshua came to save.[30] The new wine, bursting the skins and tearing the garment, should then be interpreted as the Pharisees and the Sadducees. The old skins must be preserved; the old garment must be patched because they represent old Israel. This attractive and highly innovative explanation accounts for 5:39 and avoids the anachronistic problems of the traditional interpretations, but it conflicts with statements like 5:38 and it does not fit the context. Good himself points out that it is not in concert with Matthew and Mark's versions.

David Stern, who translated the *Jewish New Testament*, suggests that Yeshua meant for us to patch up Judaism by preshrinking the cloth of messianic faith to fit the old coat of Judaism. Then he suggests that the new wineskins are actually old wineskins that have been reconditioned in order to receive the new wine. Hence the new wineskins should be read as renewed wineskins. While his interpretations are creative, they still operate under the premise of incompatibility and stretch the reader beyond the point of credibility. In addition, they don't answer the question of Luke 5:39 or address the context in which the parables are given.

CHOOSING THE TWELVE

The context of the double parable is a narrative relating how Yeshua chose His disciples. All of chapter five and the first sixteen verses of chapter six string together several stories that deal with the calling and selection of the disciples. Luke 5:1–11 records the story of the first miraculous catch of fish, during which Yeshua invites James, John, and Peter (and by inference Andrew) to become His disciples. The episode concludes in 5:11 with the fishermen leaving their boats, their nets and the miraculous catch to follow Yeshua. The narrative then turns aside to relate two short healing stories (5:17–26), but returns to the calling of the disciples with the call of Levi in 5:27–28. Like the fishermen, Levi leaves everything and follows Yeshua. Levi holds a banquet for Yeshua, and at this banquet the Pharisees level criticisms at Yeshua's disciples. They asked His disciples, "Why do you eat and drink with tax collectors and 'sinners'?"[31] They asked Yeshua, "Why don't your disciples fast and pray like John's disciples and like our disciples?"[32] Both questions are criticisms of Yeshua's disciples and His choice of company. Yeshua replies to the question on fasting with the bridegroom statements of 5:34–35 and then tells the double parable.

Following the parable, Luke 6 begins with a short story that at first seems unrelated to the concerns of choosing disciples. In the story (6:1–5), the Pharisees challenge Yeshua on Sabbath issues, but in fact it is the disciples' behavior the Pharisees criticized, not the behavior of Yeshua. They accused the disciples of breaking the Sabbath by picking heads of grain and husking them in their hands. Again the criticism is directed toward Yeshua's choice of disciples. Connected with the Sabbath observance conflict raised in 6:1–5, Luke offers a matching story in 6:6–11 that echoes and complements the first, but is clearly meant as an aside.

Returning to the call and selection of Yeshua's disciples, Luke closes the section with the final elimination round in which Yeshua chooses the Twelve (6:12–16). With the choosing of the Twelve, the disciple issue is settled.

THE CALL AND SELECTION OF HIS DISCIPLES (LUKE 5,6)

A	Calling of the First Disciples	5:1–11
-	(Aside to Healing of the Leper)	5:12–16
-	(Aside to Healing of the Paralytic)	5:17–26
B	Calling of Levi	5:27–28
C	Levi's Banquet/ Pharisees' Criticisms of Disciples	5:29–39
	Yeshua's Response and Double Parable	
D	Pharisees Accusation of Disciples of Sabbath Violation	6:1–5
-	(Aside to a Similar Sabbath Story) 6:6–11	6:6–11
E	Final Selection of the Twelve Disciples	6:12–16

We might imagine the Pharisees leaving Levi's banquet and later pondering Yeshua's words, saying, "I don't know what He meant by that, but it sounded profound." Or perhaps not.

Unlike us, the Pharisees probably knew exactly what Yeshua meant because they were familiar with the symbolism Yeshua employed in His double parable. By comparing Luke 5:36–39 with the well-known Pharisaic proverb of m.*Avot* 4:20, a whole new interpretation arises that is a natural complement to the context of the passage and is more satisfactory than those previously suggested.

LUKE 5:36–39	PIRKEI AVOT 4:20
He told them this parable: No one tears a piece of cloth from a new garment and puts it on an old garment; otherwise he will both tear the new, and the piece from the new will not match the old. And no one puts new wine into old wineskins; otherwise the new wine will burst the skins and it will be spilled out, and the skins will be ruined. But new wine must be put into fresh wineskins. And no one, after drinking old wine wishes for new; for he says, "The old is good enough"	Elisha ben Avuyah said: "He who studies as a child, unto what can he be compared? He can be compared to ink written upon a fresh [new] sheet of paper. But he who studies as an adult, unto what can he be compared? He can be compared to ink written on a smudged [previously used and erased] sheet of paper. Rabbi Yose ben Yehudah of the city of Babylon said, "He who learns from the young, unto what can he be compared? He can be compared to one who eats unripe grapes, and drinks unfermented wine from his vat. But he who learns from the old, unto what can he be compared? He can be compared to one who eats ripe grapes, and drinks old wine." Rabbi Meir said: "Do not pay attention to the container but pay attention to that which is in it. There is a new container full of old wine, and here is an old container which does not even contain new wine."

Like the larger gospel context of Luke 5–6, the *Avot* passage is comparing different types of teachers, disciples and teachings. If we allow the similes of *Avot* 4 to inform the metaphors of Luke 5, we have surprising results.[33] In *Avot*, the vessels for containing wine are not institutions, religious movements or teachings. The vessels containing the wine are individuals. The wine is the teaching that the individual consumes or contains.[34] Applying this symbolism to Luke, we could parse out 5:36–39 as follows:

New garment	previously uneducated students
Old garment	previously educated students
Patch	teaching
New wineskins	previously uneducated students
Old wineskins	previously educated students
New wine	new teaching
Old wine	previous teaching

SINGULAR MEANING: New teaching requires previously uneducated students in order to be received.

No one takes a lesson meant for a new student and tries to teach it to an old (already educated) student. If he does, he will fail to teach the new student, and the lesson meant for the new student will be rejected by the old student.

No one teaches new Torah lessons to old (previously educated) students. If he does, the new teaching will be rejected, and the student will be lost. Instead, new Torah lessons must be taught to new students. No one after receiving old teaching (previous education) wants the new, for he says, "The old teaching is better."

The *Avot* interpretation of the double parable offers several advantages. Unlike the incompatibility theory, the *Avot* interpretation is not anachronistic. It does not pit Yeshua against Judaism, nor does it imagine a conflict between new covenant grace and old covenant law. Instead, it pits Yeshua's choice of disciples against the Pharisees' choice of disciples. Unlike the incompatibility theory, the *Avot* interpretation fits the context in which the parable is found; namely, the call and selection of Yeshua's disciples. It addresses the Pharisees' criticism about fasting and answers the problems raised by 5:39.

In a similar passage in the Talmud, Rabbi Yehoshua ben Chananiah compares Torah to wine and the vessels used for storing wine to the sages that teach the Torah:

> The Emperor's daughter said to Rabbi Yehoshua ben Chananiah: "What beautiful Torah in an ugly vessel!" He replied, "Learn from the house of your father. In what is the wine stored?" "In jars of clay," she answered. "But all the common people store their wine in jars of clay! You use them too? You should keep your wine in jars of gold and silver!" She went and had the wine placed in vessels of gold and silver, and it turned sour. "Thus," said he to her, "It is the same with Torah!" She asked, "But are there not handsome people who are learned?" He replied, "If they were ugly they would be even more learned!" (b.*Nedarim* 50b)

UNSMUDGED PAPER

Luke has gone to some pains to demonstrate the unsavory character of Yeshua's choice in disciples. They are fishermen, tax collectors and "sinners." They are feasting and drinking instead of fasting and praying. They are bungling Sabbath observance to feed their stomachs. They are not pious types. They are not the kind to follow in the tradition of the disciples of Hillel and Shammai. They have not been educated with the sages. In this regard, they are like a clean slate, a fresh, unsmudged piece of paper for Yeshua to write on.

This is not to suggest that the disciples had no education. A primary education in Yeshua's day involved an extensive memorization of Scripture and knowledge of Torah. Educational standards in Galilee may have surpassed those of Judah, so even fishermen and tax collectors had received training in the Scriptures. However, only the very gifted went on to study beyond the age of twelve or thirteen, and only the truly exceptional (and perhaps wealthy) went on to become disciples of the sages.[35]

The situation with the disciples reminds me of a celebrated metal welder who was known in northeast Minnesota for his excellent work. He often remarked that he would rather teach welding to a drunk he found in a bar who had never held a welding torch in his hand than hire a welder with previous training and experience. A man who had never been taught to weld was still teachable, but a man who already knew how to weld was not.

This was the case with Yeshua's choice of disciples. The Pharisees, up to this point in the gospel narrative, were not yet opponents of Yeshua, but were probably still contemplating whether or not to become His disciples. They could not understand Yeshua's choice of disciples and were likely baffled that He had not yet approached them with the position. At Levi's banquet, they criticized the uncouth character and behavior of Yeshua's disciples. Yeshua responded with the double parable, which in essence explained to the Pharisees why they were not qualified for the job of disciple and why the lowlifes He chose to associate with were. The double parable is not a polemic against Judaism; it is an explanation of His choice of disciples. In essence, Yeshua was saying to the Pharisees, "Look, you can't teach an old dog new tricks."

We can now understand how the double parable answers the question about fasting. The Pharisees said, "John's disciples often fast and pray, and so do the disciples of the Pharisees (which is to say, "so do we"), but yours go on eating and drinking." Yeshua's statements about the bridegroom addressed the issue of fasting, but the double parable addressed the broader criticism being raised. That criticism was that Yeshua's disciples were not at all like the disciples of John or the Pharisees.

The Old Is Better

Finally, the *Avot* interpretation solves the problems raised by 5:39: "And no one, after drinking old wine wishes for new; for he says, 'The old is good enough.'" If the parable is comparing Yeshua's Torah teaching (new wine) with the Pharisee's Torah teaching (old wine), the meaning becomes clear. Disciples who have already studied Torah under the Pharisaic schools (or under John's tutelage), and have learned to interpret according to those traditions and models, are unlikely to be interested in a new approach. Those students will be apt to disregard contradictory teaching because they have already formed opinions and made judgments. They will regard the education they have already received as superior. Yeshua has chosen fishermen and tax collectors precisely because of their lack of formal education.

Luke returns to the disciples' lack of formal education in Acts 4 when the Sanhedrin questions Peter and John. In Acts 4:13, Luke writes:

> Now as [the Sanhedrin] observed the confidence of Peter and John, and understood that they were uneducated and untrained men, they were marveling, and began to recognize them as having been with Yeshua.

On that day, when two poorly educated fishermen stood before the Sanhedrin, they demonstrated the full caliber of their education under Yeshua and vindicated His choice of disciples. New garments, new wineskins and new students.

Chapter 3

THE GREAT OMISSION

Moses received the Torah at Sinai and transmitted
it to Joshua, Joshua transmitted it to the elders,
and the elders transmitted it to the prophets,
and the prophets transmitted it to the men
of the Great Assembly. The men of the Great
Assembly used to say three things, "Be diligent
in justice, raise up many disciples and make
a fence around the Torah." (m.*Avot* 1:1)

In the land of Galilee, just west of village Capernaum, a ridge of rugged hillside commanded a view of the Sea of Galilee and its shores. Springtime flowers grew there, clothed like Solomon in all his splendor. Red anemones and blue irises forced their way through the craggy soil. Eleven awkward men climbed the grassy slopes with halting strides. They seemed uncertain of where they were going, and they often stopped to glance about. They were the Eleven, formerly known as the Twelve. They had come to this place, the Eremos Heights, to find the Master.

It was on just such a sunny spring day that He had first called them to follow Him up the same grassy slopes. Hadn't He sat right over there while He taught? And wasn't it this same lonely and quiet place where they had often found Him praying in the early hours? Here He had taught them to pray and taught them the meaning of discipleship. This is the mount of the Sermon on the Mount. Now they had come to find Him again.

But where was He? Would He really appear again? Would they see Him again? They shuffled about, uncertain of what to do next.

Then they saw Him striding through the waving grass, like King Solomon himself, with the sun on His hair and the wind in

His beard. Their hearts leapt. The Master had come, and they prostrated themselves before Him.

THE FOUR IMPERATIVES HE GAVE THE DISCIPLES

Readers of the Gospels know the scene well. The encounter in Galilee is described in Matthew 28. It is the story of the Great Commission, in which Yeshua says to His disciples, "All authority has been given to Me in heaven and on earth. Go therefore and make disciples of all the nations, baptizing them in the name of the Father and the Son and the Holy Spirit, teaching them to observe all that I commanded you; and lo, I am with you always, even to the end of the age" (Matthew 28:18–20).

The Great Commission is composed of four imperatives. The disciples are to:

1. Go.
2. Make disciples of all gentiles.
3. Immerse them in the name of the Father and of the Son and of the Holy Spirit.
4. Teach them to obey everything Yeshua commanded His disciples.

The Christian faith has done a fairly good job with imperatives one and three. However, points two and four have been largely bungled. We might term those two imperatives as "the Great Omission" of our historical approach to evangelism and conversion.

We can hardly be faulted if we have missed the mark a bit on those second and last imperatives. Discipleship is an institution specific to Jewish culture. We did not know what it meant. It was not possible to make disciples out of people when we did not know what the term "disciple" meant in the context of the Judaism practiced by Yeshua and His followers. Furthermore, Christian theology became muddled with an anti-Torah bias early in its development. That muddling made it difficult for us to justify commanding gentiles to obey *everything* Yeshua commanded, especially when we ourselves believed that obedience to the commandments was legalism and somehow at odds with the truth of the gospel. Our great omission is a consequence of our separation from Judaism. It is a regrettable blunder on our part because it has shaped the character and quality of Christianity on a global scale.

Talmidim and the Art of Imitation

As He delivered the Great Commission to the eleven disciples, commanding them to make disciples of all nations, they were stretched out face down on the craggy turf before His bare feet. They understood what it meant to be a disciple. They had learned discipleship by sitting before those same feet for three years of education.

In evangelical Christianity, our image of a disciple may be a flannel-graph picture of a bearded man in a robe and sandals, or it may be a caricature of one of the Twelve who followed Yeshua. We tend to think of discipleship as a New Testament phenomenon, perhaps something Yeshua dreamed up when He chose His twelve disciples. This is wrong.

Long before the days of the Master, discipleship was a well-established institution within Jewish culture. All the great sages, the rabbis, the sages among the Pharisees and the teachers of the Torah had disciples. The Hebrew word for "disciple" is *talmid* (תלמיד). *Talmid* means "student." The plural is *talmidim* (students). We translate *talmidim* as "disciples." A *talmid*'s job was to learn everything his master had to teach. The Talmud is a written transcript of several centuries of that process.

In Judaism in the days of the apostles, the job of a disciple was well understood. A disciple's job was to become like his or her teacher. So it is written for us in the gospel of Luke, "Every [disciple], after he has been fully trained, will be like his teacher" (6:40). At its simplest, discipleship is the art of imitation. It is the art of walking after a teacher. When the disciple was fully trained, he became the teacher and passed on the teaching to disciples of his own, who in turn, when fully trained, became teachers and raised up disciples of their own.

Higher Education

Discipleship was the primary institution of higher religious education in the days of the Master. Formal Bible schools and seminaries did not exist. A young man seeking a future in teaching Torah apprenticed himself to a rabbi, just as a would-be craftsman apprenticed himself to a known master in order to learn a trade. In this case, the trade was Torah.

Even the apprentice analogy, however, falls short of describing the essence of the teacher-disciple relationship. That relationship was a powerful bond. Disciples regarded their teachers more highly than they did their own fathers.[36] They regarded themselves as servants and their teachers as masters.[37] Thus the disciples of the first century referred to their teachers as *rabbi*, meaning "revered one" or as *master*. The teacher-disciple dynamic was often expressed as a father-son relationship. In rabbinic literature, the Torah sage is the father and his disciples are called his "family." The collected words of the teachers are called "Sayings of the Fathers." A sage's school of disciples is called his "house." Therefore, the Talmud speaks of the House of Shammai, which was always at odds with the House of Hillel.

The absolute dedication and loyalty that disciples held for their teachers is incomparable to any of the pedagogic institutions of our own culture and experience. Imagine if, rather than falling asleep in your freshman composition class, you had begun to completely emulate the professor. You memorized his lectures and quoted him at every possible opportunity. You followed him to and from his home and often invited yourself to eat with him. You began to dress and act like him. You sought to absorb every possible nuance of his behavior. Obsessive? To say the least! Yet this was the prescribed mode of learning Torah in first-century Pharisaic Judaism.

The Four Jobs of a Disciple

In the days of the Master, the disciples of the sages had four major tasks to perform. These tasks describe the cultural context of the institution of discipleship that we read about in the Gospels.

1. To memorize their teacher's words

A disciple memorized his teacher's words. The oral transmission process was the only intergenerational communication practiced among the sages. The great rabbis and Torah scholars of first-century Pharisaic Judaism did not write scrolls or compose books for their students to read and study. Not that they were illiterate; they were highly literate. But in their worldview, the Scriptures were the written works. Their own teachings were meant to be passed on orally. Their disciples studied by memorizing their words. Through constant repetition, disciples memorized their teachers' words verbatim and were able to repeat them to subsequent generations. Through constant repetition, the disciples of the Pharisees committed to memory whole books of Scripture and dizzying amounts of legal argumentation.

2. To learn their teacher's traditions and interpretations

A disciple learned how his teacher kept the commands of God and interpreted the Scriptures. Every detail about the teacher was important. The disciple needed to learn how the teacher washed his hands, how he kept the Sabbath, how he fasted, how he prayed, how he gave charity, how he affixed a *mezuzah*[38] to his doorpost, how he said the blessings over food, etc. Furthermore, the way the teacher interpreted passages of Scripture, the meanings he drew out, the parables with which he elucidated, the way he explained a verse or understood a concept—each of these was of utmost importance to the disciple. Details of this sort were not just trivia. To a disciple, these were like gems and pearls meant to be gathered and treasured.

3. To imitate their teacher's actions

A disciple's highest calling was to be a reflection of his teacher. A disciple studied the things his master did. He sought to act, to speak and to conduct himself the same way in which his master conducted himself. His highest goal was to walk in the same manner as his teacher. Every disciple, after he has been fully trained, will be like his teacher.

4. To raise up disciples

Ever since the days of the Ezra and Nehemiah, the sages commanded their students, "Raise up many disciples."[39] A disciple, when finally trained, raised up his own disciples. He created a new generation of students and transmitted to them the words, traditions, interpretations, teachings, actions and behaviors of his master. The goal of discipleship was to pass the torch of Torah from generation to generation.

Choosing the Twelve

The Gospels indicate that Yeshua had many more disciples than just twelve. The first chapter of Acts mentions ten times that number, but only twelve were called to be the core students. These twelve were the ones responsible for transmitting the teaching and the message of Yeshua.

Luke's narrative says that Yeshua spent the whole night alone in the hills, deep in prayer, before making His choices for the Twelve. Each one He chose had to be the Father's choice. When morning came He was ready to call the Twelve.

He chose twelve as a microcosm for the whole of Israel. Thus the twelve disciples will be seated on twelve thrones judging twelve tribes,[40] and their names are inscribed on the twelve foundations of the New Jerusalem.[41]

Mark tells us that "He appointed twelve, so that they would be with Him" (Mark 3:14). The idea of a fellowship among a core of disciples came from the schools of the Pharisees. The disciples of the Pharisees organized themselves into small fellowships called *chaverim* (חברים). A *chaver* (חבר, which means "friend") was a fellow who lived according to the same legal standards as the rest of the fellowship. Because of the strict interpretations of the Pharisaic schools regarding laws of clean and unclean and the laws of tithing on produce before eating of it, the Pharisees found themselves unable to enjoy table fellowship at the tables of commoners. They restricted themselves to eat only at the tables of those who lived by and upheld their legal standards. Those who did so constituted a *chaverim*.

The Essenes practiced a similar community rule that allowed for table fellowship with those who had subscribed to the code and rule of their community. Those belonging to their fellowship lived a communal lifestyle in which the fraternity of the brothers was regarded as the primary family.

The *chaverim* of the twelve disciples is similar and dissimilar to both the Pharisaic model and the Essene model. While the *chaverim* of the Twelve seemed to be organized around the same social structure as the *chaverim* of the Pharisees, they were certainly not exclusive in their fellowship with others. Rigid legal standards are hardly the criteria Yeshua used in choosing His disciples. Similarities to the Essene community model include the communal mode of life and the common fraternity, but the austere and monk-like asceticism practiced by the Essenes was foreign to Yeshua and His disciples.

The *chaverim* of the Twelve was, for all practical purposes, a family. Just as the disciples of Hillel were called the House of Hillel, so too the disciples of Yeshua were a household of which He was the head.[42] They were brothers. They ate together, lived together, traveled together, worked together, prayed together and learned together. They were the new family of the Master. They were *Beit Yeshua* (the House of Yeshua).

As He selected the twelve disciples, Yeshua chose two Shimons, two Yaakovs and three Yehudahs—that is, two Simons, two Jameses and three Judases. They used epithets and nicknames to distinguish one from another. The names ring with authenticity. One is left with the impression that this was a group of men who spent considerable time with one another. Their nicknames sound more like thugs in a mafia family or the wrestlers of the World Wrestling Federation than a respectable school of sages. In our modern vernacular, the disciples' nicknames would translate to names like The Rock, Johnny Thunderhead, Big Jim and Little Jim, Matt the Taxman, The Twin, Baby-boy-lovey-kins, Simon the Terrorist and Jude the Knife. Gospel readers can derive the names of the Twelve by comparing four lists that occur in the Gospels and Acts.[43]

The Twelve included fishermen, a stone mason, a tax collector, two insurrectionists—normal men. They gave up their careers, sacrificing everything, even jeopardizing their families' financial standings, in order to follow Yeshua, to memorize His words, to learn His traditions, to imitate His actions and to raise up more disciples.

You Are Not to Be Called Rabbi

As the eleven remaining disciples lay face down before their resurrected Rabbi, He told them to "go therefore and make disciples of all the nations" (Matthew 28:19).

But there is one large difference between discipleship to the sages of Yeshua's day and discipleship to Messiah. In Matthew 23:8–10, Yeshua warns His disciples, "But do not be called Rabbi; for One is your Teacher, and you are all brothers. Do not call anyone on earth your father; for One is your Father, He who is in heaven. Do not be called leaders; for One is your Leader, that is, Messiah."

What does Yeshua mean when He tells us, "You are not to be called rabbi or father or teacher"? How does that bode for Messianic rabbis? How does it bode for teachers anywhere? What about our paternal fathers? What about our congregational elders? Does the Master mean that we should eschew all such titles? Is "Pastor" or "Reverend" permissible when "Teacher" and "Rabbi" are not? Is "Elder" permissible when "Father" is not?

The Master's words here can only be understood within the institution of first-century, teacher-disciple relationships as described above. Each disciple, when fully trained, was expected to raise up his own disciples. He then became the teacher, the rabbi, the master and the father to a new generation of disciples.

Yeshua forbade the Twelve to raise up disciples for themselves. They were not to be the teachers, rabbis, masters and fathers to the next generation of disciples. He did not want them segmenting into a School of Peter, a House of Andrew, an Academy of James. The disciples of Yeshua were never to assume the role of master, because unlike the masters of the Pharisees or the men of the Great Assembly or the sages like Hillel or Shammai, Yeshua is still alive. Followers of Yeshua are forbidden to make their own disciples because our job is to raise up more disciples for Yeshua—for we have one Teacher, the Messiah.

His words are not meant to forbid teachers among us, or elders, fathers, rabbis or leaders. Of course we have and need all of these. But we must never let our elders, fathers, rabbis, leaders or teachers take the place of our one Master. We must never become the disciples of men. Rather, we are called to be disciples of the Messiah.

Nor does our Master allow us to raise up our own disciples in order to satisfy our need for self-aggrandizement. Rather, we must raise up more disciples for Him.

The Discipleship of Paul

If any of the apostolic writers understood the institution of discipleship, it was Shaul of Tarsus (Paul). Discipled under the famous Sage Gamliel, he had spent the better part of his life learning the ins and outs of discipleship. Thus we should not be surprised to find that, as he kept the Master's Great Commission, he passed the discipleship model on to his congregations.

Perhaps as a result, Corinth was beset with problems. Paul attributed their tendency toward deviancy to a lack of qualified men who might disciple them. In his first letter to that congregation, he speaks about the dearth of "fathers" among them. He is not referring to paternal fathers.

> I do not write these things to shame you, but to admonish you as my beloved children. ... You would not have many fathers; for in Messiah Yeshua I became your father through the gospel. I exhort you therefore, be imitators of me. For this reason I have sent to you Timothy, who is my beloved and faithful child in the Lord, and he will remind you of my ways which are in Messiah, just as I teach everywhere in every church. (1 Corinthians 4:14–17)

Paul regards himself as a father to the Corinthians and to Timothy his disciple. The father-to-son language is characteristic of the Pharisaic teacher-disciple model. Furthermore, he urges the Corinthians to imitate him, thus spurring them on to live out their discipleship.

Later in the same letter, Paul refers to the oral transmission process of the teacher-disciple relationship as well as charging the Corinthians to imitate him even as he imitates Messiah. The oral traditions to which he refers are the ways and words of the Master.

> Follow my example, as I follow the example of Messiah. I praise you for remembering me in everything and for holding to the teachings [oral traditions], just as I passed them on to you. (1 Corinthians 11:1–2 NIV)

Paul's discipling activities were not limited to the congregation at Corinth. To the Philippians he wrote, "Join with others in following my example, brothers, and take note of those who live according to the pattern we gave you" (Philippians 3:17 NIV). To the Thessalonians he wrote, "You know how we lived among you for your sake. You became imitators of us and of the Master ... and so you became a model to all the believers in Macedonia and Achaia" (1 Thessalonians 1:5–7 NIV). By living out lives of discipleship to Yeshua, the Thessalonians had attracted the attention of others and won more converts to the path of discipleship. That's how it is supposed to work.

THE GOOSE AND THE GANDER

Yeshua commanded the eleven men prostrated before His feet, "Go therefore and make disciples of all the nations ... teaching them to observe all that I commanded you" (Matthew 28:19–20).

Disciples are more than just converts. Disciples are beholden to the expectations of discipleship. Yeshua's Great Commission is more than just proselytism; it is a command to raise up disciples in the name of the Master who will walk in the ways of the Master, learning His words, carrying on His traditions and raising up more disciples for Him. Paul accomplished this. He continually exhorted his converts to walk in imitation of him as he imitated Messiah.

You have probably heard the proverb "What's good for the goose is good for the gander." Paul's brand of radical discipleship could be called the Goose-Gander Model. We are the ganders and Yeshua is our goose. Whatever Yeshua said and whatever He did is good enough for us. We are to be imitators of Messiah.

THE GREAT COMMISSION

In the Great Commission, Gentile disciples are directed to obey everything Yeshua commanded the Twelve.[44] Discipleship is a call to imitation and obedience. We are called to be disciples of Yeshua, and as such, it is our job to imitate Him, obey Him and raise up more disciples for Him.

In his first epistle, John falls back on this Jewish model of discipleship as he gently coaxes his Gentile readers to take up the ways of the Master:

> The one who says, "I have come to know Him," but does not keep His commandments, is a liar, and the truth is not in him. But whoever keeps His word, in him the love of God has truly been perfected. By this we know we are in him: the one who says he abides in Him ought to walk in the same manner as He [Yeshua] walked. (1 John 2:4–6)

We need no further justification for taking up the commands of God than this: We must walk as Yeshua did. We must become His disciples.

Chapter 4

CARPENTER AMONG THE NAZARENES

And when the Sabbath had come, He began to
teach in the synagogue; and the many listeners
were astonished, saying, "Where did this man
get these things, and what is this wisdom given
to Him, and such miracles as these performed by
His hands? Is not this the carpenter, the son of
Mary, and brother of James and Joses and Judas
and Simon? Are not His sisters here with us?"
And they took offense at Him. (Mark 6:2–3)

Yeshua was from Nazareth, but He spent most of His time in
Capernaum with Peter and Peter's family. While in Capernaum, He transformed Simon Peter's home into an infirmary/
study hall. The crowd at the house was so large that space for meals
was impossible. Mark tells us, "The multitude gathered again, to
such an extent that they could not even eat a meal" (Mark 3:20).

Somehow, word of the crowds in Capernaum drifted back to
Nazareth where Yeshua's mother, Miriam, and His brothers still
lived. Nothing could be more alarming to a Jewish mother than
to hear that her son was not eating! In a panic, she summoned
the rest of her sons and set out for Capernaum to "take custody of
Him; for they were saying, 'He has lost His senses'" (Mark 3:21).
Yeshua's mother and brothers intended to bring Him back to Nazareth, where they felt He belonged.

The story occurs in the gospel of Mark immediately after
Yeshua chose the twelve disciples. Mark tells us the story to illustrate the tension between Nazareth and Capernaum and between

the family of the Master and the disciples of the Master. In Nazareth, Yeshua was just the local carpenter. In Capernaum, He was a miracle worker and rabbi.

A Visit to Nazareth

On one occasion, Yeshua did return to Nazareth. Mark 6:1 says, "Yeshua went out from there and came into His hometown." Nazareth was a small Jewish community in the upper Galilee. Like similar villages of the Middle East today, it would have been primarily a family community in which everyone was either related or once removed from being related. Nazareth was probably typical of any Jewish village in the Galilee. There was a local synagogue that also served as the village study hall (*beit midrash*, בית מדרש).

The local characters of Nazareth were undoubtedly just like the locals of any village, but there is a very real possibility that they were also descendants of the royal line of David. Villages tended to be large extended families. Children rarely left home. Families built additional wings on their houses, adding subsequent generations to the patriarchal home. In just a few generations, one or two of these large families could constitute a clan occupying a small village. There is every possibility that Joseph the carpenter's fellow townsmen were also his cousins, uncles and nephews, hence also men of the line of David.

Branchtown

As descendants of David, it would have been natural for Joseph's family clan to cling to Isaiah's prophecy of the Netzer (נצר), the promised messianic "branch" who would one day spring forth from their family.

> Then a shoot will spring from the stem of Jesse, and a branch (*netzer*) from his roots will bear fruit. And the Spirit of the Lord will rest on Him, the spirit of wisdom and understanding, the spirit of counsel and strength, the spirit of knowledge and the fear of the Lord. (Isaiah 11:1–2)

It is possible that the Davidic clan that founded the community of Nazareth named their community Nazareth (*Natzeret*, נצרת) in anticipation of the ultimate fulfillment of Isaiah's words through them. Nazareth, then, would mean "Branchtown." Under the reign of the false king Herod and the tyranny of the evil Roman Empire, the Davidic clan longed for the true Branch (*Netzer*), the Messiah who was to be born from among their kinsmen.

Every son born to the descendants of the dynasty possessed the potential of rising to reclaim the throne of their father David. Every baby boy, particularly in those days of heightened messianic expectation, was the potential *Netzer* (Branch) growing from the stump of Jesse. Thus they named their town after their great hope for Messiah.

Perhaps it is to Isaiah 11:1–2 that Matthew was referring when he said:

> [He] came and resided in a city called Nazareth, that what was spoken through the prophets might be fulfilled, "He shall be called a Nazarene (*natzri*)." (Matthew 2:23)

By the time Yeshua read Torah in the Nazareth synagogue, word of His miraculous deeds in the Capernaum vicinity had already circulated. One would expect that this Davidic clan who lived in constant expectation of a hometown Messiah would have been the first to proudly acclaim Yeshua as *Melech haMashiach* (מלך המשיח), King Messiah.

There was, however, an obstacle. To the Davidians of Nazareth, Yeshua seemed to be a far cry from *Melech haMashiach*; He was just good old Yeshy, the carpenter's son. Familiarity and intimacy proved to be blinders, which made it impossible for the Nazarenes to imagine this small-town local boy as Messiah. To them, He was simply a carpenter:

> "Is not this the carpenter, the son of Mary, and brother of James and Joses and Judah and Simon? Are not His sisters here with us?" And they took offense at Him. (Mark 6:3)

Joseph the Carpenter

Joseph was the village carpenter. Scholars often suggest that we should think of him more as a stonemason, since buildings in the Galilee were constructed of stone. In Israel, stone is the most readily available building material. The Greek term describing Joseph is *tecton*. *Tecton* is used to refer to artisans in general and includes stone, metal and wood workers, but it most often refers to woodworkers and shipwrights. It seems likely that the conventional image of Joseph as a carpenter is correct.

In Hebrew, he was probably called a *charash etz* (עץ חרש); that is, a woodworker. It was a respectable trade. It is interesting to see another early rabbi who also practiced the carpentry trade. The Talmud refers to Rabbi Abin the Carpenter.[45] When engaged in construction, the village carpenter was the builder who would have worked with the roof timbers, doors and door frames, windows and stairs and structural elements. From within his shop he would have produced furniture such as chairs and tables and stools, serving implements such as bowls and spoons, and agricultural apparatus such as yokes and hitches and plows.

The sages of the first and second centuries considered it praiseworthy to engage in a blue-collar occupation. They regarded a trade or business occupation as a complement to a life of Torah:

> Rabban Gamliel the son of Rabbi Yehudah the Patriarch said, "The study of the Torah combined together with an occupation is good, because the demands of the two of them keep sin out of one's mind; but the study of Torah that is not combined with an occupation will end in naught." (m.*Avot* 2:2)

As a responsible Jewish father, Joseph had five primary responsibilities toward Yeshua:

> A father is obligated to his son, to circumcise him, redeem him, to teach him Torah, to find a wife for him, and to teach him a trade. ... Rabbi Yehudah said, "One who does not teach his son a trade, teaches him to be a bandit." (b.*Kiddushin* 29a)

Joseph obediently circumcised Yeshua (Luke 2:21) and paid the redemption price for a firstborn (Luke 2:23). The Master had no wife, but His education in Torah is obvious from His teaching. We may be certain that Joseph also taught Yeshua the family trade.

Yeshua the Carpenter

We can deduce a thing or two about Yeshua's family situation in Nazareth. While He was growing in wisdom and stature and favor with God and men,[46] He was probably also busy providing the primary income for a large family.

After the pilgrimage to Jerusalem when the Master was twelve years old (Luke 2), His father Joseph is never mentioned again in the Gospels. His absence is conspicuous, especially in Mark 3 when mention is made of Yeshua's mother and brothers, but not Joseph. The most satisfactory way to explain Joseph's sudden disappearance from the narratives is to suppose that he died sometime between the Master's twelfth birthday and the beginning of His ministry. Whatever the reason might be, it appears that Joseph was no longer present in the family.

Had Joseph still been working his trade, it is probable that Yeshua, who showed such precocious gifting in matters of Torah at such an early age, would have been "discipled out" (so to speak) to one of the sages. With the disappearance of Joseph, however, the responsibility for the family fell to the firstborn son. Yeshua may have had to step into the role of provider and head of household at the age of thirteen or fourteen. With His widowed mother, four younger brothers and who-knows-how-many little sisters, He had many mouths to feed.

He would have been forced to set aside any opportunities to follow up on His impressive debut among the sages. Instead of learning in the academies of Hillel or Shammai, He would have had to apply Himself to the handsaw, planer and chisel.

Apparently, Yeshua picked up the family trade. Justin Martyr, an early second-century church father, reports a tradition that Yeshua was known as a carpenter skilled in agricultural implements:

> For He was in the habit of working as a carpenter when among men, making ploughs and yokes. (Justin Martyr, *Dialogue with Trypho*, 88)

His younger brother Yaakov, on the other hand, would have been free to pursue higher education. Jewish scholar Alfred Edersheim detects Shammaite leanings in the Epistle of James, and therefore suggests that Yaakov may have been discipled under Shammai.[47] We know Yaakov was respected among the Pharisees, so it is possible that while Yeshua stayed home and worked the family business, Yaakov went to study.

If Joseph died when Yeshua was fourteen or so, the youngest of the Master's sisters must have been of an age to marry within fourteen to eighteen years. At least by the time He was in His early thirties, all of His younger siblings would have been old enough to support themselves or to be married into other families. Therefore we might surmise that the so-called silent years between the age of twelve and His early thirties were spent engaged in the family carpentry trade in Nazareth, supporting His mother and brothers and sisters.

A PROPHET WITHOUT HONOR

If for sixteen years or more you had known Yeshua only as the local carpenter boy, or if for all of your life He had been merely your older sibling, it might be difficult to suddenly imagine Him as the long-promised and foretold Messiah King. John tells us, "Even his own brothers did not believe in him" (John 7:5 NIV).

Yeshua's rejection among His own family, the Davidic clan at Nazareth, is reminiscent of the legends of King David. According to rabbinic legend,[48] David was at first rejected by his brothers, who regarded him as unworthy of anointing and kingship. While in the synagogue at Nazareth, Yeshua said:

> No doubt you will quote this proverb to Me, "Physician, heal yourself! Whatever we heard was done at Capernaum, do here in your home town as well." And He said, "Truly I say to you, no prophet is welcome in his home town." (Luke 4:23–24)

The maxim "Physician, heal yourself" is preserved in the *Midrash Rabbah* as "Physician, physician, heal thine own limp!"[49] It means, "Prove yourself." Yeshua was making enormous claims. He had declared Himself to be the Messiah. The only evidence the residents of Nazareth had that might support His claim consisted of the reports of His healing ministry in Capernaum. Incredible claims require credible evidence. None, however, was forthcoming. Instead, He pointed out how both Elijah and Elisha ministered to those outside of Israel, an indictment against those within their own hometown territory who had fallen into idolatry:

But I say to you in truth, there were many widows in Israel in the days of Elijah, when the sky was shut up for three years and six months, when a great famine came over all the land; and yet Elijah was sent to none of them, but only to Zarephath, in the land of Sidon, to a woman who was a widow. And there were many lepers in Israel in the time of Elisha the prophet; and none of them was cleansed, but only Naaman the Syrian. And all in the synagogue were filled with rage as they heard these things. (Luke 4:25–28)

In the same way, Yeshua would take His Messianic ministry elsewhere. When the Master speaks of Elijah and Elisha being sent to Gentiles instead of Israelites, we are often quick to insert replacement theology into the teaching. We assume that Yeshua is using Elijah and Elisha as examples of why He will turn from the Jews and go to the Gentiles.

However, Yeshua is not rejecting a Jewish ministry in favor of a Gentile ministry; He is rejecting a Nazareth ministry in favor of a Capernaum ministry. He compares the unbelieving residents of Nazareth to the idolatrous Israelites of Elijah's day, and the widow of Zarephath and Naaman the Syrian to the more receptive residents of Capernaum. The gospel of Mark tells us, "He wondered at their unbelief" (Mark 6:6).

JOURNEY TO CAPERNAUM

For Yeshua's family, His move to Capernaum may have felt hurtful. Miriam once briefly visited Capernaum with Yeshua, but she returned to Nazareth, where her sons, daughters and grandchildren lived.[50] Miriam may have thought, *He should be in Nazareth with us, looking after the carpentry business. If He wants to do teaching and healing, that's fine, but He should do it in Nazareth with His own people.* Though His brothers did not believe in Him, Miriam knew the circumstances of His miraculous birth. She may have been the only one in Nazareth who actually believed Him to be the Messiah. But it still troubled her that He would choose to raise disciples in Capernaum while ignoring His hometown and family.

When reports came to her about the alarming crowds gathering around her son in Capernaum, she decided it was time to take matters into her own hands. Mother Miriam wanted Yeshua among His relatives in Nazareth, where His Messianic claims could be validated. Miriam planned on removing Him from Capernaum and bringing Him home, just as she had removed Him from the Temple and brought Him home when He was twelve years old. His brothers probably suspected that their older sibling had finally succumbed to their mother's delusions of grandeur. At any rate, they were not impressed with His rabble-rousing ministry or the suspicious band of disciples with whom He was hanging around. They intended to march into Capernaum and knock some sense into Him.

Arriving in Capernaum, they had no difficulty locating Yeshua. He was in Peter's house, surrounded by a crowd of people. The crowd pressed in so tightly that no one could not get through to Yeshua (unless they went through the roof). Followers and onlookers were crowded around doors and windows, trying to catch His words. Like everyone else pressing about the house, Miriam and her sons were told to take a number and wait their turn. They sent word to Him: "Tell Him His mother and brothers are waiting outside looking for Him."

Who Are My Mother and My Brothers?

Inside the house, Yeshua was seated with a circle of disciples around Him. These were the Twelve whom He had just chosen. In addition, a crowd of other disciples were gathered to hear His words. Suddenly someone interrupted. "Your mother and Your brothers are outside looking for you" (Mark 3:32).

The Master responded, "Who are My mother and My brothers?" (Mark 3:33).

No one answered. He knew they were outside, waiting to take Him back to Nazareth. But His loyalty must now lie with His disciples in Capernaum.

He looked at those seated in a circle around Him and said, "Here are my mother and my brothers! Whoever does God's will is my brother and sister and mother" (Mark 3:34–35 NIV).

He would not turn His back on His disciples. He could not turn His back from the call on His life.

When those words were reported back to His mother and brothers, they must have cut to the heart. Yeshua—their Yeshua—was rejecting them in favor of His disciples. Though the words were hurtful, they were what His family needed to hear. They still had not come to terms with who Yeshua really was or what He was about. They still thought of Him as their own, as if they could take charge of Him and talk some sense into Him. They had not yet come to a place of faith or even to a place of humility where they could follow Him instead of insisting that He follow them. Thus a rift was born between the Master's natural family and His disciple family. It is a rift still evident in John 7:2–12, where Yeshua's brothers taunt Him dismissively.

Before His ministry was completed, His mother, Miriam, began to follow in the path of discipleship. No longer just His mother, she put on the sandals of a disciple and followed Him to Jerusalem for His last Passover. A reconciliation between His disciples and the Master's natural family occurred at the cross when He gave charge of His mother to His beloved disciple John. Ironically, she who intended to "take charge of Him" and remove Him from the company of the disciples was given over to the charge of one of those disciples.

Eventually the family of Yeshua rejoined Him as part of the larger family of Messiah. The resurrected Yeshua appeared to James,[51] and James became the universally acknowledged head of the assembly of believers. His brothers became His brothers again, not just on filial terms, but as those who do God's will and place faith in God's Son. In their respective epistles, neither James nor Jude refer to themselves as "the brother of Yeshua," but as bond-servants of the Messiah.

In that respect, we all may take our places in the circle of disciples who sit at the feet of the Master. We who will follow Him and place our faith in Him are all brothers and sisters of Yeshua. We are adopted sons of the Father, and thus we are His siblings:

> For both He who sanctifies and those who are sanctified are all from one Father, for which reason He is not ashamed to call them brethren, saying, "I will proclaim your name to My brethren, in the midst of the congregation I will sing Thy praise." (Hebrews 2:11–12)

Perhaps this helps explain why the sect that followed Him came to be called Nazarenes. Even those Capernaum disciples were called Nazarenes. Just as the followers of the Chassidic dynasty that began in the city of Lubavitch, Poland, are called Lubavitchers, the followers of the man from Nazareth are called Nazarenes[52] (*Notzrim*, נצרים), a word that literally means "branches." To this day, Hebrew-speaking Jews refer to believers in Yeshua as *Notzrim*. We are the Nazarenes.

Chapter 5

THE PHARISEES
AND JEWISH TRADITION

Woe to you, scribes and Pharisees, hypocrites!
For you are like whitewashed tombs which
on the outside appear beautiful, but
inside they are full of dead men's bones
and all uncleanness. (Matthew 23:27)

Normally Christians think of Pharisees as the bad guys. Matthew 23 contains the famous passage in which Yeshua pronounces seven "woes" upon the Pharisees. Any reader of Matthew 23 unfamiliar with first-century Judaism would be convinced that the Pharisees were fairly awful human beings.

Look up the word *pharisaical* in a dictionary and you will read that a Pharisee is someone who is self-righteous or hypocritical. The Pharisees were the Orthodox Jews of the apostolic age. Orthodox Judaism, as we know it today, is a direct descendent of Pharisaism. For that reason, believers today (even within the Hebrew Roots movement) seem to consider it pious to despise Orthodox Judaism and to decry Jewish tradition.

Since it is no longer considered politically correct to speak disparagingly of all Jews, we simply disparage Judaism. We have only slightly reworked our old, anti-Semitic formulas to vilify "the rabbis"—the modern Pharisees—instead of all Jews. But what would you think if you were told that Yeshua and the apostles practiced "rabbinic traditions of men"? What would you think if you were told that Yeshua and the apostles were essentially Pharisees?

A Kara-what?

In his book *The Hebrew Yeshua vs. the Greek Jesus*, Nehemia Gordon suggests that Yeshua is best understood as an early Karaite. Was Yeshua a Karaite?

Karaite is the sect of Judaism that rejects Pharisaic tradition. In some ways, they can be compared to the Protestant reformers who proclaimed, "*Sola Scriptura!*" They reject the traditions of men and—theoretically—attempt to live according to the most literal possible reading of the biblical text. For Karaites, the Bible is supposed to be the sole authority on matters of faith and practice. No credence is granted to tradition.[53]

Given the Master's debates with the Pharisees over Sabbath restrictions, hand washing and other matters, Karaitism seems to be a natural fit for Him. Based on a cursory reading of the Gospels, it is possible to mistake Yeshua and His followers as early Karaites.

But on closer examination, it becomes clear that the Master had far more affinity with the Pharisees of His day than He did with the Karaites of His day. A careful study of Yeshua and His disciples reveals that they were scrupulously observant, traditional Jews, keeping Jewish customary laws so long as those traditions did not contradict the written commandments of God.[54]

In fact, there were no Karaites in the Master's day. Karaites did not emerge as a formal sect of Judaism until the late Talmudic age (early Middle Ages). One sect of Judaism in the apostolic age, however, closely resembled the Karaites: the Sadducees. The Sadducees were the theological archenemies of the Pharisees. The Sadducees utterly rejected Jewish tradition and traditional interpretation of Scripture. Therefore, they rejected a great deal of Pharisaic theology as well, such as the resurrection of the dead, the afterlife, and reward and punishment in the next world.

Not only were the Sadducees enemies of the Pharisees, they were also enemies of the gospel. They were the sect responsible for the crucifixion, and they were the chief sponsors of persecution of believers throughout the book of Acts. In the courtroom of the Sanhedrin, the Sadducees consistently prosecuted the believers, whereas the Pharisees sided with the believers and championed their rights. When the Pharisee Paul wanted to persecute believers, he found it necessary to betray Pharisaism in order to do it. He defied his teacher Gamliel the Pharisee and crossed party lines in order to obtain permission from the Sadducees.[55] The Sadducean-Karaites of Yeshua's day were the real bad guys of the gospel. To suggest that Yeshua and the apostles were Karaites contradicts the plain reading of the Gospels and Acts.

HYPOCRITES OR DISCIPLES?

Gospel scholars have recently come to the shocking conclusion that not all Pharisees were hypocrites. In fact, the majority of them seemed to be pretty decent fellows! If we remember one simple point regarding the Pharisees, we may avoid the trap of anti-rabbinic sentiment into which so many readers of Matthew 23 have stepped. The simple point is that Yeshua (not to mention His brother James and His apostle Paul) was, for all practical purposes, a Pharisee. His theology, His hermeneutic, His parables, His argumentation, His conclusions and even His dinner invitations were Pharisaic in origin. While we cannot be overly dogmatic that Yeshua was a Pharisee,[56] there is no other sect or form of faith in all of human history with which He shared a closer affinity. He conducted Himself as if He were one.

For example, His method of taking disciples and teaching them orally was a Pharisaic convention. We have already seen how Yeshua's concept of a core of disciples came from the schools of the Pharisees. The fellowship of the twelve disciples is patterned on the Pharisaic model. For all practical purposes, it formed a family.

In first-century Judaism, a disciple's primary job was to learn oral tradition. The sages of Yeshua's day did not write books; they taught disciples. So too with the Master. The disciples of the Pharisees, when fully trained, were charged to raise up disciples of their own. Obviously, the discipleship model of the Gospels is borrowed directly from Pharisaism.

The Pharisees themselves were never far from Yeshua theologically or geographically. He was often a dinner guest in their homes, and they were often critics of His ministry. At times, some Pharisees vehemently opposed Him. On other occasions, they cheered Him on while He thwarted the Sadducees or nailed home a point of Torah.[57] On another occasion, the Pharisees are depicted trying to rescue him from Herod.[58] The fact that the Pharisees considered

Yeshua, followed Him, discussed Torah with Him and hosted Him in their homes suggests that He was virtually a Pharisee.

PAUL THE PHARISEE

If any of the apostolic writers understood the Pharisaic institution of discipleship, it was Paul of Tarsus. Discipled under the famous Pharisaic sage Gamliel, he spent the better part of his life learning the ins and outs of Pharisaic discipleship. Some Bible students might be surprised to learn that Paul never renounced Pharisaism. Instead, near the end of his ministry, he boldly proclaims before the Sanhedrin, "I am a Pharisee, a son of Pharisees" (Acts 23:6). Paul tells King Agrippa II that he "lived as a Pharisee according to the strictest sect of our religion" (Acts 26:5). What's more, he protests to the Jews in Rome that He has done nothing against the "customs of our fathers" (Acts 28:17). "Customs of the fathers" means Pharisaic tradition. This is a clear statement proving loyalty to Jewish tradition.

In his epistles, Paul criticizes the Corinthians for deviating from accepted Jewish tradition. In contemporary Jewish practice of Paul's day, it was traditional for a married woman to indicate that she was married by covering her hair. Uncovered hair indicated an unmarried woman. It is not a commandment of the Torah for a married woman to cover her hair, but it was a widespread Jewish tradition. Paul specifically refers to a woman's head covering[59] as a matter of tradition. He opens the passage saying, "Now I praise you because you remember me in everything, and hold firmly to the traditions, just as I delivered them to you" (1 Corinthians 11:2). Even the Mishnah, an ancient collection of Jewish law and tradition, admits that a woman's head covering is a Jewish tradition and not a commandment of the Torah.

> What is an example of a wife transgressing the Torah of Moses? ... Engaging in relations with him while unclean. ... What is an example of wife transgressing Jewish tradition? Going out with her hair uncovered. (m.*Ketubot* 7:6)

In his second letter to the Thessalonians, Paul warned the believers to stay away from those who had abandoned the oral tradition that he taught and modeled while with them.

In the name of the Master Yeshua the Messiah, we command you, brothers, to keep away from every brother who is idle and does not live according to the teaching you received from us. For you yourselves know how you ought to follow our example. We were not idle when we were with you. (2 Thessalonians 3:6–7 NIV)

YESHUA AND JEWISH TRADITION

Did Yeshua keep Jewish tradition? There is no question that He did. He engaged in practices derived from both the Torah and the oral Torah. He did this deliberately and with intention. For example, before eating, He always blessed God. The written Torah only commands us to bless God after we eat.[60] Only in Pharisaic tradition do we learn to bless God before we eat. At His last Passover *seder*, He poured wine and shared it with His disciples. The Torah, however, says nothing about wine at Passover. Only in Pharisaic tradition do we find the practice of serving cups of wine as one of the elements of the Passover *seder* meal.

The gospel of Luke tells us that Yeshua customarily attended synagogue on Sabbath and read publicly from the Torah.[61] The synagogue, the synagogue prayer service, the public reading and teaching of Scripture—all of which Yeshua was accustomed to—were all standard conventions of Jewish tradition. In John 10, Yeshua celebrates Hanukkah with a trip to the Temple. Yet the Festival of Hanukkah is a traditional celebration, not a biblical one. That Yeshua wore *tzitzit* (fringes) and *teffilin* (phylacteries) is evident from the passage in which He criticizes the Pharisees for making theirs too long and too broad, respectively.[62]

In the same chapter, while lambasting them for neglecting the weighty matters of the Torah, He praises the Pharisees for tithing mint, dill and cumin.[63] Tithing on spices was not a biblical law. It was merely a convention of Pharisaic tradition. Speaking of weighty matters, Yeshua participates in a baptism-immersion ritual that, although based in the rubrics of Torah purity laws, evolved into a broader ritual because of its use in Pharisaic tradition. As *Torah Club Volume Four* demonstrates, the sayings of Yeshua are soaked with Pharisaic teaching. Many of His parables, sayings and teachings are derived directly from Hillel the Pharisee.

Many more examples could be cited that prove that Yeshua lived a life rich with Jewish tradition. Disconnecting Yeshua from the continuum of Pharisaic tradition is impossible.

For the most part, the Master's practice of Jewish tradition is simply assumed by gospel writers. Ordinarily, the gospel writers only make note of instances when Yeshua broke with religious convention. So too the Pharisees criticize Him whenever He breaks with the religious convention—often with regard to Sabbath stringencies. Reading the gospel from our perspective, we only see the points of contention. Read from outside of Judaism, the stories create the false impression that Yeshua was constantly at odds with traditional Judaism. In actuality, there are very few matters of Jewish traditional law He argues against, such as the particulars of Sabbath observance and the necessity for ritual hand washing before eating bread. Had He defied Pharisaic tradition as a whole, the Pharisees would have had far more ammunition against Him.

THE SACRED NAME

Perhaps the best example of the Master's conformance to Jewish tradition is in the matter of the pronunciation of God's name. As a matter of Jewish tradition, the name of God (Y/H/V/H) was never pronounced in the first century. Though biblical heroes like Moses and David employed the name regularly, by the days of the apostles, Jewish tradition had set aside the name of God in order to better keep the commandment of not profaning it. The command not to take the name of the Lord in vain was interpreted to mean that God's name is so holy, so set apart, so sacred, it should never be pronounced casually. By the days of the Master, only the priesthood pronounced God's name during the priestly benediction, and they obscured the pronunciation as they did so in order to protect it from profane use. Only the high priest pronounced it clearly and audibly, and he did so only on the Day of Atonement. As he did, all the worshippers in the Temple prostrated themselves.

The tradition of sanctifying the name by leaving it unpronounced is still honored in Judaism and much of the believing Torah movement today. The name of God is circumlocuted with the Hebrew *HaShem* ("the name") or Adonai ("the Lord").[64] It is never pronounced as YHWH (or Y/H/V/H), and the correct pronunciation has been lost. However, some sects believe that Yeshua and His disciples rejected this tradition and employed the pronounced name of God.

There are many difficulties with this theory that render it an almost absolute impossibility. The text of the Apostolic Scriptures provides evidence that it was not so. Yeshua Himself and all the apostolic writers retained the tradition of sanctifying the name. He taught us to pray using a standard circumlocution, saying, "Our Father who is in heaven, hallowed [sanctified, set apart] be Your name." These are clear instructions on how to address God and how to handle His name.

If Yeshua and His followers did throw off Jewish tradition, why did they continue to sanctify God's name according to the standards of Jewish tradition? In the Bible, we never see Yeshua or any of the apostles use or pronounce the name. Instead they use standard evasive synonyms like Father, Lord, God and Holy Spirit. To pronounce the name is not a violation of a biblical commandment, but it is a violation of a long-standing Jewish tradition practiced and enforced by Yeshua Himself. It would be inappropriate for His disciples to disregard His clear example. After all, a student is not above his teacher, and every disciple fully trained will be like his teacher. If the Teacher always sanctified the name by not pronouncing it, we should do so as well. We are not above our Master.

Evidence from Acts

Yeshua was not a Karaite or a Sadducee. But He commanded His disciples to heed the authority of the Pharisees, a fact attested to by every reliable manuscript of the Gospels:

> The scribes and the Pharisees have seated themselves in the chair of Moses; therefore all that they tell you, do and observe. (Matthew 23:2–3)

The book of Acts is filled with examples of the disciples keeping Pharisaic conventions and Jewish traditions. Acts 1:12 references the Pharisaic interpretation regarding the distance outside a city that a person may walk on the Sabbath. In Acts 9, the believers wash a corpse in keeping with the Pharisaic burial ritual. In Acts 10, Peter is so fixed on keeping the stringent Pharisaic tradition of not entering a Gentile's home or eating a meal prepared by a Gentile that it takes a vision from heaven to make him reconsider. When he does, he faces criticism from the rest of the apostles.

If the apostles weren't keeping Jewish tradition, why would any of those Pharisaic taboos have been a concern for them? In Acts 1:14, the believers are said to be "devoting themselves to the prayers,"[65] and in Acts 3, Peter and John are depicted participating in the daily prayers. The daily prayers arise out of Jewish tradition.

Perhaps most telling is the two Pentecost scenes (Acts 2, 21). The believers are depicted celebrating Pentecost along with the rest of the Jewish majority in the Temple according to the Pharisaic reckoning of the calendar. If the believers were truly eschewing Jewish tradition, why did they retain the Pharisaic calendar reckoning for that festival?[66] Even things as basic as their use of ritual immersion for a symbolic rite of conversion arise from Pharisaic tradition that taught that proselytes must undergo immersion.

THREE PARABLES

In Luke 15, Yeshua tells a parable in which a shepherd leaves a flock of ninety-nine sheep to pursue one lost sheep and return it to the flock. He offers the story as one in a series of three thematically linked parables. They are the parable of the lost sheep, the parable of the lost coin and the parable of the prodigal son.

◊　The Parable of the Lost Sheep　　Luke 15:1–7

◊　The Parable of the Lost Coin　　Luke 15:8–10

◊　The Parable of the Lost Son　　Luke 15:11–32

Each of these three parables is linked by a common story, theme and meaning.

Yeshua tells the three parables of Luke 15 in response to a criticism raised in verses one and two of the chapter. He is criticized by the sages for eating with, associating with and even teaching "tax collectors and sinners." The sages charge that Yeshua is guilty by association. If He eats with sinners and fellowships with sinners and chooses sinners for His disciples, He must be a sinner! This accusation is leveled at the Master several times throughout the Gospels, and it is an understandable point of contention.

Throughout the ministry of the Master, He seemed to aim sharp criticisms at the religious and the faithful while at the same time generously offering warmth, hospitality and gentle teaching to the irreligious and lawless of society. To the religious and observant Jews of the Master's day, it must have seemed as if Yeshua spurned those who strove to live lives according to God's instruction, while He coddled those who lived in open rebellion to God.

The Pharisees were at a loss to explain His seemingly irrational behavior. Here was a man who claimed to be a prophet of God, and more than a prophet, but rather than rebuking the sinners, He rebuked the righteous!

On one occasion, Yeshua attempted to explain His dualistic approach to ministry. When a group of Pharisees criticized Him for eating with tax collectors and sinners, He said, "It is not those who are well who need a physician, but those who are sick. I have not come to call the righteous but sinners to repentance" (Luke 5:31–32). We should not read sarcasm into the Master's words. He genuinely meant what He said. He was less interested in the religious and righteous of Israel because they were already on the path of Torah. He was concerned with the irreligious. He had not come to seek the righteous, but sinners.

This explains why Yeshua was sharply critical of the religious of His day. He regarded them as the healthy and the righteous of Israel. Therefore, He held them to a much higher standard and was quick to point out hypocrisy and pretense. His criticisms, however, were not a rejection of the religious. Rather, they were corrections and rebukes.

On the other hand, when He was among the irreligious, He did not rebuke them as He did the Pharisees and teachers of Torah. The irreligious were outside the domain of Torah. It does no good to rebuke someone for disobeying a law he or she does not believe in. Therefore He sought to first entice people to repent and return to obedience to the Father. He needed to bring them into the kingdom before holding them up to the standards of the kingdom.

But the Pharisees and teachers of the Torah interpreted this behavior as hostility toward themselves and love for lawlessness. Therefore they criticized Him, saying, "He hangs out with bad company."

This is the situation to which the parable triplet of Luke 15 is addressed.

LOST SHEEP, COIN AND SON

Luke 15 begins with just such a conflict. We read, "Now all the tax collectors and the sinners were coming near Him to listen to Him. Both the Pharisees and the scribes began to grumble, saying, 'This man receives sinners and eats with them.'" [67]

Yeshua attempts to explain His mission to seek and save the lost of Israel by retelling the famous story of Moses seeking after the lost sheep. The Master tells the story this way. He says:

> Suppose one of you has a hundred sheep and loses one of them. Does he not leave the ninety-nine in the open country and go after the lost sheep until he finds it? And when he finds it, he joyfully puts it on his shoulders and goes home. Then he calls his friends and neighbors together and says, "Rejoice with me; I have found my lost sheep." I tell you that in the same way there will be more rejoicing in heaven over one sinner who repents than over ninety-nine righteous persons who do not need to repent. (Luke 15:4-6 NIV)

In the parable, the lost sheep of Israel are symbolic for the "sinners and tax collectors." The context makes that obvious. Yeshua is the shepherd like Moses. The ninety-nine remaining sheep are the righteous of Israel who do not need to repent, present company of Pharisees and teachers of the Torah included. Yeshua explains that just as the shepherd leaves the flock in order to pursue and rescue the one lost sheep, so too He leaves the religious and observant in order to pursue and rescue the irreligious and lawless of Israel.

In Luke 15, He tells the parable of the lost coins and then the parable of the prodigal son. The meaning of the three parables is the same. They are explanations of why the Master is engaged in seeking after the lost of Israel.

The prodigal son represents the "sinners and tax collectors." The faithful son represents the observant and religious of Israel. The father who goes to meet the prodigal and then prepares a banquet for him represents Yeshua, who is pursuing the irreligious and lawless of Israel. He tells the parable to caricaturize the bitter attitude harbored by the Pharisees and the teachers of the Torah toward those who are turning to repentance. Indeed, they are jealous just like the loyal son, because the Master seems to disregard them and spend all of His attention on these people of ill repute.

Each of these parables concludes with a scene of rejoicing. If there was any doubt about the meaning of the parables, Yeshua makes the meaning explicit in verse 7, when He says, "I tell you that in the same way there is more rejoicing in heaven over one sinner who repents than over ninety-nine righteous persons who do not need to repent."

SEVEN KINDS OF PHARISEES

How then do we explain the rancor with which Yeshua attacks the Pharisees in the Gospels? His scathing rebukes are best understood as an internal criticism of Pharisaic Judaism. Notice that He never offers similar rebukes to the Sadducees or the Herodians, who were far more wicked than the Pharisees. The matter may be compared to a mother who rebukes her own children with harsh words and an occasional swat on the seat, but turns an indifferent eye to the misdeeds of the neighbor's children. The neighbor's children are of no concern to her. They are not within her purview. It is because Yeshua is so close to the Pharisees in theology and practice that they fall under His immediate concern.

The fact that there were hypocrites among the Pharisees does not discredit their teaching. The writings of the Pharisees freely admit to the presence of rank hypocrisy and pretentiousness among some members of their sect. In his Jewish New Testament commentary, David Stern has compiled and translated a delightful fusion of passages from the Gemara of both Talmuds to illustrate this point. Remember when reading Stern's quotes that these words were written by disciples of the Pharisees themselves:

> There are seven kinds of Pharisees: the "shoulder" Pharisee, who ostentatiously carries his good deeds on his shoulder so all can see them; the "wait-a-moment" Pharisee, who wants you to wait while he performs a mitzvah; the bruised Pharisee, who runs into a wall while looking at the ground to avoid seeing a woman; the "reckoning" Pharisee, who commits a sin, then does a good deed and

balances the one against the other; the "pestle" Pharisee, whose head is bowed in false humility, like a pestle in a mortar; the Pharisee who asks, "What is my duty, so that I may do it?" as if he thought he had fulfilled every obligation already; the Pharisee from fear of the consequences if he doesn't perform the commandments; and the Pharisee from love. (Talmud)[68]

In the words of the Pharisees themselves, seven out of eight Pharisees are of ignoble character. Have the Baptists, Lutherans, Episcopalians, Catholics, Adventists, Messianics or any other sect of our faith ever produced such an honest self-critique? Yes, there were bad Pharisees, and the Master soundly chastised them. But Yeshua's critique of the Pharisees is consistent with their own.

Yeshua was not a Karaite, but neither was He shy about shoving aside Jewish tradition when it stepped on the commandments of God or trod over the backs of human beings. Unlike the Pharisees, He did not allow Jewish tradition to be elevated to the same level as Scripture. He was quick to discard any traditions that contradicted the Word of God. He placed compassion above the stringencies of tradition, and He rebuked hypocrisy and pretense whenever He saw it. But He did all of this from within traditional Judaism and as a part of traditional Judaism. If He were in the flesh among us today, He would look to us like an Orthodox Jew. In fact, He is an Orthodox Jew.

Chapter 6

NONE GREATER THAN JOHN

> Truly I say to you, among those born of women
> there has not arisen anyone greater than John the
> Baptist; yet the one who is least in the kingdom
> of heaven is greater than he. (Matthew 11:11)

When the Gospels are removed from their original context, passages are often obscure and subject to gross misinterpretation. Yet when examined in light of a traditional Jewish reading, difficult passages come alive with new meaning and clarity.

Matthew 11 and its parallel in Luke 7 are fraught with several obscure and difficult sayings. In that passage, the Master discourses regarding His older cousin John the Baptist (John the Immerser) and comments on His relationship with him. The passage raises several questions. Was John losing His faith in Messiah? Why did Yeshua contrast John against a reed blown in the wind? How is the least in the kingdom greater than John? What does it mean that the kingdom suffers violence? Did the Torah end with John? What does flute playing have to do with anything? When read in light of the broader Jewish context, however, the entire passage snaps into focus.

JOHN IN PRISON

Herod Antipas arrested John the Immerser. How did it happen? Herod Antipas, the son of Herod the Great, was tetrarch over the Galilee. Though Herod Antipas enjoyed listening to John,[69] Josephus tells us that Herod perceived John's popularity with the crowds as a threat.[70] John's condemnation of Herod's marriage to his sister-in-law resulted in his arrest. John found himself imprisoned far away from the living waters of the Jordan where he had carried on his ministry. Herod put him in chains in the dungeon of

Macherus, a fortress overlooking the lifeless and poisoned waters of the Dead Sea.

As John sat alone in his prison cell, his voice echoing off the dungeon walls, he may have cried out, "The One coming after me will baptize with fire! His winnowing fork is in His hand, and He will clear the threshing floor, burning up the chaff with unquenchable fire." He may have recalled his own words roaring beside the Jordan, "Repent, the kingdom of heaven is already here!" Perhaps in those quiet moments he may have asked himself, *If the kingdom is already here, why am I in chains?*

When John's disciples came to him, he eagerly plied them for news about Yeshua. "What's happening out there?" he must have asked them. "Is Messiah raising His army? Has He begun His terrible judgment?"

"Not exactly," they could have replied, then related to him the latest news of Yeshua. "The last time we saw Him, He was eating at a big party for tax collectors in Capernaum." John must have wondered what kind of kingdom this was! He possibly mused about what was taking Yeshua so long.

So he sent his disciples to ask Him, "Are You the Expected One, or shall we look for someone else?" (Matthew 11:3). Was John having a moment of doubt about the identity of Yeshua? Could he have questioned the validity of Yeshua's ministry? Surely not. After all, John had seen the heavens open and the dove descend on the Master. He had heard the heavenly voice speak, saying, "This is My beloved Son, in whom I am well-pleased" (Matthew 3:17). John himself testified:

> I have beheld the Spirit descending as a dove out of heaven, and He remained upon Him. And I did not recognize Him, but He who sent me to baptize in water said to me, "He upon whom you see the Spirit descending and remaining upon Him, this is the One who baptizes in the Holy Spirit." And I have seen, and have borne witness that this is the Son of God. (John 1:32–34)

Two Messiahs

If John did not doubt Yeshua's identity, what is the meaning of his question? He asked, "Are You the Expected One, or shall we look for someone else?" The answer may be found in the writings of a small community across the Dead Sea from Macherus. It is the community of Qumran. Among those writings we find references to their belief in the possibility of two different Messiahs. The two messianic figures of the Qumran community are known as the Priestly Messiah (possibly called the Teacher of Righteousness) and the Davidic Messiah. It is probable that the Qumran community influenced John's theology.

The two-Messiah theory was not limited to Qumran. Although we don't know how old the concept is, a firmly rooted belief is expressed in later rabbinic literature that there would be two Messiahs. The first Messiah is the suffering Messiah who suffers for Israel's sins and eventually dies while fighting for Israel's redemption. He comes as a fulfillment of those prophecies that point to a Messiah of enduring pain and sorrow. "Man of sorrows"—what a name! In rabbinic literature, He is called "Messiah ben (son of) Joseph" because His mission of affliction is compared with the weeping character of Joseph, who underwent rejection, trial and pain to save his brothers.

In rabbinic literature, the second Messiah is called "Messiah ben (son of) David." He is the ruling, kingly Messiah who will complete the redemption begun by Messiah ben Joseph. He comes as a fulfillment of those prophecies that point to a Messiah of victory and salvation. He will avenge Messiah son of Joseph's death and, in some legends, even resurrect him from the dead.[71]

We cannot say with any certainty that John knew this type of eschatology or had developed these kinds of ideas, but it seems likely that the possibility of two different Messiahs had occurred to him. What if Yeshua was the suffering-servant Messiah son of Joseph? What if the kingdom had not begun yet? What if the kingly Messiah son of David was yet to arrive? What if this was not the end of the world, but only the beginning of the end? John sent his disciples to inquire of Yeshua, "Are you the Expected One (that is, Messiah ben David), or shall we look for someone else?" Are you the only one, or should we expect another?

GO AND REPORT WHAT YOU SEE

We often miss a great deal of what the Gospels attempt to communicate because we are unfamiliar with the conventions of first-century Judaism. Yeshua's response to John's query is a good example of this. In the first century there were no printing presses, and copies of the Scriptures were extremely rare and valuable. Only a very wealthy family would have possessed even a single scroll of one of the books of the Bible. Most often, whole communities would pool their resources to produce copies of the Scriptures. These community scrolls would be kept in the local synagogue. They were neither convenient to access nor portable. Thus the primary education of Jewish children was the word-for-word memorization of the Scriptures. At age five, Jewish children began to memorize.

The memorization of large passages of the Scriptures (even whole books of Scripture) resulted in a highly developed mode of communication for religious Jews. They were able to reference a particular passage or prophecy by citing only a few key words. It is a methodology well attested to in the argumentation and teaching of rabbinic literature.

Thus, when Yeshua tells John's disciples to report to John that "the blind receive sight and the lame walk, the lepers are cleansed and the deaf hear, the dead are raised up, and the poor have the gospel preached to them" (Matthew 11:5), He is citing at least two important passages about the advent of the kingdom of heaven from the book of Isaiah. John would have known these passages well.

Let's look at those passages as John recites them in the darkness of the Macherus dungeon and muses over the meaning of Yeshua's cryptic response to his question.

> Encourage the exhausted, and strengthen the feeble. Say to those with anxious heart, "Take courage, fear not. Behold, your God will come with vengeance; the recompense of God will come, but He will save you." Then the eyes of the blind will be opened and the ears of the deaf will be unstopped. Then the lame will leap like a deer, and the tongue of the mute will shout for joy. For waters will break forth in the wilderness and streams in the Arabah. The scorched land will become a pool and the thirsty ground springs of water; in the haunt of jackals, its resting place, grass becomes reeds and rushes. (Isaiah 35:3–7)

As John sat enchained within Macherus, prisoner in a land of hot burning sands beside the lifeless waters of the Dead Sea, these words of Isaiah were words of hope and affirmation. Streams in the desert. The burning sand becoming a pool. The thirsty ground bubbling springs. Living water in a dead land.

In his rabbinic commentary on the New Testament, Jewish New Testament scholar Tobias Lachs quotes a passage from midrash that quotes this passage of Isaiah to prove that healing the infirm is one of the signs of Messiah:

> Not only this but all who suffer affliction will be cured in the world-to-come ... as it is written, "Then will the lame leap like a deer" (vs. 6) and "then will the eyes of the blind be opened (vs. 4)." (*Tanchuma Metzorah* 7 [24a])

The Master's answer to John's disciples contains explicit references to a second passage from Isaiah.

> The Spirit of the Lord God is upon me, because the Lord has anointed me to bring good news to the afflicted; He has sent me to bind up the brokenhearted, to proclaim liberty to captives and freedom to prisoners; to proclaim the favorable year of the Lord and the day of vengeance of our God; to comfort all who mourn. (Isaiah 61:1–2)

Liberty for captives and freedom for prisoners; Isaiah's words must have sounded very hopeful indeed to John as he sat in the darkness of the Macherus dungeon. But if Messiah was about to initiate the day of vengeance and the release of captives and the final judgment, what did He mean by His obscure postscript, "blessed is he who keeps from stumbling over Me?" (Matthew 11:6).

Yeshua must have known that in His cousin John's case there would be no "liberty to captives" or "freedom to prisoners." His allusions to Isaiah coupled with His word of caution in Matthew 11:6 seem to convey the cumulative message, "Yes, I am the One who was to come. Don't let your disappointment break your faith." The kingdom had indeed arrived, but it was not the final apocalyptic event that John had anticipated ... not yet at least.

A Bent Reed

As John's disciples leave to bring back Yeshua's message, He asks the crowd rhetorically, "What did you go out into the wilderness to see? A reed shaken by the wind?" (Matthew 11:7). In the Talmud, the sages warn against obstinacy and pride, saying that a man should endeavor to bend like a reed:

> Our Rabbis have taught: A man should always be gentle as the reed and never unyielding as the cedar. (b. *Taanit* 20a)

Yeshua used the same metaphor to teach the reverse of that principal. A man should not bend under the pressure to compromise God's Torah. Jewish New Testament scholar David Flusser explains Yeshua's obscure question as reference to the popular fable of "The Oak and the Reed." In that fable, everyone expects that the mighty oak is stronger than the tiny, frail reed, but the oak is broken off:

> Which is more powerful, the reed or the oak? The first response is the majestic oak. But in a storm with violent gusts, the oak is broken while the reed is merely shaken. In such a storm, the flexible reed proves stronger than the mighty oak.[72]

In matters of Torah, John was no flexible reed. The smart thing for John to do would have been to bend like a reed and look the other way, ignoring Herod's immoral marriage. But like a rigid oak tree, he would not bend under the political pressure. Thus he was broken down by the wind. John was not a reed bending in the wind, nor was he a politician wearing fine clothes in kings' palaces. John was a prophet—a real prophet!

Yeshua tells them that John is the one "about whom it is written: 'Behold, I will send my messenger before your face, who will prepare Your way before You'" (Matthew 11:10). The Master quotes Malachi 3:1, an explicit reference to the anticipated coming of Elijah to proclaim the messianic advent.

Among Those Born of Women

Yeshua goes on to say:

> Among those born of women there has not arisen *anyone* greater than John the Immerser! Yet he who is least in the kingdom of heaven is greater than he. (Matthew 11:11, emphasis mine)

Traditional Christian thought has taken this to be evidence of two dispensations. That is, the Old Testament dispensation of law ends with John (who was the greatest of that dispensation), but a believer in the New Testament dispensation of grace is greater than even John. The short way of saying this is simply, "Even the worst Christian is better than the best Jew." This is a deeply misguided interpretation.

Does the Master mean to imply that John is not in the kingdom of heaven? Obviously not. Rather His words are typical of His reversal-of-expectation style. His concern is with the least, the poor in spirit, the brokenhearted and the meek. John is the greatest of all human beings, He says, but greatness in the kingdom is not measured by human standards. Who, then, is the greatest in the kingdom? The children, or those with a childlike spirit.[73]

There is another possibility, however, that merits some thought. The Greek word translated as "the least" in Luke 7:28 is comparative in form ("the littler").[74] As the gospel story has thus far progressed, John has been clearly portrayed as the forerunner, the older cousin who proclaims the message of the kingdom before Yeshua's ministry begins. Yeshua comes after John, and in regards to His fame and general acceptance with the people, He was at that time still second to John. Thus the term "the littler" could well be meant to refer to Himself. If so, it would parallel John's statements about Yeshua. Consider the following possible translation.

> I tell you, among those born of women there is no one greater than John; yet the one who is younger in the [proclamation of the] kingdom of God is greater than he. (Luke 7:28, my translation)

This would parallel John's own words, "He who is coming after me is mightier than I" (Matthew 3:11; Luke 3:16). Might Yeshua have been referring to this well-known saying of the Immerser and subtly be telling the crowd that He Himself was the one who comes after John? He certainly had come to be regarded as the one carrying on John's ministry and message of the kingdom, so much so that after the Immerser's death, He was mistaken for a resurrected John. Even in the annunciations, the birth narratives and the ministry descriptions, the gospel writers always introduce Yeshua second to John. John is the forerunner who prepares the way. Thus Yeshua refers to Himself as "the lesser" in the kingdom of heaven because He came second and carries on the work John began. In actuality, however, this seemingly "lesser" in the kingdom is infinitely greater than John.

Some will find this interpretation difficult to accept. The difficulty stems from our reluctance to allow Yeshua to refer to Himself as "the lesser in the kingdom" or as "the least in the kingdom." Such self-abasement, however, is consistent with His teaching. He came to serve. He came humbly, as a servant. The great reversal of expectation is that He (who appears to be the lesser) is actually the greater, even the greatest.

THE KINGDOM SUFFERS VIOLENCE

The Master goes on to say:

> From the days of John the Baptist until now the kingdom
> of heaven suffers violence, and violent men take it by
> force. (Matthew 11:12)

Prior to Dr. David Flusser's outstanding research, Yeshua's words regarding the kingdom suffering violence and the violent taking it by force seemed enigmatic at best and dangerous at worst. Those words have been used to justify militant Christianity and the slaughter of innocents in the name of the gospel. If we try to understand them as our English translations render them, they contradict Yeshua's previous statements about the meek, the humble, the peacemakers and the persecuted inheriting the kingdom.

In his book *Jesus, Rabbi and Lord*, Robert Lindsey suggests that the Greek word *biazetai*, translated as "suffers violence" in Matthew 11:12, might have originally been the Hebrew *poretz* (פרץ). *Poretz* means "breach-maker." Dr. Flusser made the connection between the term *poretz* and Micah 2:12–13:[75]

> I will surely assemble all of you, Jacob, I will surely gather
> the remnant of Israel. I will put them together like sheep

in the fold; like a flock in the midst of its pasture they will be noisy with men. The breaker (*poretz*) goes up before them; they break out (*partzu*), pass through the gate and go out by it. So their king goes on before them, and the Lord at their head. (Micah 2:12–13)

In Micah's metaphor, the breaker (*poretz*) is a shepherd. The remnant of Israel is compared to sheep penned up in a sheepfold for the night. The sheepfold, typical of Judean shepherding (as practiced by the Bedouin even today), is constructed by making a low rock fence along a cliff wall or hillside. The pen is crowded because of the multitude of sheep. In the morning the shepherd uses his staff to break down some of the rocks to make an opening for the sheep to come out. As the sheep pour forth from the sheep pen to follow the shepherd, they continue to dislodge the rocks and break the opening wider and wider, thus literally breaking through to follow the shepherd. In rabbinic literature, this Micah passage is traditionally associated with the coming of Messiah.[76]

Flusser cites a midrash from Radak that interprets the *poretz* of this passage to be Elijah, who opens the way for the shepherd-king Messiah to lead the flock. When we employ the midrashic values of Micah 2:12–13 to interpret Matthew 11:12–13, the passage leaps to life. Yeshua is not sanctioning violence as a means of advancing the kingdom; rather, He is comparing John to the prophet Elijah, who breaks open the gate in the sheepfold, and the kingdom to the sheep breaking out of the sheepfold.

The kingdom of heaven	the sheep pen
Suffers violence	is being broken open [by John the breaker]
The violent men	those pushing their way into it
Take it by force	burst through [the opening] into it

SINGULAR MEANING: Ever since John began his ministry, people have been pouring into the kingdom.

Yeshua's listeners would have been familiar with the terminology. They probably would have understood the *poretz* as a messianic reference or a reference to Elijah. Yeshua adds, "And if you care to accept it, John himself is Elijah who was to come" (Matthew 11:14).

PROPHESIED UNTIL JOHN

Yeshua goes on to say, "For all the prophets and the Torah prophesied until John" (Matthew 11:13). John, He tells them, is the culmination point of all the prophets because he is the one who prepares the way for Messiah. Thus all the prophecies (about the coming of Messiah) pointed to the age of John: the beginning of the days of the Messiah. John the Immerser is the culmination point because he is the last prophet before that day. He comes as the promised Elijah-character to herald the advent of Messiah.

Yeshua says, "For all the prophets and the Torah prophesied until John." The meaning of His words is made clearer by comparing them with a parallel statement in the Talmud:

> Rabbi Hiyya bar Abba said in the name of Rabbi Yochanan: "All the prophets prophesied only for the Days of Messiah; but as for the World to Come 'no eye has seen [O God, what he has prepared] on behalf of those who wait for him.'" (*Sanhedrin* 99a, citing Isaiah 64:4)

Read in a Semitic sense, the word *until* in the passage would most likely be the Hebrew preposition *ad* (עד), which also carries with it the sense of having an end point in mind. Thus John and all the other prophets prophesied with the goal of Yeshua in mind. For example, in Psalm 110:1 the Davidic King is told, "Sit at my right hand until (*ad*) I make your enemies a footstool for your feet." Here the word "until" must mean, "Sit at my right hand until (*ad*) with a view to the time when I make your enemies a footstool for your feet." The *until* does not mark the end of the Davidic King's sitting at God's right hand, but merely a goal of his sitting there.[77]

WE PLAYED A FLUTE FOR YOU

Both John and Yeshua came preaching the same message: "Repent, because the kingdom of heaven is now." Yeshua compared the last generation before the destruction of the Temple to children sitting in the marketplace, saying, "We played the flute for you, and you did not dance; we sang a dirge, and you did not mourn" (Matthew 11:17). What does that mean?

New Testament scholar Dr. David Flusser's sharp insight into the words of the Master unravels this otherwise obscure saying. Brad Young draws on Flusser's work to relate the old fable of "The Fisherman with the Flute."

The fisherman invites some fish to hear the tune of his flute and dance. But when the fisherman plays, the fish refuse to dance. After they are caught in the net, the fish dance as they squirm this way and that without hearing the fisherman's tune. "Dance now without any music," the fisherman tells the fish. "It would have been better for you to have danced some time ago when I was supplying music for the dance." The saying of Jesus is an echo of this fable, which was widely circulated.[78]

This children's story was perhaps proverbial on the lips of children. The fish ignore the fisherman's music and will not dance. In the same way the generation has ignored the warnings of John and Yeshua. John played a dirge: "Judgment is about to begin!" Yeshua's flute was His ministry of healing and miracles performed among them. The generation ignored both flute and dirge. Yeshua warns them, "It would have been better for you to have repented some time ago when John and I were telling you to repent." He makes this explicit as He denounces Korazin, Bethsaida and Capernaum for ignoring the calls to repentance.

EATING WITH THE MASTER

The Master's comments on John the Immerser continue in Luke 7. John came as a stern prophet, practicing extreme asceticism; Yeshua came as a man of the common people, eating and drinking. Yet neither John nor Yeshua were heeded:

> For John the Baptist has come eating no bread and drinking no wine; and you say, "He has a demon!" The Son of Man has come eating and drinking; and you say, "Behold, a gluttonous man, and a drunkard, a friend of tax collectors and sinners!" Yet wisdom is vindicated by all her children. (Luke 7:33–35)

Apparently, Yeshua's critics labeled Him as a drunkard and a glutton. The situation is reminiscent of the situation in Luke 5 where the disciples of the Pharisees and the disciples of Yochanon the Immerser criticized Him and His disciples for not fasting. Quite the opposite of fasting, they were enjoying a sumptuous feast with ample food and drink at Mattityahu Levi the tax collector's home. Occasional attendance at a banquet certainly does not make one a glutton and drunkard, but Luke does reveal that Yeshua seemed to enjoy eating and drinking. He depicts Him eating often.

Obviously, to Yeshua, eating and drinking were more than just necessary biological functions. He delighted in sharing a meal with others. The *Jerusalem Talmud* says, "A man will have to give an account on the judgment day of every good and permissible thing which he might have enjoyed and did not" (y.*Kiddushin* 66d). The *Babylonian Talmud* records the opinion of Rav Shmuel: "Whosoever fasts [merely for the sake of self-affliction] is called a sinner" (b.*Taanit* 11a).

WISDOM AND HER CHILDREN

The Master concludes His discourse on John the Immerser by saying, "Yet wisdom is vindicated by all her children" (Luke 7:35). In Hebrew the word *wisdom* is not always a good thing. Bivin and Blizzard point out that unlike the English language, where wisdom always has a positive connotation, the Hebrew *chachmah* (חכמה) might be used in either a positive or negative sense. For example, the best wisdom of a fool is still foolishness. *Chachmah* in Hebrew is similar to our word *philosophy*. It is the "wisdom" of His critics that Yeshua is criticizing in this passage.

Bivin and Blizzard explain that when Yeshua says, "Wisdom is vindicated by all her children," (Luke 7:35) He is saying simply and clearly in Hebrew idiom, "You can tell whether wisdom is real wisdom or stupidity by the consistency or inconsistency of its arguments. Since your arguments are so inconsistent, it is a clear indication of your stupidity."[79]

The context for the remark is in regard to the criticisms lodged at Yeshua and John the Immerser. John lived a life of austere asceticism and the "wisdom" of the generation accused Him of having a demon because of it. Yeshua Himself rejected asceticism, and the "wisdom" of the generation accused Him of being a glutton and a drunkard. Yeshua points to the obvious contradiction of such "wisdom."

Wisdom is proved right or wrong by her children, and the contradictory nature of these two examples prove the wisdom of the generation wrong. The conclusions reached by their wisdom constitute the children of their wisdom, and since the conclusions are contradictory, the wisdom is proven to be folly.

In the end, it turns out that the obscure and difficult sayings of Matthew 11 and Luke 7 regarding John and Yeshua and their relationship with each other are far less difficult and obscure when read in light of their traditional and historical Jewish context.

Chapter 7

THE VILLAIN
WHO WOULD BE KING

Now it took place in the days of Herod Antipas, the
Herod Antipas who reigned from Galilee to Perea,
in those days as the king sat on his royal throne
which was in Tiberius, in the thirtieth year of his
reign he gave a banquet. (Esther 1:1–3—sort of)

The apple does not fall far from the tree. Just as King Herod the
Great tried to kill the infant Yeshua, his son Herod Antipas set
his sights on killing the Master.

Herod Antipas wanted to be king of the Jews like his father had
been, but in reality he was only a lowly tetrarch. A man hoping to
be regarded by the Jewish people as king could not afford to let a
legitimate Son of David rise to power.

His father, King Herod the Great, died shortly after his infamous slaughter of the Bethlehem innocents. His kingdom was
divided between three of his sons. Herod Archelaus and Herod
Antipas were the sons of his Samaritan wife. To Archelaus he gave
Judah and Jerusalem. To Antipas he gave Galilee and Perea (the
land east of the Jordan). His third heir, Herod Philip, received territories to the northeast, which included the tribal holdings of Dan
in the region of Caesarea Philippi and Mount Hermon.

Archelaus was deposed by Rome shortly after coming to power.
He was replaced by a Roman procurator, and his territory of Judea
was made into a Roman province. His brother Antipas continued
as the tetrarch over the Galilee and Perea into the days of the Master's ministry. The sordid tale of his family affairs, the tragic story
of his execution of John the Immerser and his ultimate encounter

with the real King of the Jews forms much of the backdrop against which the Gospels are set.

"HEROD WANTS TO KILL YOU"

Even when he is not expressly mentioned, Herod Antipas is lurking behind the scenes of the Gospels. His arrest of John the Immerser was the event that signaled the beginning of the Master's ministry in Galilee.[80] Galilee was Herod Antipas's territory. He ruled from his palace in Tiberias, a Galilean city of his own making. The city was built just ten years before the events described in the Gospels. Antipas named it after Emperor Tiberius as part of his continuing campaign to curry favor from Rome and be declared king like his father had been before him.

The site he chose to build on was a rocky projection above the western shore of the Sea of Galilee not far from some natural hot springs. Yeshua based His ministry out of the nearby fishing village of Capernaum. Though Tiberias was a major metropolitan center not more than twelve miles down the shore from Capernaum, Yeshua and His disciples never set foot in Tiberias. There was good reason to avoid it—the site Herod Antipas chose to build on was a Jewish cemetery. Antipas disregarded the Torah mandates regarding clean and unclean, disregarded the sanctity of the tombs there, and built right over the top of them. Any traditionally observant Jew entering the city would have been ritually defiled and been required to undergo purification with the ashes of a red heifer.[81] Like other traditional Jews of their day, Yeshua and His disciples avoided Tiberias.

The Master's general policy of keeping His identity concealed, His frequent admonitions to those He healed to "tell no one," His occasional tactical retreats to Phoenicia, Caesarea-Philippi and the Decapolis, and His reluctance to assemble large crowds can all be attributed to the watchful, nearby presence of Herod Antipas. The Master was none too eager to meet him, but Antipas wanted very much to meet Yeshua. In Luke 13:31, some of Yeshua's allies from among the Pharisees warn Him, "Go away and depart from here, for Herod wants to kill You." It was not a vain threat. Herod Antipas had already offed the head of John the Immerser. In fact, Mark tells us that Herod Antipas was fearful of Yeshua because he at first thought the young, charismatic miracle worker might be John the Immerser raised from the dead.[82]

HEROD AND JOHN

Herod Antipas had put John the Immerser to death. How did it happen?

Mark tells us that Herod Antipas liked to listen to John.[83] Apparently, Antipas enjoyed a good sermon. But John's preaching had been making him nervous. The constant political and religious unrest among the Galileans made the possibility of revolution an ever-present danger. Antipas knew that as the local Roman puppet ruler, he would be the first target of any popular uprising. It seemed to him that the ministry of John the Immerser might be the flash point of such an uprising.

Josephus tells us about the political threat John's ministry presented to Herod Antipas.

> When the crowds grew around John, because they were aroused to the highest degree by his sermons, Herod became alarmed. Eloquence that had so great an effect on mankind might lead to some form of sedition, for it looked as if they would be guided by John in everything they did. Herod decided therefore that it would be much better to strike first and be rid of him before his work led to an uprising. (Josephus, *Antiquities*, 18.5.2)

Herod Antipas had been watching John carefully, looking for a reason to arrest him. John provided the reason by offending Herod's new wife.

YOUR BROTHER'S WIFE

Herod Antipas had originally married a Nabatean princess. The Nabateans were an industrious people who had settled in the ancient territories of Edom. The amazing canyon city of Petra was one of their cities. Antipas' marriage to the daughter of Aretas IV, the Nabatean king, is an example of the political marriages common among monarchs. King Aretas ruled over the broad territory referred to at the time as Arabia. Politically, it was an excellent move for the lowly tetrarch.

Herod Antipas and the Nabatean princess were married many years and might have lived happily ever after had not Antipas made a trip to Rome, where he lodged with his stepbrother Herod Philip. (Note that this was a different Herod Philip from the one mentioned above.) While staying in Philip's house in Rome, Antipas was introduced to Philip's wife Herodias and their teenage daughter, Salome (*Shulamit*). Shulamit is a feminine form of *shalom*, so in English, we would translate her name as "Peace."

Doubtless, both Herodius and Salome were beautiful. Antipas fell madly in love with the mother and maybe a little bit with the daughter as well. While a guest in his brother's house, he found himself coveting his brother's wife. Herodius was both his sister-in-law and his niece. She was the niece of her husband Philip and of her guest Antipas because she was the daughter of Aristobulus (another of the sons of Herod who had not survived their father's paranoia). Thus she would have been the sister of Herod Agrippa, who appears in the book of Acts.

The Herod family's egocentric and limited nomenclature is evident in that almost all of the sons received the first name of Herod, and even this unfortunate woman is stuck with the feminine form: Herodius.

I imagine Herod suggested to her, "Wouldn't you rather be married to a king?" Of course, he was just a tetrarch, but he fancied himself a king.

Herod Antipas promised Herodius that he would divorce his wife if she would leave her husband (his stepbrother), travel to Galilee and marry him. Herodius liked the idea of being called "Queen Herodius." She agreed to the plan.

Antipas returned to his palace in Galilee to await the arrival of his new wife-to-be. But before his dastardly plan was even set in motion, the Nabatean princess, his current wife, heard about the scheme. She was not pleased with the new arrangements. Without telling him that she knew of his intentions to divorce her and marry another, she fled to the fortress Macherus by the Dead Sea.

Macherus was an imposing Hasmonean-era fortress that had been rebuilt and fortified by Herod the Great. He installed an elaborate palace. When the Jewish Revolt broke out in 66 CE, zealots took over the site and held it until 72 CE. But in the days of Herod Antipas, it was a useful garrison with royal accommodations.

Herod's Nabatean wife took refuge at Macherus. From there she sent word to her father, King Aretas. He dispatched his army to rescue her and brought her back to his territory.

That wasn't how Antipas had hoped things would work out, but he married Herodius all the same. His new bride brought her teenage daughter, Salome, along with her.

FEMME FATALE

John the Immerser declared the marriage invalid by Torah. "It is not lawful for you to have your brother's wife" (Mark 6:18), he announced to Antipas. Josephus agrees with John's assessment of the Herod/Herodius union. As a commentary on the morality of the situation he wrote:

> Herodius took it upon her to confound the laws of our country, and divorced herself from her husband while he was alive, and was married to Herod Antipas, her husband's brother by the father's side. (Josephus, *Antiquities*, 18.5.4)

This may be the situation Yeshua had in mind when He said, "Whoever divorces his wife [in order to marry] another woman commits adultery against her; and if she herself divorces her husband [in order to marry] another man, she is committing adultery" (Mark 10:11–12).[84] John's condemnation of the marriage was probably more direct. He undoubtedly quoted Leviticus 18:16, "You shall not uncover the nakedness of your brother's wife; it is your brother's nakedness." Thus, as he rebuked Herod Antipas, he declared, "It is not lawful for you to have your brother's wife." Indeed, it was a transgression of the Torah.

Herod Antipas probably found the famous preacher's stinging rebuke irksome. But when Herodius heard what John had said, she was furious. She demanded that Antipas have him arrested. Antipas was already looking for a pretense on which to arrest the popular prophet. He readily complied with his bride's wishes and had John brought in chains to the fortress Macherus by the Dead Sea, the same fortress to which his previous wife had fled.

John languished in the dungeons of Macherus for a long time. Herod Antipas probably did not intend to kill him. To do so would have been an invitation for civil unrest and criticism. Besides, Mark tells us that Antipas respected John, "for Herod was afraid of John, knowing that he was a righteous and holy man, and kept him safe" (Mark 6:20).

His new wife, Herodius, on the other hand, had every intention of seeing John dead. The motivation behind her unbridled hatred is patently obvious. John's condemnation of her marriage had branded her an adulteress. But besides her personal embarrassment over the situation, John's rebuke devastated her dreams of being a queen. She had hoped her husband would be elevated to the station of king over Judea, Galilee and Perea. She was hoping he would be the next Herod the Great and that she would be the mother of a new line of kings over Israel. Due to John's preaching, any children they bore for the throne of Judea would be regarded as *mumzer* (ממזר, illegitimate). There was no hope for her children to be accepted as monarchs as long as they were regarded as *mumzers*. John had ruined her public image and destroyed her aspirations to be a queen spawning a dynasty of Jewish kings.

Despite his new wife's insistence, Herod Antipas refused to have John executed. Instead, he chose to imprison John in the faraway fortress of Macherus, probably in order to protect him from any assassination attempts by his lovely wife.

Big Party in Tiberias

When Herod Antipas's birthday came, he threw a big party and invited all his high officials to his palace in Tiberias. Undoubtedly he was anxious to show off his beautiful new wife and teenage stepdaughter. As part of the entertainment, Herod Antipas's new stepdaughter danced for him and his officials. Salome's seductive dance moves so agitated her stepfather that he rashly swore to give her anything she asked, even up to half his kingdom. It was a generous offer. She might have done very well for herself. Instead she asked her mother to advise her. Herodius had only one thing in mind. There was nothing she wanted more than John's head.

Salome returned and requested the head of John on behalf of her mother. Antipas was reluctant to comply but felt compelled to because of the presence of his dinner guests.

Josephus tells us that Salome applied her feminine wiles to another of her great-uncles. She was eventually married to the much older Herod Philip, the tetrarch over Banaeus.

The Megillah of Esther and the Death of John

There is a connection between the gospel story of King Herod Antipas' birthday party and the story of Esther. As the gospel of Mark tells us the sad tale of the unfortunate demise of John the Immerser, several allusions to the *Megillah* (scroll) of Esther should bring the *Purim* story to our minds. The two stories share several fascinating parallels that the gospel writer wants us to recognize.

Both stories begin with a large party. Herod invites "his lords and military commanders and the leading men of Galilee" (Mark 6:21). Ahasuerus (often translated Xerxes) invites "all his princes and attendants, the army officers of Persia and Media, the nobles, and the princes of his provinces" (Esther 1:3). Both Herod and Ahasuerus are frustrated would-be kings. According to the *Midrash Rabbah*,[85] Ahasuerus wanted to sit on the throne of Solomon but was not able to because he was not of Davidic descendant. The same is true of Herod. All his aspirations to be declared King of the Jews by Tiberius Caesar were disappointed. Like his father King Herod, his claim to the throne was illegitimate in that he was neither of the line of David nor a true Jew.

Both stories involve a trophy wife. Ahasuerus requests his wife Vashti to be brought before him "with her royal crown in order to display her beauty to the people and the princes, for she was beautiful" (Esther 1:11). At his birthday party, Herod was showing off his new wife as well. Both stories have a bawdy dance. In the traditional midrashic telling of the story of Esther, Vashti is requested to appear before the officials wearing her crown ... and nothing else! Hence her refusal. In the story of Herod's birthday, his stepdaughter danced to please the dinner guests. (One can imagine.) Both stories have a fabulous offer. In the story of Esther, Ahasuerus offers Queen Esther, "Even up to half the kingdom" (Esther 5:3). In the Gospels, Herod Agrippa makes the identical offer to his teenage stepdaughter Salome. Herod's party ends on a sour note when his wife requests the head of John on a platter. Ahasuerus's party ends on a sour note when the head of Vashti is brought to him on a platter.

> He said to him, "Your Highness, but say the word and I will put Vashti's head on a platter. ... [The king] gave the order and they brought in her head on a platter. (*Esther Rabbah* 4:9, 11)

Through these allusions, the writer of the gospel of Mark probably wants us to take confidence in the sovereign hand of God even as he tells his sad and sordid tale. Just as God used the debauchery of one king's drinking party to work salvation for the Jewish people, so too He used the death of John the Immerser to prepare the way for Messiah.

The Tomb by the Sea

The narrative of Mark 6 sounds as if John's execution was immediate and his head was brought in on the day of the party. If the party was in Tiberias, however, and John was still being held in Macherus, several days would have been necessary for the execution orders to arrive at the Dead Sea fortress and for the head to be returned to Galilee. Roman-style parties (like those of the Persian kings) lasted for days. It may have been as many as six or seven days later—as the revelries continued—that the gruesome token arrived for display.

When John's disciples heard about his execution, they retrieved his body and buried him in a tomb.[86] We can imagine the somber scene as the Immerser's body is laid in a cave tomb among the lifeless, barren cliffs of the Dead Sea. We can hear his disciples weeping the *Kaddish* (the traditional mourner's prayer) over their teacher's body. *"Yitgadal v'yitkadash sh'mei rabbah!"* they cry to heaven. "Exalted and sanctified be Your great name!"

The Punishment of Herod

According to Josephus, Herod Antipas was right to be nervous about killing John. Punishment followed quickly. His ex-father-in-law, Aretas of the Nabateans, raised up an army to punish Herod Antipas for cheating on his daughter. Aretas had some territorial disputes to settle as well, but avenging his daughter's honor was at the forefront of the battle. Herod Antipas sent out his entire army to answer the challenge. Several of his mercenaries (borrowed from Herod Philip the Tetrarch), however, betrayed him and joined the forces of Aretas. As a result of their treachery, Herod Antipas's entire army was wiped out. He was humiliated and had to appeal to Tiberius Caesar, like a child tattling to his mother when thrashed by a neighborhood bully. Regarding the ignominious defeat of Herod Antipas's army, Josephus relates the following:

Now some of the Jews thought that the destruction of Herod's army came from God, and very justly, as a punishment of what he did against John, that was called the Baptist: for Herod killed him, who was a good man. (Josephus, *Antiquities*, 18.5.2)

In his martyrdom, death and burial, John finished his job as forerunner of the Messiah. Yeshua was soon to follow.

HEROD THE FOX

Yeshua spent the years of His ministry dodging Herod Antipas. When crowds of followers grew to dangerous sizes, He would slip away before attracting the attention of Antipas's authorities. As the prominent members of the Pharisaic party began to galvanize their position against Yeshua, they "began taking counsel with the Herodians against Him, as to how they might destroy Him" (Mark 3:6). The Pharisees who remained loyal to Yeshua warned Him of the danger. "Go away and depart from here, for Herod wants to kill You" (Luke 13:31).

Yeshua responded cavalierly, "Go and tell that fox, 'Behold, I cast out demons and perform cures today and tomorrow, and the third day I reach My goal' ... for it cannot be that a prophet should perish outside of Jerusalem" (Luke 13:33–34). The Master was saying that He would not be arrested in Galilee because He knew His suffering would be in Jerusalem. But why did He refer to Herod Antipas as a fox?

In English proverbs, we often use the fox as an example of a clever schemer. He is metaphoric for intelligence and craftiness. Not so in Yeshua's time. By calling him a fox, Yeshua was probably referring to a rabbinic proverb that says, "When the fox is in his hour, bow down to it."[87] The proverb has the same effect as the English proverb, "Every dog has his day." In other words, Herod may be a fox being honored for a day, but he is still just a fox, hardly worthy of respect. In another place in the Talmud, we are told that the "scratch of a fox's claw is of no consequence";[88] so too Herod Antipas' threats are of little concern to Yeshua. He knows His destiny lies in Jerusalem. When He arrived in Jerusalem, He found Himself standing before Herod after all.

THE WOULD-BE KING MEETS THE REAL KING

Luke records for us an important encounter between Yeshua and Herod Antipas on the day of the crucifixion. It is important for its symbolic meaning. Herod is the would-be king of the Jews. Yeshua is the true King.

Shortly after questioning Yeshua, Pilate sent Him off to face Herod. Herod would have been in Jerusalem for the Passover to do his "duty" as a Jew (even though he wasn't Jewish by pedigree) and celebrate a *seder*. Luke tells us that prior to this incident, there was considerable tension between Herod and Pilate. "They had been enemies," Luke says (23:12). Their enmity may have stemmed from the incident reported in Luke 13:1 where Yeshua was told about "the Galileans whose blood Pilate had mixed with their sacrifices." Those Galileans were citizens under Herod Antipas' domain and jurisdiction. By rights they should have been sent to Herod Antipas to be dealt with, not butchered in the Temple. Pilate's indiscriminate slaughter of Herod's citizens was an affront to Herod's authority. Herod Antipas probably shed no tears over the death of those Galileans, but we can be sure he was angered by Pilate's impudence.

When Pilate heard that Yeshua was a Galilean, he saw an opportunity to be rid of the whole troublesome affair and to win some affection with Herod Antipas at the same time. By sending Yeshua to Herod Antipas, he was in essence acknowledging Herod's jurisdiction. It was a diplomatic gesture, even an apology for over-stepping his bounds. Yeshua became a token Galilean.

Luke tells us that Herod Antipas was greatly pleased to see Yeshua. "He had wanted to see Him for a long time, because he had been hearing about Him and was hoping to see some sign performed by Him" (Luke 23:8).

Herod Antipas was, no doubt, delighted with the turn of events. Yeshua was sure to be executed, which was what he had wanted. But even better, he would not have to bear the responsibility. There would be no political repercussions for him because he could blame Pilate and the Judeans.

Herod tried to interrogate the Master, but Yeshua refused to answer his questions. "He questioned Him at some length; but He answered him nothing" (Luke 23:9). No magic tricks were forthcoming. The Master held the would-be king in such disdain that He did not even grant him the dignity of speaking to him.

Luke tells us that Herod and his soldiers performed a mock coronation by dressing Yeshua in a royal robe before sending Him back to Pilate.

Herod Antipas mocking the kingship of Yeshua is ironic considering that he strove all his life to win the title of king of the Jews. When face to face with the real King of Israel, he is foolish and clownish, plying for miracles and making a mockery of royalty he does not begin to understand.

Herod returns Yeshua to Pilate, returning the gesture of goodwill. Luke tells us, "Herod and Pilate became friends with one another that very day" (Luke 23:12).

THE CROWN OF ISRAEL

Herod continued as tetrarch over Galilee well into the apostolic era. His prestige-hungry wife, Herodius, continued to nudge Antipas to acquire the title of king. At last, many years later, he and his wife made a trip to Rome to formally request the title from Caesar Gaius Caligula. However, unbeknownst to the would-be monarchs, Herodius's brother Herod Agrippa had sent letters to Caesar ahead of them, accusing Antipas of treason. Rather than receiving the title of king, Antipas ended up being deposed and his dastardly brother-in-law, Agrippa, received his territories.

Josephus comments on the unexpected reversal with these words: "Thus did God punish Herodius …, and [He punished] Herod also for giving ear to the vain discourses of a woman" (Josephus, *Antiquities*, 18.7.2). Herod Antipas probably would have been better off sticking with his Nabatean wife. He never did achieve the crown he sought, nor did he recognize the rightful owner of that crown when he met Him.

Chapter 8

LET THE DEAD BURY THE DEAD

These are the precepts whose reward a person
will have in this world and in the world to come.
Honoring one's father and mother, acts of
devotion, early attendance at the study hall in the
morning and in the evening, hospitality to guests,
visiting the sick, providing [financial assistance]
for a bride [to be married], escorting the dead [to
burial], concentration in prayer, bringing peace
between a man and his companion, and the study
of Torah is equal to all of them. (b.*Shabbat* 127a)

As Yeshua moved through the cities of Galilee proclaiming the
kingdom, He was followed not only by His disciples, but often
by large crowds. On one occasion when His disciples and an enthu-
siastic crowd were following Him, they came to the small village
of Nain. (See Luke 7:11.)

A VILLAGE CALLED NAIN

On the northern slopes of the hill of Moreh in the ancient tribal
territory of Issachar, a modern Arab village called Nein marks the
location of ancient Nain. According to the *Midrash Rabbah*, the
town of Nain derived its name from Genesis 49:15. Describing the
territory of Issachar, it says, "He saw that a resting place was good,
and that the land was pleasant (*na-eimah*, נעמה)."

A short distance away, on the south side of the hill, is the
ancient village of Shunem, where Elisha the prophet lodged in the
Shunamite's house in 2 Kings 4.

There, in Shunem, Elisha performed the miracle for which he is
most famous, the resurrection of the Shunamite's son. The fame of

that miracle probably had not dissipated, even after nine hundred years. No doubt the villagers of Nain were fond of recalling the story of how Elisha the prophet had resurrected the Shunamite's son right there. It was their own piece of local lore to tell to strangers and to connect themselves with the Hebrew Scriptures.

Two Processions

As the Master and His disciples drew near to the gates of Nain, they saw a procession of mourners leaving. Jewish burial customs dictate that burial happen on the day of death if at all possible. Thus the young man laid out on the bier had probably not been dead for more than twenty-four hours. In keeping with Galilean funeral customs, the burial procession was led by the women. The men of the community carried and followed the open bier. Professional mourners and musicians trailed behind it.[89] Jewish cemeteries were always outside the city walls. Thus the funeral procession was leaving the city gates as Yeshua and His procession were drawing near to enter.

In first-century Judaism, escorting the dead was a *mitzvah* (commandment) and a duty incumbent upon everyone:

> Rechava said in the name of Rav Yehudah, "Whoever sees a corpse being carried to burial and does not accompany is the one of whom it is written [in Proverbs 14:31], "He who oppresses the poor shows contempt for their Maker." But what if he does accompany the dead? Then what is his reward? Rav Assi says, "To him applies the passage [in Proverbs 19:17] that says, 'He who is kind to the poor lends to the LORD, and he will reward him for what he has done.'" (b.*Berachot* 18a)

According to the law, custom, convention and courtesy of the land, Yeshua and His procession of disciples and followers should have stepped aside for the funeral procession, allowed it to pass, then followed it to the cemetery. The duty of escorting the dead was incumbent upon them even though they were strangers. According to Jewish custom, even the study of Torah should be interrupted for the sake of escorting the dead.[90]

The grief and shock was fresh and acute among the women who led the procession. Yeshua easily picked out the mourning mother. "She was a widow; and a sizeable crowd from the city was with her" (Luke 7:12). Her tragedy was compounded by the fact that without a husband or other children, she had lost her sole hope of provision and standing in the community. Luke tells us the Master "felt compassion for her" (7:13). She, not the dead man, was the intended beneficiary of the ensuing miracle.

Her story is similar to that of the widow at Zarephath, who the Master spoke of in Luke 4:26. In that story, the prophet Elijah resurrected the widow's son. As the geography and the circumstances of the miracles of Elijah and Elisha converge in the gospel narrative, the resurrection of the widow's son is almost inevitable.

A COLLISION COURSE

Instead of stepping aside to let the procession pass and then following them to the cemetery, Yeshua approached the procession head on. With His disciples and followers trailing behind Him, He said to the widow, "Do not weep" (7:13). Then He passed her by and touched the bier, bringing the whole procession to a sudden halt. Both the procession of the funeral and the procession of the Master came to a dead stop on the road outside the gates of Nain. Failing to yield the right-of-way to a funeral procession created a severe breach of etiquette, a major cultural faux pas.

Yeshua's seeming impudence is rooted in His identity. The Talmud, in its concern to legislate every possible contingency, discusses what to do when one procession meets another. The priority almost always goes to the funeral procession. Everyone is supposed to make way for a funeral procession. The only exception is the procession of a bride on her wedding day and the procession of the king of Israel. In those two cases, the funeral procession must stop and make way.

> Our Rabbis taught, "One should require a funeral procession to stop to make way for a bridal procession, and both a funeral procession and a bridal procession should stop to make way for the King of Israel." (b.*Ketubot* 17a)

In Luke 7, the King of Israel brought a funeral procession to a halt. He touched the bier and said, "Young man, I say unto you, 'Arise!'"

A Great Prophet among Us

The dead man sat up and began to talk. Luke is clearly influenced by the stories of Elijah and Elisha as he crafts this narrative. The Greek phrase "and he gave him back to his mother" finds an exact parallel in the Greek LXX version of 1 Kings 17:23:

> And he brought him down from the upper chamber into the house, and gave him back to his mother; and [Eliyahu] said, "See, your son lives." (1 Kings 17:23, LXX)

The parallels to Elijah and Elisha were not lost on the people of Nain. Their favorite local legend had just been reenacted before their very eyes. A second son of Shunem had been awoken from death. A son had been returned to a widow mother. The people declared, "A great prophet has arisen among us" (Luke 7:16).

Of course there were skeptics. "The boy was only in a swoon," they probably said. But the witnesses to the event were not dissuaded by the predictable skepticism. They told everyone what had happened, and if anyone doubted it, he could make the trip to Nain himself and meet the boy and his mother. Word of the resurrection miracle spread as far as Judea.

Let the Dead Bury the Dead

The resurrection at Nain brings to mind another time when Yeshua violated funerary customs. Once a man came to the Master and said that he would like to join the disciples as soon as he had buried his father. But Yeshua said to him, "Follow Me, and allow the dead to bury their own dead" (Matthew 8:22).

This seems puzzling. Is the Master really telling the man to neglect the important commandments of honoring father and mother and burying the dead? Surely not, for He criticizes the Pharisees for even a legal infraction of the commandment to honor father and mother.[91] Consider the following passage from the Talmud.

> These are the precepts whose reward a person will have in this world and in the world to come. Honoring one's father and mother, acts of devotion, early attendance at the study hall in the morning and in the evening, hospitality to guests, visiting the sick, providing [financial assis-

tance] for a bride [to be married], escorting the dead [to burial], concentration in prayer, bringing peace between a man and his companion, and the study of Torah is equal to all of them. (b.*Shabbat* 127a)

The above list of important commandments includes the honoring of father and mother and the burial of the dead. It is an impossibility that Yeshua would have encouraged the man to neglect such important commandments. The solution to His puzzling directive can be understood only in the context of first-century burial customs. In first-century Judaism (as is preferable in Judaism today), burial was performed on the day of death. Thus the man's father must have already been entombed at the time of the conversation with Yeshua. After entombment of a parent, first-century Jews observed a year of semi-mourning, during which they recited the *Kaddish* daily, just as is done today. After the completion of the year, they opened the tomb, gathered the dead parent's bones and placed them in a stone box (called an ossuary). Then the tomb was ready to be used again.

When the man approached Yeshua, he was probably requesting to finish out the year of waiting to rebury his father before following Yeshua. The Master regarded the request as an unnecessary objection to the urgent call of discipleship. No dishonor would be accorded to his father by having another member of the family gather the bones for the ossuary.

Note from the above Talmud passage that Torah study was considered to be of equal importance to honor of father and mother and the burial of the dead. Following Yeshua as a disciple was a call to Torah study, a *mitzvah* equivalent to all the *mitzvot*. In Matthew 10:37, Yeshua warns His disciples, "He who loves father or mother more than Me is not worthy of Me; and he who loves son or daughter more than Me is not worthy of Me."

Yeshua urged the man to become a disciple and join the procession of the King. The procession of the King of Israel—the King of the Jews—takes precedence over even a funeral procession.

Chapter 9

THE HIGH MOUNTAIN

THE FEAST OF SUKKOT AND THE TRANSFIGURATION

Enter, exalted and holy guests, enter exalted
holy patriarchs to be seated. ... In the shade
of the Holy One, Blessed is He ... in Sukkot
you shall dwell, be seated, exalted guests,
be seated; be seated, guests of faithfulness,
be seated. (*Ushpizin* Liturgy for Sukkot)

In Mark 9:1, the Master tells His disciples that some would not taste death before seeing Him come in His glory. This is a problem. Assuredly, all twelve of the disciples tasted death, and the Master still has not come in His glory.

He told them this just after dashing all their hopes to the ground. Without riddles or parables, Yeshua told them that His plan was to go to Jerusalem to be arrested, to suffer, to die and to rise again. This news was terribly frightening to the disciples; it didn't seem to make any logical sense. They anticipated the kingdom of Messiah to come with gratuitous displays of power. They expected Messiah, the King of the Jews, to wrest back the throne of David. In contrast, Yeshua told them to expect arrest, suffering and death.

Lest they lose heart completely, He spoke of a time yet coming, "when [the Son of Man] comes in the glory of His Father with the holy angels" (Mark 8:38). Magnificent glory and holy angels are more what one would hope for from a messianic advent. Perhaps the disciples asked, "When will this happen? How soon?"

Yeshua responded with another cryptic and troubling answer. He said, "Truly I say to you, there are some of those who are standing here who will not taste death until they see the kingdom of God after it has come with power" (Mark 9:1).

The gospel narrative immediately sets apart three disciples from the Twelve. The Zavdai brothers (James and John), along with Shimon Peter, are taken up onto a high mountain and given an amazing encounter with the Master in His glory. Are we to understand that these three disciples were granted a foretaste of the "kingdom of God ... come with power"?

The Coming Kingdom

Each year, Torah-keeping disciples of Yeshua experience a similar foretaste of the kingdom of God in the annual celebration of the festival of *Sukkot* (סכות, Tabernacles). The Hebrew word *sukkah* means "a small shelter, stable or hut." These temporary, tent-like structures are often translated as "tabernacles" in our English Bibles. *Sukkot* is plural for *sukkah*. The festival is so named because Israel is commanded to annually build such dwelling places as reminders of the years when they lived in huts and booths, following God in the wilderness.[92]

Many beautiful traditions are attached to the annual festival of Sukkot. For example, it is traditional to invite guests into one's *sukkah* for a festive meal each night of Sukkot. Among the list of invitees are Abraham, Isaac, Jacob, Joseph, Moses, Aaron and David. Each one is specifically invited to come into the *sukkah*. A chair is set at the *sukkah* table for one of these exalted guests each night of the festival. Obviously, Abraham, Isaac, Jacob, Joseph, Moses, Aaron and David are all unlikely to actually attend the meal, since they are all dead. That, however, is the point of the ritual. The Feast of Sukkot anticipates the messianic age[93] when the dead will be raised to life again and we will all, indeed, sit at the table with the aforementioned in the kingdom of heaven. Sukkot celebrates a time when all nations will ascend to Jerusalem bearing tribute to King Messiah, and each man will rest under his own vine and fig tree. Interestingly, the Gospels' descriptions of the transfiguration of Messiah are layered with Sukkot imagery.

The High Mountain

Yeshua took His three chosen disciples upon a high mountain. The traditional location of the Mount of Transfiguration is Mount Tabor.

However, Mount Tabor was populated, and it even boasted military fortifications during the first century. It could hardly have been the lonely and isolated high mountain of the Gospels. Additionally, the Gospels set the context of the story in Caesarea Philippi, which lies at the base of Mount Hermon, far from Mount Tabor. The geography of the story dictates the interpretation. Snow-capped Mount Hermon is the high mountain of Caesarea Philippi. While at Caesarea Philippi, Yeshua had deeply alarmed His disciples with His talk of suffering and dying in Jerusalem. Their paradigmatic expectation of Messiah as a military and political conqueror prevented them from seeing Yeshua for who He truly was.

On arriving in the region of Mount Hermon, He asked them pointedly, "Who do people say that I am?" (Mark 8:27)

"Some say Elijah; and still others, one of the prophets," they replied. But on the high mountain, they would learn that He is greater than Elijah, even greater than Moses. He is more than a prophet.

MOSES AND ELIJAH

The Master took the three disciples up the mountain with Him. There they beheld Him in His Father's glory. The text of Mark says, "He was transfigured before them" (Mark 9:2). A metamorphosis is the process of substantially changing (or transfiguring) from one physical state to another. They saw Him in a form in which they had never seen Him. Their eyes were opened to His glory. "His garments became radiant and exceedingly white, as no launderer on earth can whiten them" (Mark 9:3).

Moses and Elijah appeared with the Master as the requisite two witnesses.[94] They are metonies for the Torah and the Prophets, respectively. Moses recorded the Torah, and as the archetypal prophet, Elijah represents the rest of the Hebrew prophets. In that sense, Moses and Elijah can be understood to represent the testimony of the whole Hebrew Bible. Yeshua refers to this testimony frequently.[95]

The *Midrash Rabbah* anticipates Moses and Elijah to herald the advent of Messiah:[96]

> The Holy One, blessed be He, said to Moses, "Moses, by your life, just as you have given your soul for Israel in This

World, so in the Future to Come, when I bring them the prophet Elijah, the two of you will come as one. ... In that hour [Moses] will come and comfort Israel. (*Deuteronomy Rabbah* 3:17)

In terms of life and death, Moses and Elijah form an interesting pair. Whereas Moses died, Elijah did not. In the story told in 2 Kings 2, Elijah was swept into the sky in a whirlwind. Because he never died, he frequently makes cameo appearances in Jewish literature and folktales. One never knows when Elijah might show up. A place is set for him at the Passover table, and a chair is usually prepared for him at the circumcision ritual in case he should pop in. Elijah did not taste death.

The presence of Moses (who died) and Elijah (who did not) on the high mountain with Yeshua constitutes testimony from both the living and the dead. Messiah is "Lord both of the dead and the living" (Romans 14:9).

THREE SUKKOT

Shimon Peter suggests they should build shelters (סכות, *sukkot*) for the three men. Mark comments on Shimon Peter's awkward suggestion by saying, "He did not know what to answer, for they became terrified" (Mark 9:6). There is a ring of authenticity in Mark's comment. It is the type of thing one might expect to hear in an anecdotal retelling of the events where Shimon Peter was present. We can almost hear Shimon Peter's voice as he tells Mark the story. "I didn't know what to say! We were terrified. What would you say?"

The Jewish tradition to invite guests into the *sukkah* at the Feast of Sukkot includes the invitation of notable personages from the Hebrew Scriptures? In traditional Judaism, Moses himself is annually invited to enter the *sukkah*. How strange it must have been for Peter to find himself living out this ritual by offering to build *sukkot* for Moses and Elijah.

Mark tells us, "Then a cloud formed, overshadowing them, and a voice came out of the cloud, 'This is my beloved Son, listen to Him!'" (Mark 9:7). The voice from the cloud is meant for the benefit of Shimon Peter, James and John (and of course all of us who read their story). The voice addressed them directly, explicitly declaring

Yeshua to be Messiah, Son of God, the Beloved One, the Prophet like Moses, to whose words they must listen. Their hopes were not in vain. They were following the right man—even if it meant following Him to Jerusalem, arrest, suffering and death.

Sons of Thunder

Of the three disciples who ascended the high mountain and witnessed the transfiguration, two of them were brothers: *Yaakov* (James) and *Yochanon* (John). *Yaakov* and *Yochanon* are collectively known as the sons of *Zavdai* (Zebedee), but Yeshua calls them the "Sons of Thunder" (בני רעם, *bnei raam*).[97]

Just as He gave *Shimon bar Yonah* the name "Rock" (i.e., *Petros*), He assigned the two sons of Zavdai the name "Sons of Thunder." We don't know why. Some have supposed that the name might have been a reflection on the boisterous character of the two brothers, based upon their desire to call down fire on a village of Samaritans. Yet perhaps the story of the high mountain can offer us a clue to the meaning of this nickname.

While on the high mountain, James, John and Peter shared the amazing experience of hearing God's voice address them directly from within a cloud of glory. The sages of the apostolic era referred to the experience of hearing God's voice speak from heaven as hearing a *bat-kol* (בת קול); literally, the "daughter of a voice." The idiom is meant to express an echo effect. Since God's true voice would be infinite, filling all time and space, one hearing God speak from heaven actually hears only an echo of His true voice.

In the Gospels, the *bat-kol* is heard by John the Immerser and Yeshua at His immersion. It is heard on the Mount of Transfiguration. And it is heard a third time on the day of the Master's triumphal entry. On this third occasion it was heard by a large crowd in the Temple area just days before Passover. Some discerned the word, "I have glorified [My name] and will glorify it again," whereas others supposed that they had merely heard the sound of thunder.

> The multitude therefore, who stood by and heard it, were saying that it had thundered. (John 12:28–29)

The revelation of God's voice is closely associated with the sound of thunder. In Exodus 20, God's voice is heard speaking from Mount Sinai amidst peals of thunder. In Revelation 10, John hears seven voices speak from seven peals of thunder. We may well expect that the *bat-kol* heard atop the high mountain on the day of the Master's transfiguration sounded like thunder in the ears of the disciples.

> A bright cloud overshadowed them; and behold, a voice out of the cloud, saying "This is My beloved Son, with whom I am well pleased; listen to Him!" And when the disciples heard this, they fell on their faces and were much afraid. (Matthew 17:5–6)

This encounter with the *bat-kol* may explain the Master's nickname for the sons of Zavdai. By referring to them as the "Sons of Thunder," He may have been hearkening back to their experience with the thunder on the Mount of Transfiguration.

In Hebrew, a son can mean "one who is obligated." The term *bar-mitzvah* literally means "son of the commandment" but implies "one who is obligated" to keep the commandments. By calling these brothers "Sons of Thunder," the Master may have been speaking of their obligation to heed the voice of thunder that they heard atop the high mountain. Specifically, the voice said, "This is My beloved Son, with whom I am well pleased; listen to Him!" (Matthew 17:5)

By obeying the voice they heard in the thunder, they were literally "Sons of Thunder"—those obligated to the Voice.

THE FEAST OF CLOUDS

The cloud of glory is also associated with the Festival of Sukkot. Based upon the Aramaic version of the Torah, some of the sages referred to the Feast of Sukkot as the Feast of the Clouds; specifically, the cloud of glory that sheltered Israel in the wilderness. The Talmud records one opinion that the *sukkot* in which the Israelites of the wilderness lived were none other than the cloud of glory that went before the hosts of Israel.

> R. Eliezer said, "It has been taught: 'I had the Israelites live in Sukkot.' These Sukkot were clouds of glory." (b.*Sukkah* 11b)

This association is based on the Aramaic translations of the Torah called *Targums*. The Targums translate the Hebrew *sukkah* (סכה) with a word than can mean "clouds" (*metalaya*, מטליא). The double meaning of the Aramaic word led the sages to interpret the structures of the Feast of Booths as symbols for the cloud of glory (i.e., the Divine Presence) that overshadowed Israel in the wilderness.

In the transfiguration narrative, the cloud of glory appears immediately after Shimon Peter offers to build three *sukkot*. If we were Aramaic speakers, the connection between the *sukkot*, the Feast of Sukkot, and the cloud of glory would be more obvious.

In addition, the interpretation equating the *sukkah* and the cloud of glory may stem partly from Isaiah 4, where the prophet Isaiah invokes sukkot imagery when he speaks of messianic Jerusalem.

> Then the LORD will create over the whole area of Mount Zion and over her assemblies a cloud by day, even smoke, and the brightness of a flaming fire by night; for over all the glory will be a canopy. There will be a *sukkah* to give shade from the heat by day, and refuge and protection from the storm and the rain. (Isaiah 4:5–6)

Isaiah's cloud over the New Jerusalem is obviously borrowed from the Torah's wilderness narratives. He calls it a *sukkah*. Thus the wilderness cloud of glory that led Israel through the desert, rested on Mount Sinai, and filled the Tabernacle is specifically connected with both the Festival of Sukkot and the messianic age to come.

SOME WILL NOT TASTE DEATH

What did the Master mean when He said, "Some who are standing here will not taste death before they see the kingdom of God come with power?" The three who ascended the high mountain actually did see the Master basking in the Father's power and glory. In a sense, these three disciples were granted a foretaste of the "kingdom of God come with power" because they saw the King in His splendor, clothed in the power and glory to be revealed when He comes. They experienced a miniature version of that coming day and hour, annually rehearsed in the rituals of the Festival of Sukkot.

Similarly, it is our privilege, year after year, to celebrate Sukkot, building our *sukkot*, inviting guests, and anticipating that day when we will see the Son of Man revealed in His Father's glory. In that day, we will no longer taste death.

Chapter 10

ACROSS THE GREAT DIVIDE

In the middle of the journey of our life I came
to myself within a dark wood where the straight
way was lost. How hard a thing it is to tell of that
wood, savage and harsh and dense, the thought
of which renews my fear! So bitter is it that death
is hardly more. (*Dante's Inferno*, Canto 1:1)[98]

Every human being has stood, at one time or another, lost and
confused in Dante's dark wood, where the questions of life are
more terrifying than death itself. And what is the greatest question of life but the passage from life to death? Even believers must
confess to some bewilderment in the midst of these trees. We prove
our uncertainty by the various antithetical theologies we possess
regarding the existence of the soul, life after death and the resurrection of the dead.

Ironically, most of our confusion stems from our reading of the
Bible. We turn there to find answers, but when we try to understand
the Master's words outside the matrix of the first-century Judaism,
we only become more puzzled. Oftentimes, when encountering
terminology or concepts unfamiliar to us, we fill in the theological
blanks as best we can.

The parable of the rich man and Lazarus in Luke 16 provides a
case in point. In that story, the two characters find themselves on
opposite sides of a great divide. The rich man is in Hades, where he
is in severe torment, while Lazarus is safe in a place called Abraham's Bosom. But what is Hades? And what is Abraham's Bosom?
What awaits the soul of man beyond the grave? How do we know
if there is a soul that goes on after death?

The Rich Man and Lazarus

Yeshua began his story by saying, "There was a rich man who was dressed in purple and fine linen and lived in luxury every day" (Luke 16:19 NIV). The description suggests a man who lived without regard to Torah. Deuteronomy 22:11 says, "You shall not wear a material mixed of wool and linen together," yet the man wears purple[99] and linen every day. He has no regard for the *mitzvot*. His wealth and fancy garments are more important.

Lying near the rich man's gate is a starving beggar named Eliezer. He is called Lazer for short, and with the Greek masculine suffix he is known to us as Lazarus. The Master tells us that Lazarus longed to eat from the rich man's table, but He does not say he ate. Dogs came and licked his sores, showing him more mercy than the rich man. Finally the beggar died, and angels carried him to Abraham's Bosom, which is to say, to Abraham's side.

The Harrowing of Hell

Where was Abraham's Bosom? One creative explanation is that Abraham's Bosom was Limbo, a place of waiting just on the edge of hell, where all the Old Testament saints were supposedly penned up and left to wait until Messiah's resurrection. According to this theology, when Messiah died and began the new covenant, He opened the gates of Limbo (Abraham's Bosom) and let out all the righteous who had lived before Him. They followed Him out of Abraham's Bosom and into heaven.

The advantage to this explanation is that it created a theological buffer zone between the old covenant and the new covenant. It allowed us to believe that prior to the death and resurrection of Yeshua, no one could have gained admittance to heaven. For the expositors, it was a convenient way of allowing their Old Testament heroes into the new covenant paradise while keeping the rest of the Jews in hell.

In this belief system, Abraham's Bosom was a sort of kinder, gentler realm of hell. One can travel to that outermost circle with Dante Alighieri and the ghostly shade of the long dead, first-century, Roman poet Virgil in Dante's *Divine Comedy* and meet Dante's "Virtuous Heathen." In *Inferno*, Virgil explains:

> I was new in this condition when I saw a mighty one come
> here, crowned with a sign of victory. He took from among
> us the shade of our first parent, of Abel his son, and of
> Noah, of Moses, law-giver and obedient, of the patriarch
> Abraham, and of King David, of Israel with his father ...
> and many others. ... And I would have thee know that
> before these no human souls were saved.

Thus, according to Dante (who was dutifully reporting the popular church theology), faithful Israelites who died prior to the resurrection received a fate no better than Socrates and Plato. They were consigned to Limbo.

It is astonishing how this old church mythology has survived in modern Protestant circles. It is still a common belief that at His death, Yeshua marched into that gloomy netherworld of moping spirits, kicked in the doors, and led the "Old Testament heroes" out and up to paradise. Some explain the enigmatic resurrection of Matthew 27:52–53 as the transition point at which the souls of those Old Testament saints were released from "Abraham's Bosom."

PARADISIO

But if the place of Abraham's Bosom is not Limbo, where and what is it? Christian Talmudist Jonathan Lightfoot was one of the early voices to protest the Limbo explanation of Abraham's Bosom. He did so by taking the term back to its Jewish origin. In his *Commentary on the New Testament from the Talmud and Hebraica* he wrote, "If our Saviour had been the first author of this phrase, then might it have been tolerable to have looked for the meaning of it amongst Christian expositors; but seeing it is a scheme of speech so familiar amongst the Jews, and our Saviour spoke no other than in the known and vulgar dialect of that nation, the meaning of it must be fetched thence, not from any Greek or Roman lexicon." [100] Lightfoot argues that we should not look for an interpretation arising out of Christian theology; rather, we should try to understand Yeshua's words as those listening to Him would have understood. How was He understood by the disciples, the crowds and the Pharisees? What did the terminology mean to them?

One of the central tenants of faith among the Pharisees was that there is a place of reward and a place of punishment that which souls go after death. The place of reward was, of course, paradise. The word *paradise* (*pardes*, פרדס) is a Persian loan word that appears in both Hebrew and Greek to describe the place of the soul's reward after death. It entered Latin and English (*paradisio* and paradise) in similar form. According to the broad view of the Pharisees, the souls of the righteous wait in paradise for the resurrection of the dead, at which point they will be returned to their bodies.[101]

Several other terms for paradise appear in rabbinic literature, including the Garden of Eden (*Gan Eden,* גן עדן) and the term "under the throne of glory" (*tachat kiseh hakavod,* תחת כסא הכבוד). A Talmudic tradition[102] records the names of seven heavens, each one a subsequent and ascending level into the precincts of paradise. The belief in seven heavens is attested to by Paul, who claims to know a man (himself, no doubt) who was once caught up to the third one.[103]

Pharisaic Judaism believed in a place of reward, and the place was known by several names. To be in Abraham's Bosom meant to be with Abraham. Abraham's Bosom was simply another term for paradise. In Jewish literature, "going to Abraham" is idiomatic for going to paradise. In the Talmud, the term "Abraham's Bosom" is used to speak euphemistically of the death of Rabbi Yehudah the Prince. "Today he sits in the bosom of Abraham" (b.*Kiddushin* 72b).[104]

It is also common in rabbinic literature to speak of the souls of the righteous as being "carried by angels" into paradise. In the *Midrash Rabbah,* an angelic escort is sent to fetch the soul of Moses, but Moses' soul will yield only to God Himself.[105]

As Yeshua described the soul of Lazarus being carried by angels to Abraham's Bosom, He was using the common terms and idioms of Pharisaic theology to describe the death of the righteous. The paradise to which Lazarus was escorted is the same paradise of which Paul the Pharisee spoke when he said that "to be absent from the body [is to be] at home with the Lord." [106]

The Pharisaic belief in the separation of the soul from the body at death and its return to the body at the coming resurrection of the dead is well expressed in the following blessing from the daily prayers:

> My God, the soul You placed within me is pure. You created her, you shaped her and you breathed her into me and You keep her within me, and in time You will take her away from me only to restore her to me again in the time to come. As long as the soul is within me I will thank You Lord my God and God of my fathers, Master of all work, Lord of all souls. Blessed are You Lord, who restores souls to dead bodies. (Traditional Morning Blessings)

In this blessing we see that the soul, which is breathed into the human body by God, is withdrawn at the time of death, held until the resurrection, and then returned to the body at the moment of the resurrection. Revelation 6 describes the host of disembodied souls of the martyrs crying out before God, "How long, O Lord, holy and true, will You refrain from judging and avenging our blood on those who dwell on the earth?" (Revelation 6:10).

H. E. DOUBLE-TOOTHPICKS

Yeshua continued the story, saying, "The rich man also died and was buried" (Luke 16:22). Note that He does not say that the rich man's soul was carried anyplace by angels. He says he died and was buried. The rich man finds himself "in Hades ... being in torment."

When our gospel text says "hell" or "hades," we should keep in mind that those are Greek language translations for the Hebrew Gehennah,[107] but "hell" and "hades" do not equal Gehennah. Hades is the mythological place of the dead, the realm of the underworld.

In Greek mythology, we visit the realm of the dead with Orpheus to discover a place of misery and torment ruled by the despotic Greek god Hades; hence, the term. The word *hell* seems to rise from an old Anglo-Saxon word describing the shadowy realm of the dead.[108] Confusion with the Greek mythological concepts of Hades gave rise to the church's popular Dantesque vision of souls in torment being whipped by demons, which are all ruled over by satan in hell. Biblically, however, satan is not the god of the underworld, nor is hell his kingdom. Rather, he is described as the "the prince of the power of the air." [109] The pit of fire is his final destiny, not his realm.[110]

Neither hell nor hades was a part of Yeshua's vernacular. They are Greek translations of the Hebrew term *Gey-Hinnom* (גי־הנום); i.e., Gehennah. In several instances, the gospel writers don't even try to translate Gehennah into Greek but opt to simply transliterate the Hebrew. The word *Gey-Hinnom* (גי־הנום) literally means "Valley of Hinnom." [111] The Valley of Hinnom is one of the three valleys that comprise the topography of Jerusalem. In the days of the Judean monarchy, children were sacrificed to Molech in that valley. King Josiah defiled its ritual status by turning it into a garbage dump.[112] Apparently refuse was still burned in the Hinnom valley even in the days of the Master. With such an evil reputation and the continual burning of the garbage fires, the name of the valley came to be euphemistic for God's eternal garbage dump.

By the time of the Master, the name Gehennah had come to mean the place of torment and purgation, where the souls of the dead received their comeuppance. It is a dry and waterless place of unending thirst.

The rich man begs Abraham to allow Lazarus to "dip the tip of his finger in water and cool off my tongue." The thirst of the rich man is similar to the *Jerusalem Talmud*'s description of a tax collector in Gehennah:

> He saw the tax-collector, and his tongue sought to drink at the brink of a river; he tried to reach the water, but he could not. (y.*Sanhedrin* 6.9, 23c {32})[113]

Like the torments of Tantalus, the tax collector tries to lap at the water, but it is just beyond his reach.

WHERE THE WORM DOES NOT DIE

Belief in paradise, Gehennah, and even the existence of the soul was not universal among first-century Judaism. The Sadducees rejected all these notions as Pharisaic balderdash. They were rigid literalists who accepted only the authority of the written Torah. Since they could find neither Abraham's Bosom nor the fires of Gehennah anywhere mentioned in the Torah of Moses, they rejected them both. "Humph," they snorted. "Enough with your traditions of men."

Perhaps the rich man in Luke 16 is to be understood as a Sadducee, which is why he begs to be allowed to return to warn his five brothers of their error. Abraham chides him, saying, "They have the Torah and the Prophets."

The Pharisees attempted to bring proof for the existence of Gehennah by quoting from the Torah and the Prophets. For example, the last verse of the book of Isaiah says:

> And they shall go forth and look on corpses of those who have transgressed against Me. For their worm shall not die, and their fire shall not be quenched; and they shall be abhorrence to all mankind." (Isaiah 66:24)

They explained that the "dead bodies" of those who rebelled referred to the souls of the damned in Gehennah. There the fire was not quenched and the worm did not die.

Yeshua uses the same passage to describe Gehennah.[114] The following midrash assumes Isaiah 66:24 is a description of Gehennah:

> Rabbi Acha warns us, "Be among those who are doing the looking, as it is written, 'And they will go out and look upon the dead bodies of those who rebelled.' ... Do not be among those who are looked upon of whom it is written, 'Their worm will not die, nor will their fire be quenched.'" ... Gehinnom and Gan Eden: What is the distance between them? No more than a handbreadth. Rabbi Yochanan said, "A wall runs between them." The Rabbis say, "They are parallel, so that one should be visible to the other." (*Ecclesiastes Rabbah* 7:23, quoting Isaiah 66:24)

But is it reasonable to say that the souls in Gehennah can see the souls of those in paradise and vice versa? Apparently so.

Another classic Pharisaic proof text used to describe Gehennah is Psalm 112:10. There, the wicked in Gehennah are described as gnashing their teeth at the sight of the righteous. Yeshua draws on Psalm 112's teeth-gnashing image seven times across the Gospels as He describes the fate of those consigned to Gehennah:[115]

> The wicked man will see it and be vexed; he will gnash his teeth and melt away; the desire of the wicked will perish. (Psalm 112:10)

> Rabbi Nehemiah said, "When the wicked ascend from Gehennah and see the righteous sitting peacefully in the Gan Eden they are ashamed. Hence it is written, 'The wicked man will see and be vexed, he will gnash his teeth.'" (*Leviticus Rabbah* 32:1, quoting Psalm 112:10)

Just as in the above *midrashim*, the rich man and Lazarus are visible one to the other, but they are separated by a great divide. Abraham explains to the rich man, "Between us and you there is a great chasm fixed, in order that those who wish to come over from here to you may not be able, and none can cross over from there to us" (Luke 16:26).

Gehennah and *Gan Eden* run parallel. But no one can cross over from one to the other. No one can cross the great divide.

WE HAVE ABRAHAM AS OUR FATHER

In the days of the Master, there were some who believed the Jews would receive an automatic "get out of Gehennah free" pass from Abraham. That seems to be the sentiment that compelled John the Immerser to rebuke the people, saying, "Therefore bear fruits in keeping with repentance, and do not begin to say to yourselves, 'We have Abraham as our father'" (Luke 3:8). The following two quotations, one from the Midrash and one from the Talmud, both attest to a common belief that Abraham would not allow a Jewish soul to suffer in Gehennah:

> Rabbi Levi said, "In the Hereafter Abraham will sit at the entrance to Gehennah, and permit no circumcised Israelite to descend therein." (*Genesis Rabbah* 48:8)

> What does the passage [in Psalm 84:6] mean that says, "Passing through the Valley of Weeping"? It means that there are some who are sentenced to suffer in Gehennah, but our father Abraham comes, brings them up to himself, and receives them to himself." (b.*Eiruvin* 19a)

Perhaps it was on the basis of this folk-belief that Yeshua has the rich man in the parable appeal to Abraham for mercy. If those listening to Yeshua's parable were depending upon Abraham to deliver them from Gehennah, the parable was aimed at them.

LIFE AFTER DEATH

In telling us this parable, the Master isn't making things up, nor is He revealing secret information about the afterlife. This is not a peek behind the veil. The terminology He used was very familiar to His listeners. The belief in Abraham's Bosom as paradise and Gehennah as the place of torment was a well-established theological assumption. If Yeshua meant to correct them or dispel these beliefs, He would not have told this story in those terms.

The Bible is not ours to freely interpret for our theological convenience. We do not have the right to explain Gehennah away or to replace the meaning with Dante's mythological landscapes and pictures of demons in tights, whipping souls. To do so is presumptuous. The Master wasn't speaking in riddles for us to guess at the meaning. He was speaking in the common, everyday terminology of first-century Pharisaic Judaism. If we want to know what He believed and taught about these issues, we must look there for the meanings.

Throughout the Gospels, Yeshua's statements regarding life after death—the immortality of the soul, the sentence of the soul, the angelic escort of the souls of the righteous, the immediate punishment and reward of the wicked and the righteous, the proximity of Gehennah and paradise, and the presence of Abraham at the entrance to paradise—are in keeping with that of traditional Pharisaism. If Yeshua knew any of those beliefs were wrong, why would He endorse them by incorporating them into the parable? Why did He endorse them over and over throughout His teaching, often quoting or alluding to the same proof texts that the Pharisees used? Clearly He endorsed them because He believed them.

I would rather have Yeshua guide me out of Dante's dark wood than trust myself to Virgil. If anyone knows what's beyond the veil, it is Yeshua.

A PARABLE ABOUT REPENTANCE

Yeshua does not tell this parable to teach us about life after death. He assumed that his listeners already understood those basic principles. He was speaking to a Jewish audience with general Jewish expectations. The issues of life and death are incidental to the story. The parable is not about the afterlife, repentance, and the ultimate results of repentance.

The Master uses the parable to teach us that the Torah and the Prophets are the means by which we should be inspired to repent. The rich man's five brothers had the Torah. They had the Prophets. If they would listen and obey the Torah and the Prophets, they would repent. Repentance would keep them out of the place of torment and allow them to join Abraham in paradise.

The rich man objects, "They won't listen to the Torah. Send Eliezer to warn them. Send a ghost. A man come back from the dead. A resurrection. A miraculous intervention."

> But he [Abraham] said to him, "If they do not listen to Moses and the Prophets, neither will they be persuaded if someone rises from the dead." (Luke 16:31)

Yeshua's words apply to the majority of our world as well. We did not listen to Moses or the Prophets, and we did not listen to one who came back from the dead: Yeshua Himself.

The Master's parable is meant as a warning. What will become of us if we ignore Moses and the Prophets? If we reject Moses and the Prophets, will we really listen to the resurrected Messiah? The parable teaches that if Torah is not adequate to bring us to repentance, nothing will be. Our hearts will be so hard, we will even turn away from the gospel of the resurrection of Messiah.

The matter is similar to a parable that appears in the *Midrash Rabbah*. In this parable, a man consigned to Gehennah sees an old colleague of his in paradise and complains that this is unfair since they were both criminals. The angels explain to him that his colleague is in paradise because he repented:

> The angels said (to the man in Gehennah), "You fool ... you also had the opportunity of repenting and you did not take it." When he heard this, he said to them, "Permit me to go and repent now!" And they answered him and said, "You fool! Do you not know that this world is like the Sabbath and the world from which you have just come is like the eve of the Sabbath? If a man does not prepare his meal on the eve of the Sabbath, what shall he eat on the Sabbath?" (m.*Ruth Rabbah* 3:3)

Chapter 11

HOUSE OF THE WATER DRAWING

Reb Berekiah said in the name of Rabbi
Yitzchak: "The Latter Redeemer [Messiah] will
be like the First Redeemer [Moses]. The First
Redeemer made a well to rise in the wilderness,
so will the latter Redeemer bring up water,
as it is stated [in Joel 3:18], 'And a spring will
go out from the house of the LORD to water
the valley.'" (*Ecclesiastes Rabbah* 1:28)

For most of His ministry, Yeshua concealed His Messianic identity from the masses. Not until the Festival of Booths, six months before His crucifixion, did He publicly declare Himself Messiah. The story as told in John chapter 7 begins in Nazareth and concludes in the Temple courts of Jerusalem.

During the High Holiday, six months before He suffered, Yeshua was in His hometown of Nazareth. His younger brothers Yaakov, Yosi and Yehudah were present, and along with the other men of Nazareth, they were making their plans for the Sukkot (Feast of Booths) pilgrimage. The Torah commands that every Israelite male is to make the pilgrimage to the Temple for Sukkot.[116] In the days of the Master, when the Temple still stood, that commandment was still binding. The men in the village were already preparing for the journey to Jerusalem.

But at that time Yeshua's brothers were not yet His disciples. After all, they had grown up with Him. He was their older brother and, from their perspective, He was mostly unremarkable. As a result, not even His brothers believed in Him (John 7:5).

They chided Him regarding the pilgrimage, saying:

> Depart from here, and go into Judea, that Your disciples
> also may behold Your works which You are doing. For no
> one does anything in secret, when he himself seeks to be
> known publicly. If You do these things, show Yourself to
> the world. (John 7:3–4)

Their criticism of Yeshua's ministry packed some truth. For the previous several years, Yeshua had conducted His miraculous ministry somewhat clandestinely. Rather than seeking recognition as a public figure (i.e., Messiah), He warned those He healed to "tell no one." He retreated from crowds and hushed the voices that sought to proclaim His identity. His brothers interpreted the secrecy as evidence that He was less than He claimed to be. They suspected He was simply extending the charade as long as He could.

THE APPOINTED TIME

Yeshua responded, "My time is not yet at hand. ...Go up to the feast yourselves; I do not go up to this feast because My time has not yet fully come" (John 7:6, 8). His answer contains two meanings. In the immediate and literal sense, He is telling His brothers that the time in which He intends to leave for the festival of Sukkot has not yet arrived. He will not travel with their pilgrimage caravan. The message implied behind His words is that the right festival (the appointed time) for Him to go public had not yet arrived. He is referring, of course, to the Passover (still six months away), when He would be publicly hailed as King Messiah—King of the Jews— during the triumphal entry, and subsequently crucified. When that fateful Passover did arrive, He referred to it as "My appointed time." [117] In John 7, the time for that grand entry and unveiling of His public ministry was not yet ripe.

Yeshua waited until after His brothers and the Nazareth pilgrims had embarked. He even acted as if He were not planning to attend the festival. When at last the way was clear, He and His disciples made a private pilgrimage. Arriving in Jerusalem, they kept a low profile for the first half of the eight-day feast.

Yeshua stayed among the pilgrims encamped on the Mount of Olives.[118] He and His disciples must have built their *sukkah* (festival booth) on those slopes, perhaps even in the garden Gethsemane. Their little hut was only one among the hundreds of such shacks built for the occasion. There, under the shelter of the *sukkah*, Yeshua and the disciples ate their meals together. The roof of their tiny hut, like all such festival booths, was partially open to the sky, allowing the brilliant light of the full moon to shine inside.[119]

On the third or fourth day of the festival, He began to teach publicly in the Temple.

YOU SHALL REJOICE

The festival days were all joyful occasions, but the feast of Sukkot was especially so. It was called the "Season of our Rejoicing" in accordance with the verse that states, "You shall rejoice before the LORD your God for seven days" (Leviticus 23:40).

The Mishnah describes the festival of Sukkot (Booths) as it was celebrated in the days of the apostles. The festival transformed the entire city of Jerusalem. Pilgrims and native Jerusalemites built booths on rooftops and in every public courtyard. Galileans crowded into the city, as at Passover time. A festive atmosphere of joy and revelry was everywhere, but nowhere more so than in the Temple.

During Sukkot, the priesthood followed the daily sacrifices with an ancient ceremony called the *Beit HaShoevah* (בית השואבה)—"House of the Water Drawing." It was essentially a water libation poured over the altar, but by the days of the Master, it had become a ceremony of great joy and celebration: [120]

> Anyone who has not seen the rejoicing of the House of
> the Water Drawing has never seen rejoicing in his life.
> (m.*Sukkot* 4:10)

On each day of Sukkot, the rejoicing began when the priesthood completed the afternoon sacrifice, and it continued for the rest of the day and all of that night. The Levites led worship music with flutes, harps, lyres and cymbals. Whoever could play a musical instrument did so, and whoever could sing sang. Those without such talents stomped their feet, slapped their thighs, clapped their hands, leapt or danced—each to the best of his ability. All night long they sang songs and hymns of praise. In the Temple courts, the priests constructed four gigantic towers, each bearing four golden lamps. Young priests climbed to the tops, carrying with them immense containers of oil with which they filled the giant lamps. Once lit, the lamps burned all through the night, transforming Jerusalem into a blazing city of light. The Mishnah reports that there was not a courtyard in all of Jerusalem that did not glow with light.[121]

While the people sang and danced, the famous sages and holy men of the generation entertained the crowds by clapping, stamping and dancing along with the music. The rabbis performed acrobatics and juggled flaming torches as part of the festivities.

To increase the joy, Deuteronomy 14:26 prescribed spending one's tithe money on food or liquor or whatever delicacies one might desire for the purpose of eating and rejoicing in the presence of the Lord. In short, it was an all-night party all week long.

The Ceremony

The Water Drawing was a ritual beseeching of God for adequate rainfall in the coming year. Each day, just before dawn, two priests with trumpets emerged from the Temple gates. They sounded the *tekiah, teruah, tekiah* blasts on their *shofarim* to alert the crowd that the water drawing procession was about to begin. A column of priests, led by a priest carrying a golden pitcher, passed through the midst of the reveling worshippers and out through the Lower Gate of the Temple. As they left the Temple, they sounded the trumpets again. They turned and descended into the city of David and came to the great stepped Pool of the Sent One (*Shiloach* , שילוח, Siloam). They sounded the trumpets again and used the golden pitcher to draw living water from the pool before returning to the Temple.

Torah refers to naturally flowing water that has not been artificially manipulated by plumbing (such as rivers, springs, lakes, pools and rainwater) as living water (*mayim chayim,* מים חיים). The water the priests used for the libation was *mayim chayim.*

By the time they had drawn the water, the sun had risen and the morning sacrifice was underway. The assembled worshippers, bearing the four festival species of herbage[122] (willow, palm, myrtle and citron), filled the Temple courts. Others carried giant willow and palm branches. Together, all the worshippers circled about the altar, chanting, "*Hoshanah,*" which means, "Save us now!"

People would gather young willow branches and throw them along the sides of the altar, with their heads bent over the altar. They blew on the shofar a tekiah, teruah, tekiah. Every day they would walk around the altar one time and say, "Hoshanah! Save now, we beseech thee, O LORD! We beseech thee, O LORD, send prosperity now." [Rabbi Yehudah says,] They prayed, "Save us we pray! Save us we pray!" And on the seventh day of the willow branch they walk around the altar seven times. (m.*Sukkot* 4:5, quoting Psalm 118:25–27)

The priest sent to draw the water returned to the Temple. When he and his procession reached the Temple, they blew the trumpets again to signal that the time for the libation had arrived. After the morning sacrifice was completed, the priest with the golden pitcher ascended the altar ramp. Again they sounded the trumpets. Everyone strained to catch a glimpse of the water being poured out over the altar.

They sounded the trumpets one last time, silencing the crowd, as the priest poured out the water. He lifted the golden pitcher high into the air for everyone to see and emptied its contents into a special receptacle in the altar.

Following the Water Drawing and a few additional festival sacrifices, the worshippers dispersed to eat and drink and, according to Rabbi Yehoshua Chananiah, to study Torah. A few hours later, it was time to reassemble for the afternoon prayers and sacrifice, after which the entire production all began again with another all-night praise-and-worship service staggering into the morning Water Drawing ceremony. They hardly had a chance to sleep:

It was taught: Rabbi Yehoshua ben Chananiah [the priest] said, "When we used to rejoice during the House of the Water Drawing, our eyes saw no sleep." How is that possible? "The first hour we were busy with the morning continual burnt offering. After that we finished the morning prayers. After that we offered the additional festival sacrifices, followed by the prayers that accompanied the additional sacrifices. Then to the House of Study, and from there we went eating and drinking. By then it was time for the afternoon prayers accompanied by the afternoon continual burnt offering, and after that the Rejoicing at the House of the Water Drawing" [which went on all night]. ...What he really meant was this: "We did not enjoy a proper night's sleep," because they dozed on one another's shoulders. (b.Sukkah 53a)

Three or four days into this week-long marathon celebration, Yeshua began to publicly teach in the Temple courts, probably in the early afternoon, before the evening's revelries began again. "But when it was now the midst of the feast Yeshua went up into the Temple, and began to teach" (John 7:14). The famous sages and teachers had a long-standing custom of using the festivals as an occasion to teach Torah publicly in the Temple courts. When Yeshua took His place in the Temple, He was entering the arena of the sages and discoursing alongside them. The people wondered if this might be an implied endorsement of Yeshua. They said, "Look, He is speaking publicly, and they [the sages] are saying nothing to Him. The rulers do not really know that this is the Messiah, do they?" (John 7:26).

Hoshanah Rabbah

As the festival week reached its crescendo, John writes, "Now on the last day, the great day of the feast" (John 7:37). The last day, the great day of Sukkot, is the seventh day of the festival. The Mishnah calls it *Hoshanah Rabbah* (הושנא רבה), which means "Great Salvation." It is so called because on each day of the festival the worshippers encircled the altar with palms in hand while singing, "*Hoshanah*, do save, we beseech You; O Lord, we beseech You, do send prosperity!" (Psalm 118:25) On the seventh day of the festival they encircled the altar seven times, preparing for the final water libation. The worshippers shook their palm branches to create a rushing sound like wind and rain. They regarded the entire celebration as a fulfillment of the passage in Isaiah (12:3) that says, "Therefore you will joyously draw water from the springs of salvation." The rejoicing and ecstatic worship of the previous days culminated in this seventh and last water-libation ceremony. *Hoshanah Rabbah* made for the highest point of the festival. It was the big *Hoshanah*.

As the worshippers were making their seven circuits around the altar, the priest ascended the altar to pour out the seventh and last water libation of the festival. The trumpet blasts signaled to the crowd that the priest was ready. Imagine the moment of silence descending upon the Temple courts as the priest raised the golden pitcher above the crowds to pour out the libation on the altar. One can almost see the morning sun glinting on the gold, the breathless anticipation of the people and the sparkle of the water as the priest poured it onto the altar. It was likely at that moment that Yeshua shouted out, breaking the holy reverie, "If anyone is thirsty, let him come to Me and drink. He who believes in Me, as the Scripture said, 'From his innermost being will flow rivers of living water'" (John 7:37–38).

Many translators suggest that we should read the last pronoun of Yeshua's declaration as referring to Himself; thus, the streams of living water (*mayim chayim*) flow from within Yeshua. If so, His declaration may be read as follows:

> If anyone is thirsty, let him come to Me. And let him drink who believes in Me. As the Scripture has said, "From His [Messiah's] innermost being will flow rivers of living water."

The Springs of Salvation

Where does Scripture say that streams of living water will flow from Messiah's innermost being? No such passage exists, at least none that we know of. But the concept is definitely biblical, and several illustrative passages could be cited.[123] But the verse Yeshua is probably referencing is Isaiah 12:3, the text after which the water-libation ceremony is named. When spoken in Hebrew, the name Yeshua (Salvation) is obvious in Isaiah 12:3, "Therefore you will joyously draw water from the springs of salvation (Yeshua)" (Isaiah 12:3).

John explains that the water Yeshua referred to is the outpouring of the Holy Spirit. In Judaism, the endowment of the Holy Spirit is traditionally associated with the outpouring of the Sukkot water libation. The *Jerusalem Talmud* also equates the water-libation ceremony with receiving the Holy Spirit. Therein, Yehoshua ben Levi declares, "Why did they call it 'The House of the Water Drawing'?

Because it was from there that they drew the Holy Spirit, according to the Word [in Isaiah 12:3]: 'Therefore you will joyously draw water from the springs of salvation'" (y.*Sukkot* 55a).

Yeshua was publicly declaring Himself to be the wellspring of salvation—that is, Messiah.

THIS IS THE MESSIAH

Apparently the crowds understood Yeshua's public declaration as a Messianic claim. On hearing His words, the people declared, "This certainly is the Prophet." Others were saying, "This is the Messiah." [124]

Gospel commentators have puzzled over Yeshua's triumphal entry into Jerusalem at Passover. They wonder why the people met Him with palm branches and shouts of "Hoshanah!" The puzzling part is that both palm branches and *hoshanahs* are part of the Sukkot water-libation rituals, not Passover. Some commentators have suggested that the gospel writers confused the Sukkot rituals with Passover and placed those elements on the wrong festival.

The explanation for the people's strange reception of Yeshua at the triumphal entry is in John chapter seven, where Yeshua makes His loudest and most public declaration of Messiahship. In this context, the people were singing the *hoshanah* acclamations and waving palm branches. The people's reception of Yeshua at the following Passover is in response to His declaration here at Sukkot. The palm branches and shouts of *hoshanah* are the pilgrims' way of saying, "Finish what you started at Sukkot. We believe in you. You are the Messiah." By the end of Passover that year, even His brothers believed in Him.

Chapter 12

HEIR TO THE VINEYARD

A parable: "A king had a field which he leased
to tenants. When the tenants began to steal
from it, he took it away from them and
leased it to their children. When the children
began to act worse than their fathers, he
took it away from them and gave it to the
grandchildren. When these too became worse
than their predecessors, a son was born to
him." (*Sifre on Deuteronomy,* Piska 312)

The chief priests, scribes and the elders were the religious leaders of the day. As heads of the priesthood and leaders on the
Sanhedrin, they occupied a God-given place of authority over the
Temple, Jerusalem and Judaism in general. The Torah has plenty
to say about this. The priests were given charge of the Tabernacle/
Temple and the assemblies therein. They were to be the teachers of
Torah as well. The Sanhedrin's authority is established in Exodus
18, Numbers 11 and Deuteronomy 17. The Master referred to their
authority as "the seat of Moses" (Matthew 23:1–2); i.e., the place
of authority in which the words of Moses were interpreted and
applied, primarily in laying down the accepted *halachah* (legislation) based upon the words of Moses.

They were the custodians of God's people. Hence they were
only doing their job in questioning the young maverick rabbi from
Nazareth. They could not let just anyone enter the Temple courts,
claim to be Messiah, and stir up the people into a dangerous, revolutionary Messianic fervor. "Tell us by what authority You are doing
these things, or who is the one who gave You this authority?" (Luke
20:2) they demanded. Yeshua answered their inquiry with a dis-

arming question about the authority of another maverick prophet: John the Immerser. When they could not answer His question, He told them a parable. The parable relates the story of a vineyard owner and the difficulty he has in finding good help.

> A man planted a vineyard and put a wall around it, and dug a vat under the wine press and built a tower, and rented it out to vine-growers and went on a journey. And at the harvest time he sent a slave to the vine-growers, in order to receive some of the produce of the vineyard from the vine-growers. And they took him, and beat him and sent him away empty-handed. And again he sent them another slave, and they wounded him in the head, and treated him shamefully. And he sent another, and that one they killed; and so with many others, beating some and killing others. He had one more to send, a beloved son; he sent him last of all to them, saying, "They will respect my son." But those vine-growers said to one another, "This is the heir; come, let us kill him, and the inheritance will be ours!" And they took him, and killed him and threw him out of the vineyard. What will the owner of the vineyard do? He will come and destroy the vine-growers, and will give the vineyard to others. (Mark 12:1–9)

SYMBOLISM OF THE PARABLE

Most of the symbolism of the parable is fairly straightforward. The owner of the vineyard is God. The owner's beloved son and heir can only be a reference to Yeshua. The owner's servants are clearly the prophets whom God has sent over the centuries to warn Israel. "Though the LORD has sent all his servants the prophets to you again and again, you have not listened or paid any attention," the prophet Jeremiah declared.[125] Jerusalem was the city that "kills the prophets and stones those who are sent to her," the Master lamented in Matthew 23:37.

The parable of the vineyard is one of Yeshua's most pointed stories. The Temple authorities to whom He addressed it certainly got the point. Mark 12:12 tells us, "They understood that He spoke the parable against them." Subsequent generations of gospel readers have been less astute. The interpretation of the parable of the vineyard is often tainted by unwarranted theological assumptions.

REPLACEMENT THEOLOGY

The parable of the vineyard is most often explained as an illustration of how Christianity replaces Judaism. The vineyard is understood to be the kingdom of heaven. The wicked tenants are the Jews. Thus the Jews are thrown out of the kingdom, and their place as God's elect is given to others. This interpretation seems to find support in Matthew's telling of the parable. In Matthew 21:43, Yeshua ends the parable with: "Therefore I say to you, the kingdom of God will be taken away from you and given to a people, producing the fruit of it." (Matthew 21:43) In retribution for killing His servants and His Son, the Owner of the vineyard punishes the wicked tenants and gives the kingdom to another nation; namely, the Gentiles. By this we are to understand that the Jews are replaced by Christians in God's kingdom. This reading of the parable is heavily colored by the assumptions of Replacement Theology.

REPLACEMENT THEOLOGY INTERPRETATION OF
THE PARABLE OF THE VINEYARD

Owner of the vineyard	God
Vineyard	Kingdom of heaven
Wicked tenants	Jews
The owner's servants	Prophets
The owner's son	Yeshua
New tenants	Christians

SINGULAR MEANING: After years of contending with Israel, God deemed the crucifixion of Yeshua as the last straw. He takes away the kingdom from the Jewish people and gives it to Gentile Christians.

The Replacement Theology interpretation of the parable of the vineyard is so ubiquitous that it normally passes completely unchecked. However, there are two primary problems with this interpretation.

The first problem is one of context. Yeshua's parable comes as a response to a question posed to Him by the Temple officials about authority. They demanded to know by whose authority Yeshua was teaching. The Replacement Theology interpretation ignores the question posed and the gospel context. But how is that relevant to the situation in Mark? Questions regarding the Jewish people and the Christian religion are not at all in view in Mark 12. Those issues are not even remotely connected to the confrontation between Yeshua and the Temple authorities.

The second problem with the Replacement Theology interpretation is in the symbolic meaning of the vineyard and the tenants. Parables are supposed to be understood symbolically. They are illustrations used to make a singular point. But if we misunderstand the symbols, we are likely to misinterpret the parable. The interpretation that equates the wicked tenants to the Jews and the vineyard as equaling the kingdom of heaven is highly unlikely. The best way to demonstrate the error, and to correct our reading of the parable, is to compare it with similar rabbinic parables and a very similar parable in Isaiah chapter 5 that uses the same language and several of the same metaphors.

The Rabbinic Understanding

Yeshua's parables are best understood when compared to the larger body of rabbinic teachings found in classical Jewish literature. Illustrating the teaching of Torah by way of parables was the conventional medium of Yeshua's day.

The image of Israel as God's vineyard is common in rabbinic writings. Lightfoot brings the following example from the *Tanchumah*, a collection of traditional rabbinic material from the Talmudic era. Here the vineyard symbolizes the house of Israel (i.e., the people of Israel).

> The matter may be compared to a king that had a vineyard; and there were three who were enemies to it. What were they? One cut down the branches. The second cut off the branches. And the third rooted up the vines. That king is the King of Kings, the Blessed LORD. The vineyard of the

LORD is the house of Israel. The three enemies are Pharaoh, Nebuchadnezzar, and Haman. (*Tanchumah*)[126]

There are many other examples. We will consider a few of them. In the *Midrash Rabbah*, Rabbi Yehudah emphatically declares:

> The vineyard of the Holy One, blessed be He, is none other than Israel, as is proved by the text, "The vineyard of the LORD Almighty is the house of Israel, and the men of Judah are the garden of His delight." (*Leviticus Rabbah* 32:1, quoting Isaiah 5:7)

The wicked tenants set over the vineyard find a parallel in rabbinic literature. Commenting on the verse in Song of Songs (8:11) that says "Solomon had a vineyard in Baal Hamon; He entrusted the vineyard to caretakers," the *Midrash Rabbah*[127] homiletically declares that the vineyard is Israel, and the tenants are foreign powers that take authority over Israel, such as Nebuchadnezzar.

An even more dramatic parallel is found in *Sifre*, a Mishnaic-era commentary on Deuteronomy, which preserves a parable with similar elements, including the king's son. Here the wicked tenants are foreign nations, and the vineyard is the land of Israel. The king's beloved son symbolizes the people of Israel:

> A parable: A king had a field which he leased to tenants. When the tenants began to steal from it, he took it away from them and leased it to their children. When the children began to act worse than their fathers, he took it away from them and gave it to the grandchildren. When these too became worse than their predecessors, a son was born to him. He then said to the grandchildren, "Leave my property. You may not remain in it. Give me back my portion, so that I may repossess it." (*Sifre on Deuteronomy* Piska 312)

The following midrash by Shimon bar Yochai, an early-second-century sage, is even more pertinent to understanding the symbolism Yeshua used. In Bar Yochai's version, not only is the vineyard Israel, but those who tend the vines are Israel's political and religious leaders:

> Why was Israel likened to a vineyard? In the case of a vineyard, in the beginning one must hoe it, then weed it, and then erect supports when he sees the clusters forming... So also Israel—each and every shepherd who oversees them must tend them as he would tend a vineyard. (Midrash on Proverbs 19:21)[128]

According to Shimon bar Yochai's version, the vineyard represents Israel, and the tenants represent the religious authorities over Israel. In all of the above examples, Israel is symbolized by a vineyard. The Vineyard = Israel equation, so common in rabbinic literature, springs primarily from a parable written centuries before by the prophet Isaiah.

Isaiah's Song of the Vineyard

In Isaiah chapter 5, the prophet makes a parable comparing Israel to a vineyard planted by God. The vineyard owner selected a plot of ground, dug around it, removed its stones and planted a choice vine. Each of these preparations is a familiar element of agriculture in the rocky soil of Israel's hill country. The vineyard owner then built a tower in the middle of the vineyard and dug a pit for a winepress within the vineyard. When everything was completed, the owner waited for his vine to bear fruit. It did not. "He expected it to produce good grapes, but it produced only worthless ones" (Isaiah 5:2).

As Isaiah unpacks the parable's symbolism, we are told that God is the owner/husbandman, Israel is the vineyard, and the fruit He anticipated was justice and righteousness.

> For the vineyard of the LORD of hosts is the house of Israel and the men of Judah His delightful plant. Thus He looked for justice, but behold, bloodshed; For righteousness, but behold, a cry of distress. (Isaiah 5:7)

Both Yeshua's vineyard illustration and its rabbinic parallels draw heavily on the Isaiah 5 passage. In fact, when the introduction of Yeshua's parable is examined against the Greek LXX version of Isaiah 5:1–2, the language is often verbatim.[129] The allusion is explicit.

Yeshua's listeners and Mark's readers were both meant to make the connection between the parable and Isaiah 5.[130]

CONTEXTUAL INTERPRETATION OF THE PARABLE OF THE VINEYARD	
Owner of the vineyard	God
Vineyard	Israel
Fruit of the vineyard	Righteousness
Wicked tenants	Religious authorities present
The owner's servants	Prophets
The owner's son	Yeshua
New tenants	New religious authorities

SINGULAR MEANING: Despite the call of the prophets and Yeshua Himself, repentance has not been forthcoming. Therefore, a day of reckoning is coming when the religious-political authorities over Israel are going to be toppled and replaced.

Yeshua's parable has an affinity with the Isaiah parable in more than just language. The symbolic values are also the same. In both parables, God is the owner and planter of the vineyard. In both parables, the vineyard is Israel. Isaiah spells it out for us: "The vineyard of the LORD of hosts is the house of Israel and the men of Judah His delightful plant" (Isaiah 5:7).

THE WICKED TENANTS

If the vineyard symbolizes Israel, how do we explain Matthew 21:43, where Yeshua says, "Therefore I say to you, the kingdom of God will be taken away from you, and given to a nation producing the fruit of it"? As we have seen, the term "kingdom of heaven" refers to the active rule and reign of God. It is the authority of the King. The authority of the kingdom, which has hitherto been vested in the wicked tenants, is to be taken away from them and given to others.

The wicked tenants are those in authority over the vineyard; i.e., Israel. The religious leaders, primarily the Sadducean-dominated priesthood and Sanhedrin, are the wicked tenants Yeshua was speaking about, and they knew He was talking about them.

In the days of the Master, the priesthood of Israel had become largely corrupt. It was dominated by the Sadducees and controlled by the wealthy, Romanized power elite. The corrupt Yosef Caipha (Caiaphas) was the man on top of the priesthood.[131] In the parable, the Master compared the priestly authorities to wicked husband-men who had failed in their responsibilities to tend the vineyard and rebelled against the owner of the vineyard. They are the ones from whom the kingdom is taken—not the Jewish people.

This explanation answers to the context. Yeshua told the parable of the vineyard in response to the chief priest's question about authority. "By what authority are you doing these things?" they asked in Mark 11:28, "and who gave you authority to do this?" Just as the vineyard owner's son has authority above that of the tenants, so too Yeshua has authority above that of the present religious leaders.

The parable also warns about the impending judgment of Israel. The call of the prophets and even the words of Yeshua had gone unheeded. Rather than repenting, the religious authorities planned on doing to Yeshua what their predecessors did to the prophets. Therefore, a day of reckoning was coming when they would find themselves removed from their position of authority and replaced by new leadership.

In light of this explanation, we should understand the parable as follows: "Despite the call of the prophets and Yeshua Himself, repentance has not been forthcoming; therefore, a day of reckoning is coming when the religious-political authorities over Israel are going to be toppled and replaced."

Keys to the Kingdom

The Replacement Theology explanation is illegitimate. It is not the Jewish people who are being replaced in the parable; it is the corrupt religious and political authorities of first-century Jerusalem. The vineyard in which they have been employed is Israel. Through the parable, Yeshua was telling those authorities that their term of service is ending. In Matthew's version, we are told that the vineyard owner "will bring those wretches to a wretched end, and will rent out the vineyard to other vine-growers who will pay him the proceeds at the proper seasons" (Matthew 21:41).

But who are the new vine-growers? Who are these "others" who are given authority over Israel? The Gospels seem to indicate that the new tenants are the disciples and elders of the believing community. In the messianic era, "when the Son of Man will sit on His glorious throne," the twelve disciples "shall sit upon twelve thrones, judging the twelve tribes of Israel" (Matthew 19:28). The Twelve are given the "keys of the kingdom of heaven" and the authority "to bind and to loose" (Matthew 16:19), terminology that implies the authority to make legal decisions.

An honest, historical review of the situation must admit that the authority over Israel did not land with the community of disciples, at least not initially. But just as Yeshua said, authority over Israel was wrested away from the corrupt and morally bankrupt leadership of His day. The Jewish revolt and subsequent Roman occupation brought a sudden end to the powerful elite who had misruled the people for so long. Those wretches came to a wretched end indeed.

THIS IS THE HEIR

Ultimately, the parable is meant to answer the initial question posed to Yeshua in Mark 11. The religious authorities had asked Him, "By what authority are You doing these things or, who gave You this authority to do these things?" (Mark 11:28) The parable of the vineyard answers the question while making a statement about the nature of God-given authority.

The parable is meant to remind the religious leaders that their authority is derived only from God. That authority comes with accountability. They are supposed to be caring for Israel like hired vine-dressers caring for a vineyard. Since they are merely hired men, they can be replaced. Yeshua's authority, on the other hand, is inherited. He is the heir. He represents the owner of the vineyard because He is His Son.

Through the parable of the vineyard, Yeshua answers their question in a roundabout manner. They asked, "By what authority are You doing these things?" Through means of the parable, He answers, "I do them by the same authority that initially gave you authority over Israel; namely, God. But whereas your authority is tenuous in that you are merely hired help who can and will be replaced, My authority is inherent in that I am the Owner's Son."

In the year 70 CE, the tenancy over the vineyard of Israel changed hands. The religious elite of Yeshua's day were supplanted. A new leadership emerged from the ruins. For almost two thousand years, these new custodians have preserved the identity of Judaism. They are the sages and rabbis of the generations, and they are worthy of respect as the caretakers of Israel proper. Ultimately, however, they too are only hired vine-dressers; they are not the owners of the vineyard. They have been given temporary authority over the vineyard until the true owner returns from His long journey. When the Son returns, the authority over the vineyard will return to Him. In that day, "the Son of Man will sit on His glorious throne," and the twelve disciples "shall sit upon twelve thrones, judging the twelve tribes of Israel" (Matthew 19:28).

Chapter 13

THE STONE THE BUILDERS REJECTED

If a stone falls on a pot, woe to the pot! If a
pot falls on a stone, woe to the pot! In either
case, woe to the pot! (*Esther Rabbah* 7.10)

Yeshua asked them, "Did you never read in the Scriptures, 'The stone which the builders rejected, this became the chief cornerstone; this came about from the LORD, and it is marvelous in our eyes'?" (Matthew 21:42) It was a rhetorical question. Of course the Temple authorities had read the passage. Not only had they read that verse before, they had sung it in the Temple while slaughtering their Passover lambs every year. They had sung it in their homes at every Passover *seder*. They had sung it as part of their liturgies for the festival of Sukkot. It is Psalm 118:22–23, part of the festival liturgy called the *Hallel* (הלל). *Hallel* means "praise." The *Hallel* is a series of Psalms (113–118) beginning and ending with the words "Praise the Lord"—*Halleluyah*.

The words of the *Hallel*, particularly Psalm 118, are closely associated with Passover. They are sung at the conclusion of the Passover *seder* meal. The *Hallel* is almost certainly the hymn Yeshua and His disciples sang at the conclusion of the Last *Seder*.[132] Psalm 118 is the grand finale of the *Hallel*, and Yeshua quoted from Psalm 118 when He asked His critics, "Did you never read in the Scriptures, 'The stone which the builders rejected, this became the chief cornerstone; this came about from the LORD, and it is marvelous in our eyes'?"

THE JEWISH INTERPRETATION

Psalm 118 is a messianic acclamation psalm. It was probably used in first-Temple Judaism to celebrate a king's triumphant return from battle. The story in 2 Chronicles 20 of King Jehoshaphat's triumph employs passages from this psalm. The chronicler describes the king's joyous return from battle as he and the army entered Jerusalem. "They came to Jerusalem with harps, lyres and trumpets to the house of the Lord" (2 Chronicles 20:28).

Jewish tradition purports that Psalm 118 is a psalm heralding the messianic redemption. Other old traditions held that the psalm refers to David's rise to the throne. Radak reconciles these two interpretations by suggesting that the psalm speaks simultaneously of the rise of David to the throne and the future advent of Messiah.[133] It is further believed that Psalm 118 will be sung to welcome the Messiah when He arrives. Therefore, the classical Jewish interpretation of the psalm projects the imagery into the realm of messianic interpretation.

According to these opinions, the phrase "I shall not die but live, and of the works of the Lord" (Psalm 118:17) refers to the resurrection. "This is the Lord's doing; It is marvelous in our eyes" (118:23) refers to the amazement of the nations when Israel is catapulted to greatness. "This is the day which the Lord has made" (118:24) refers to the appointed time when God will send Messiah. "O Lord, do save, we beseech thee; O Lord, we beseech Thee, do send prosperity" (118:25) is interpreted as a plea to God that He might send Messiah immediately.

When the Master entered Jerusalem for that last Passover, the crowd met Him with shouts of acclamation drawn from Psalm 118: "Hosanna! Save us now! Blessed is He who comes in the name of the Lord!" The gospel writers obviously regarded this psalm as finding its fulfillment in the passion story of Yeshua. They quote it widely in the Apostolic Scriptures and especially in the narratives of the final week leading up to the crucifixion. In a sense, it is as if the solemn and joyous tones of Psalm 118 form the background music for the dramatic events that lead up to the crucifixion.

After being welcomed in Jerusalem with acclamations from Psalm 118, Yeshua spent His time teaching in the Temple courts. While teaching, He clashed with the Temple authorities, who were seeking some way to discredit His teaching and His claim to Davidic kingship. After one particularly sharp confrontation, He challenged them with a seemingly cryptic citation from Psalm 118.

Yeshua said to them, "Have you not even read this Scripture: 'The stone which the builders rejected, this became the chief cornerstone; this came about from the LORD, and it is marvelous in our eyes'? And He who falls on this stone will be broken to pieces; but on whomever it falls, it will scatter him like dust" (Mark 12:10–11, followed by Matthew 21:44, both quoting Psalm 118:22–23).

THE STONECUTTING TRADE

To understand the meaning of the Psalm's imagery and why it was significant in the mouth of Yeshua, one needs to know something of the ancient crafts of stonecutting and masonry. In the land of Israel, stone is the most readily available building material. Buildings are primarily constructed of stone. The archaeology of first-century Judea reveals an amazing sophistication of masonry and stonecutting. Herodian-era blocks are still readily identifiable in standing structures. Each stone was cut to exacting specifications. They were so carefully and perfectly fitted together that they required no mortar.

Such precision would have been especially necessary when building an arch. In the architecture of the Middle East, the arch bore much of the weight of the structure above it. Made without mortar, each stone of an arch needed to be fitted precisely to form the correct angle of arching and exert consistent pressure on the adjacent stones. Should a stone be misfitted, the structural integrity of the entire building could be compromised.

Psalm 118 invokes this imagery. We are meant to imagine a team of masons cutting stones for such an arch when one of the stones is accidentally mis-cut. Realizing that the stone is the wrong shape for that part of the arch, they toss it onto a scrap heap of cracked and misfit stones—useless rubble. As the work proceeds, they prepare to cut the final piece, the capstone (*rosh pinah*, ראש פינה) of the arch, the one on which all the other stones will press in order to support much of the structure. Looking about for a suitable stone to form into the capstone, the masons discover the stone they had earlier discarded as a misfit. The once seemingly useless stone, it turns out, is perfect for the capstone. The stone the builders rejected has become the most important stone of all.

DAVID THE KING

At least as early as Rabbi Yonaton (early second century), in whose name the tradition is reported,[134] the stone (*even*, אבן) the builders rejected is identified as referring to King David. The Talmud explains that just as the odd-cut stone was initially rejected by the builders, so too David's father and brothers did not consider him a candidate for anointing. They did not even present him before Samuel the prophet. In their opinion, he was not worthy king material.

Eliyahu Kitov brings a tradition that expands upon this legend. He says that David's father and brothers suspected him of being born out of infidelity and disregarded him as a candidate for the kingship on that basis. Though there is no indication in the text of 1 Samuel that this was true, Yeshua's conception and birth were similarly shrouded in rumor and scandal.[135] Thus, according to rabbinic interpretation of Psalm 118, the "stone the builders rejected" refers to David, and his rise to "capstone" refers to his rise to the throne of Israel.

Following the same line of interpretation, one *Targum*[136] on Psalm 118 reads the Hebrew word for "stone" (*even*, אבן) as "son" (*ben*, בן) and renders the passage as "the son the builders rejected."[137] According to this interpretation, it was David's father, Jesse, who, upon seeing the prophet anoint his son David as king, declared, "The stone [son] the builders rejected has become the capstone." David's brothers, upon seeing the prophet anoint their youngest brother king, declared, "This is the LORD's doing; it is marvelous in our eyes."[138]

It is possible that Yeshua meant to invoke the tradition of the early rejection of David when He scolded the Temple authorities, saying, "Have you never read…" If the rejected stone was popularly understood to be David, the passage became an apt rebuke. It is as if Yeshua said to them, "Just as David was at first rejected, but later was recognized as God's choice of messiah, so too you are rejecting Me."

The Rejection of Yeshua

The use of the passage becomes more meaningful when we realize that the word "builders" is a term the sages homiletically applied to themselves.[139] They referred to themselves as the "builders" of Israel. Yeshua referred to Himself as the stone the builders (i.e., scribes and teachers of Torah) rejected.

This analogy enabled the early apostolic community to explain the mainstream rejection of their Messiah. It also gave them a glimpse of hope for a future when all Israel would recognize the chief cornerstone to be Yeshua. Like David (who was once a lowly shepherd and later regarded as an outlaw), they believed that Yeshua would one day rise from obscurity and rejection to universal recognition. Just as an oddly cut stone (*even*, אבן) might be tossed aside by builders as they fit together an arch, so too Yeshua was rejected by the religious authorities and mainstream Judaism. Just as the builders might later reconsider the stone they had tossed aside and thought disqualified, only to discover it was the perfect fit for the capstone (*rosh pinah*, ראש פינה) that completes the structure and provides it the integrity to remain standing, so too the rejected and crucified Yeshua turned out to be the living Messiah and anointed King of the Jews.

An Apostolic Midrash

Shimon Peter was confident about the identity of the stone. Early in the apostolic ministry we find him declaring to the curious crowds in the Temple, "[Yeshua] is the stone which was rejected by you the builders, but which became the very cornerstone" (Acts 4:11). Obviously the Master's words had not been lost on him. By the time he wrote his first epistle, the capstone image of Psalm 118 had been further developed. He linked it with two "stone" passages from Isaiah to form a complex midrash about the Messiah.

> As you come to Him, the Living Stone—rejected by men but chosen by God and precious to Him—you also, like living stones, are being built into a spiritual house to be a holy priesthood, offering spiritual sacrifices acceptable to God through Yeshua the Messiah. For in Scripture it says: "See, I lay a stone in Zion, a chosen and precious cornerstone, and the one who trusts in Him will never be put to

shame." Now to you who believe, this stone is precious. But to those who do not believe, "The stone the builders rejected has become the capstone," and, "A stone that causes men to stumble and a rock that makes them fall." They stumble because they disobey the message— which is also what they were destined for. (1 Peter 2:4–8, citing Isaiah 28:16, Psalm 118:22–23 and Isaiah 8:14 NIV)

In this passage, Shimon Peter uses typical rabbinic methodologies to link together three otherwise disparate and unrelated passages. He combines the three passages on the basis of certain keywords common to all three. The rabbis often employed this method of biblical cross-reference where a scripture is used to define another to further search out a passage. Each of the passages quoted by Shimon Peter contains the keyword *even*, which means "stone." Psalm 118 and Isaiah 28:16 both refer to the *even* as a capstone (*pinah*, פינה). In the world of rabbinic logic, the two passages may therefore be used together to uncover further meaning. This type of hermeneutical engineering is typically referred to as *midrash*. *Midrash* means "searched out." By combining Psalm 118, Isaiah 8:14 and 28:16 on the basis of their common keywords, Shimon Peter has searched out a messianic meaning—he has created a midrash.

> The stone (*even*) the builders rejected has become the capstone (*pinah*); the Lord has done this, and it is marvelous in our eyes. (Psalm 118:22–23 NIV)

> See, I lay a stone (*even*) in Zion, a tested stone, a precious cornerstone (*pinah*) for a sure foundation; the one who trusts in Him will never be dismayed. (Isaiah 28:16 NIV)

> He will be a stone (*even*) that causes men to stumble and a rock that makes them fall. And for the people of Jerusalem He will be a trap and a snare. (Isaiah 8:14 NIV)

The common words *even* and *pinah*, and the proactive placement of the stone by God, link the three passages. The meaning Peter has searched out is that the celebrated capstone will be a stone of stumbling for some. Yeshua will not be received by everyone; some will reject Him. For those who believe in Him, He will be a sure foundation, but for those who do not, He will be a stone of stumbling. Yet even their rejection of Yeshua is ordained by God, for it is God who placed the precious stone in Zion; therefore, all things are according to His purpose.

It is a brilliant piece of midrash, but Shimon Peter isn't really the author of it. It was Yeshua Himself who originally made the connection between the capstone and the stumbling stone. In His challenge to the Temple authorities, He told them, "He who falls on this stone will be broken to pieces" (Matthew 21:44).

Daniel's Crushing Stone

Yeshua drew in yet another *even* (stone) passage into His midrash. He told the Temple authorities, "Everyone who falls on that stone will be broken to pieces; but on whomever it falls, it will scatter him like dust" (Luke 20:18). The falling stone that crushes those it falls on is borrowed from a stone passage written by the prophet Daniel.

> You continued looking until a stone was cut out without hands, and it struck the statue on its feet of iron and clay, and crushed them. ...The God of heaven will set up a kingdom which will never be destroyed, and that kingdom will not be left for another people; it will crush and put an end to all these kingdoms, but it will itself endure forever. Inasmuch as you saw that a stone was cut out of the mountain without hands and that it crushed..." (Daniel 2:34; 44–45)

In the interpretation of the Daniel passage, the stone cut out from the mountain symbolizes the kingdom of God. Through a midrashic connection, Yeshua understood the rock cut out of the mountain as the rock that the builders rejected and the rock that God would lay in Zion and the rock men would stumble over. He understood all of the above to refer to Himself.

Yeshua and Shimon Peter weren't the only ones to make midrash on Psalm 118. Rabbinic literature preserves a similar interpretation that combines the rock the builders rejected with the crushing rock from Daniel's apocalyptic vision. In the *Midrash Rabbah*, however, the symbolism has been somewhat reassigned. The people of Israel are regarded as the rejected stone upon/under which others will be crushed.

Rabbi Shimon ben Yose ben Lakunia said, "...Israel is compared to stones, as it says [in Genesis 49:24] 'because of the Shepherd, the Rock of Israel,' and [in Psalm 118:22] 'The stone the builders rejected.' But the other nations are compared to pottery, as it is written [in Isaiah 30:14], 'It will break in pieces like pottery.' If a stone falls on a pot, woe to the pot! If a pot falls on a stone, woe to the pot! In either case, woe to the pot! So too, whoever tries to attack [Israel] receives his comeuppance because of them. That is why it says in the dream of Nebuchadnezzar [in Daniel 2:34], 'a rock was cut out, but not by human hands. It struck the statue on its feet of iron and clay and smashed them.'" (*Esther Rabbah* 7:10)

In the same way, Yeshua is a dangerous stone. Those who trip over Him are shattered, and those He falls upon are crushed and scattered like dust.

BETWEEN A FATHER AND SON

In his book *The Messiah in the Old Testament*, Risto Santala tells the following story about Psalm 118:22.

A certain young student, while supervising the building of a high-tension electricity line on the slopes of Mount Carmel, chanced to find a torn New Testament, which had been thrown into the undergrowth. His father was a teacher of the Talmud in a local college and so the son was also well-acquainted with the rabbinic literature. Straight away on his first reading he realized that [Yeshua] was the Deliverer he had been searching for in the Old Testament and in his father's writings, and only two weeks later he confessed his faith to his father. The latter then offered him money, a house, and even a wife, if he would only give up his conviction.

Our student had not yet left home at Passover time. After eating the [Passover *seder*], it was the custom to sing the *Hallel* psalms, and when they had sung psalm 118, the youngest member of the family, a boy of 19, asked his father, "What is this stone?" Father went completely silent. "Dad, what is the stone which the builders have rejected?" Once more the head of the family remained silent, even though he always answered the Passover evening questions. "Dad, what is the stone which has become the cornerstone?" the boy asked a third time. At that our believing student requested permission to reply, and his father nodded. The young man's answer was enigmatic: "It is what is between father and son!"

Being accustomed to [rabbinic] riddles the rest of the family understood immediately who he was talking about. "Stone" in Hebrew is *even* [אבן]; reading the first part of this (in Hebrew characters) three-letter word, we read the word *av* [אב], "father", reading the latter part from the middle gives *ben* [בן], "son". Of course, everyone [at the table] knew then that [Yeshua] had come between this father and his firstborn son.[140]

This anecdote contains within it some of the pain of the rejected stone. The Son (*ben*, בן) of the Father (*av*, אב) is the stone (*even*, אבן) the builders rejected. But herein is also hope. Those same builders will one day acknowledge this stone to be the chief cornerstone. Yeshua will one day ascend to the throne of David in the sight of all mankind. Then we will all declare, "This is the Lord's doing. It is marvelous in our eyes."

Chapter 14

THE KING IN DISGUISE

YESHUA'S LOST HIGH HOLIDAY PARABLES

A blast will be sounded … and all the
dwellers of the earth will cross before You
like the members of a flock. Like a shepherd
shepherding his flock … thus You will pass and
count and number and visit the souls of all
flesh. (Traditional Prayer for Rosh HaShanah)

Several apocryphal and bogus gospels purport to contain "the lost teachings of Jesus." The majority of those sources are hardly worthy of mention. Most of them came from second- and third-century heretical sects of Christianity that had lost sight of the historical Yeshua and His teachings. But we may be in possession of two "lost parables" of Yeshua right in the gospel of Matthew. These parables are thematically linked to the High Holidays.

In Jewish tradition, the High Holidays of the Feast of Trumpets (*Rosh HaShanah*)[141] and the Day of Atonement (*Yom Kippur*) are regarded as days of judgment. Rosh HaShanah, the civil New Year, is comparable to the end of the heavenly fiscal year, so the tradition arose that God reviews the books at the end of each year. According to the classical Jewish explanation, God convenes the heavenly court on Rosh HaShanah, and the books of judgment are opened before the court. Everyone's deeds are recorded therein to be scrutinized by the Judge. The names of the righteous are written in the Book of Life; the names of the wicked are written in the Book of Death. Ten days later, on Yom Kippur, God seals the verdict, and the books are closed.

The decision is based largely upon the accumulation of one's merits or sins over the previous year. A preponderance of merit results in one's name being written in the Book of Life. Hence the traditional greeting in Jewish congregations on Rosh HaShanah is "May you be inscribed in the Book of Life for a sweet year."

SHEPHERD AND JUDGE

This imagery of judgment is akin to the imagery of Matthew 25, wherein a shepherd is recorded as separating sheep and goats (sheep on the right, goats on the left) and a king is found separating righteous and wicked subjects (righteous on the right, wicked on the left).[142] Similar to Matthew 25, the Mishnah expresses the same High Holiday judgment concept in terms of a flock passing before their shepherd. God is presented as a shepherd causing sheep to pass under His staff—counting, calculating, reckoning and separating them:

> At Rosh Hashanah all flesh passes before Him like the members of a flock. (m.*Rosh Hashanah* 1:2, cf b.*Rosh Hashanah* 16a)

Rabbi Yehudah the Prince recorded the Mishnah less than a century after the days of the Master. It is the written version of much older orally transmitted material. Based simply on this mishnaic image of God judging all mankind like a shepherd causing sheep to pass before him, the medieval Rabbi Amnon of Mainz composed a prayer, which has become one of the central liturgies of the High Holiday synagogue service:

> And with a great shofar, a blast will be sounded ... and angels will hasten ... and all the dwellers of the earth will cross before You like the members of a flock. Like a shepherd shepherding his flock, passing his sheep beneath his staff, thus You will pass and count and number and visit the souls of all flesh." (*Unesanaeh Tokef* from the Rosh HaShanah Liturgy)

The haunting imagery of God standing like a shepherd, pasturing His flock, making sheep pass underneath His staff, sounds so similar to the scene described in Yeshua's parable of the sheep and the goats that one would suspect Rabbi Amnon was plagiarizing the Gospels. He wasn't. Rabbi Amnon had reason to be bitter toward Christianity. The church tried to force him to convert, and, as the story goes, when he refused, the inquisitors chopped his feet and hands from his body, one joint at a time. He was then released to live his life as a cripple, after which he wrote the prayer. Rabbi Amnon wasn't borrowing imagery from the Gospels; he was borrowing it from the Mishnah. The obvious affinity with Yeshua's parable of the sheep and the goats may imply that Yeshua was familiar with a similar pre-mishnaic tradition:

> But when the Son of Man comes in His glory, and all the angels with Him, then He will sit on His glorious throne. All the nations will be gathered before Him; and He will separate them from one another, as the shepherd separates the sheep from the goats; and He will put the sheep on His right, and the goats on the left. (Matthew 25:31–33)

Two Lost Parables

Two parables seem to be missing from the text of Matthew. This is not to suggest that the gospel of Matthew is somehow deficient or that the lost parables were included in an earlier version of Matthew. Instead, we find some pieces of parables in Matthew 25 that seem to be excerpts from longer teachings. Two seeming parable fragments are fused together to form the famous parable of the sheep and the goats of Matthew 25:31–46. Admittedly, the material communicates strongly enough as it is written in Matthew. No improvement is necessary. But one cannot help but wonder if there might have been a longer version behind these parable fragments.

In Matthew 25, the parable of the sheep and the goats is told in conjunction with an immediate explanation. The explanation, however, sounds suspiciously like a different parable. The dramatic shift from one metaphor set (shepherd, sheep and goats) to another (king, kind citizens and unkind citizens) is disconcerting. It is also atypical of Yeshua's storytelling style. Nevertheless, it is obviously the same subject matter. The imagery of shepherd, sheep and goats transfers smoothly into imagery of the king, the righteous and the wicked. The latter explains the former. But might these have been originally two separate parables?

Yeshua commonly employed series parables (a string of two or three parables told back to back) to drive home a single point. For an example of a series of three thematically linked parables told back to back, see the parable of the lost sheep, the parable of the lost coin and the parable of the lost son in Luke 15. Each of these parables is linked by a common story, theme and meaning. Matthew 25:31–46 may have been taught originally by Yeshua as two separate parables: the parable of the sheep and the goats and the parable of the king in disguise.

THE SHEEP AND THE GOATS

There is not really a parable of the sheep and the goats in Matthew; there is only some metaphoric language employing those symbols. The text lacks several important conventions of the parable form. For example, rather than beginning with the stock parable introduction ("To what can it be compared?"), the passage begins with the words "When the Son of Man comes." We find ourselves in the explanation of the parable without ever hearing the parable.

To better understand the problem, we need only compare it to the full-length text of the parable of the wheat and the tares' in Matthew 13:24–30. Like many rabbinic parables, the passage begins with a stock introduction: "The kingdom of heaven can be compared to ..." That statement of simile, even when it is implied rather than stated, makes a story a parable. The comparative language is absent from the parable of the sheep and the goats. Instead, it literally reads as the Son of Man coming in glory and sorting real sheep from goats. Not a very likely scenario.

In contrast, the parable of the wheat and the tares is presented without breaking the allegory to explain the symbolism. An explanation of the parable is offered later in the passage.[143] In the explanation, Yeshua speaks of the coming of the Son of Man and explains the meaning of the various components of the parable. The explanation, however, is a separate literary unit from the parable.

The sheep-and-goat piece, on the other hand, begins like the explanation of a parable we have not yet heard. Like the explanation of the wheat and the tares, it starts off explaining things in terms of the coming of the Son of Man: "When the Son of Man comes in His glory ..." Aside from this explanation, an actual parable of sheep and goats is absent from the text.

The confusion might arise from Matthew's abbreviated style. Matthew is notorious for condensing his material. It is possible that he so truncated the original teaching that he omitted the sheep and goats parable (if one ever existed) and left us only with the Master's explanation of it. If there ever was an original parable of the sheep and the goats, it might have sounded something like this:

> To what can the kingdom of heaven be compared? The kingdom of heaven will be like a shepherd who kept both sheep and goats. While he pastured them in the day, the sheep and the goats mingled with one another. When he returned to lead them home he wanted to separate the two flocks. First he gathered them all before him, and then he separated them, putting the sheep at his right hand and the goats at his left.

In light of Matthew's probable "lost parable," we can parse out the imagery of the symbolism as follows.

The shepherd	Yeshua
The mixed flock	all nations
The sheep	the righteous
The goats	the wicked

SINGULAR POINT: Not everyone who appears to be in the kingdom is a genuine citizen of the kingdom; when Yeshua returns He will sort one from another.

THE KING IN DISGUISE

Just as we have surmised that there may originally have been a parable of the sheep and the goats, so too there may have been a parable of the king in disguise. In Matthew 25:34–46, Yeshua describes a king who separates the subjects of his kingdom on the basis of whether or not they fed him, clothed him and cared for him while he was disguised in their midst. When the king separates the citizens, he places the righteous on his right and the wicked on his left, just as the shepherd placed the sheep on his right and the goats on his left. But when did the citizens have the opportunity to care for the king? Why didn't they recognize him?

We are provided with Yeshua's explanation of the symbolism ("to the extent that you did it to one of these brothers of Mine, even the least of them, you did it to Me"), but we are not given the original story. The separating of sheep and goats has nothing to do with the circumstances implied by the king's answer. Neither sheep nor goats can be held responsible for feeding and clothing the needy.

For that reason and those cited earlier, we may surmise that there might have been an original parable of the king in disguise. If there were, it is also absent from Matthew's text. Instead, Matthew preserves Yeshua's explanation of the parable along with the "moral of the story," but we are left to imagine what the original parable might have been.

A strong traditional source for such a parable is the legend of King Solomon's exile. Jewish literature alludes to the legend often. It shows up in a variety of sources, so it must have been well known.[144] In fact, it was probably such a popular story that Yeshua didn't even need to retell it. He simply drew imagery from it in Matthew 25 and everyone recognized the characters.

In that story, wise King Solomon foolishly opts to dabble in the occult. He is punished for his hubris by a nasty encounter with a demonic spirit.[145] The demon flings him far from Jerusalem, then takes on his shape and assumes the throne. The real King Solomon is reduced to wandering from city to city, begging for food. Though he protests that he is the true king and that the man on the throne is an imposter, his claims are disregarded as lunacy. No one believes him. Some have pity on him and feed him; others drive him away. The King of Ammon at first allows him to serve as kitchen help but later exiles him to the wilderness to starve.

Meanwhile, back in Jerusalem, the Sanhedrin becomes suspicious about the apparent king's recent strange behavior. They investigate the matter. Realizing what has happened, they banish the evil imposter and begin a search for the real king. In the end, Solomon is returned to his throne and everyone lives happily ever after, as they say in fairy tales.

Once restored to his throne, Solomon was in a position to reward those who had shown him kindness and to punish those who had mistreated him while he was among them as a beggar.

Yeshua's parable of the king in disguise follows similar lines. When the King is returned to His throne, His subjects are dismayed. "Lord, when did we see You hungry, and feed You, or thirsty, and give You drink? And when did we see You a stranger, and invite You in, or naked, and clothe You? And when did we see You sick, or in prison, and come to You?" (Matthew 25:37–39) The original parable Yeshua told (if there was an original parable) may have begun something like this:

> To what can the kingdom of heaven be compared? The kingdom of heaven is like a king who was banished from his throne and wandered through his kingdom, begging from place to place and from door to door. Though he cried out earnestly, none recognized him. Some showed the man mercy, but others sent him away. When at last he was restored to his throne, he sent his servants to summon all his subjects before him. To those who had treated him kindly while he was in exile he said, "Come and take your reward, for I was hungry and you gave me something to eat."

ACTS OF LOVING-KINDNESS

Though we no longer possess the parable, we still possess the meaning of it. The criteria by which we will be judged are based upon how we treat the downtrodden among us. Feeding the hungry, sating the thirsty, clothing the naked, visiting the sick and the imprisoned are examples of what the Talmud calls acts of loving-kindness (*gemilut chasidim*, גמילות חסדים).[146] Such acts are regarded as higher than all sacrifices and as more meritorious than all the commandments.[147] Along these lines, we can parse the imagery of the parable as follows:

The King	Yeshua
Those on His right	those who performed acts of loving-kindness for others in need
Those on His left	those who did not perform acts of loving-kindness for others in need
The least of His brothers	the hungry, the thirsty, the naked, the sick and the imprisoned
The reward	the messianic kingdom and eternal life
The punishment	Gehennah

A midrash on Psalm 118:19 sounds surprisingly similar to the parable of the king in disguise. Psalm 118:19 reads, "Open for me the gates of righteousness." Why does it say "gates of righteousness"? Is there more than one gate? *Midrash Shocher Tov* explains the significance of the plural usage.

> In the future, they [i.e., the angels] will ask a man, "On which mitzvah did you concentrate?" If he answers, "I fed the hungry," they will tell him, "This is the gate for those who fed the hungry; you may enter!" If a man answers, "I gave drink to the thirsty," they tell him, "This is the gate of those who gave drink to the thirsty; you may enter!" The same will happen to those who clothed the naked, provided homes for orphans, practiced loving-kindness or concentrated on any of the [commandments]." (*Midrash Schocher Tov* on Psalm 118:20)

The Least of His Brothers

Like the sheep-and-goat imagery, the king in disguise parable naturally lends itself to the themes of the High Holy Days. The coming of the Son of Man and the final judgment of all nations are related to Rosh HaShanah and Yom Kippur. Every Rosh HaShanah, we gather to hear the shofar blown in anticipation of the coming of the King and His coronation. In so doing, we should remember the lesson of Yeshua: The King wears many disguises. As we look forward to Messiah's advent, we should remember the old Yiddish proverb, "The Messiah you're expecting will never come; the Messiah that's coming, you never expected."

In the narratives of the book of Genesis, there is a motif of concealed identity that culminates in the story of Joseph. Unlike the story of Solomon, where the beggar is actually King Solomon, in Joseph's story the king is your brother.

Near the end of the story, Joseph reveals his true identity to his brothers with the words "I am Joseph." [148] Prior to that moment they never suspected that the Gentile prince was their brother. This is the great reversal of the book of Genesis.

At the end of the age, Yeshua tells us, there will be another great reversal. This time, however, it will be all nations that are gathered before the King. This time, the surprise will fall upon the nations, who in utter dismay will protest to the King and say, "Master, when did we see You hungry and feed You, or thirsty and give You something to drink? When did we see You a stranger and invite You in, or needing clothes and clothe You? When did we see You sick or in prison and go to visit You?"

Notice that in Matthew 25:32 the subject of the coming judgment is "all nations," a term that usually implies the Gentile nations, as contrasted with Israel. It is the nations that stand in judgment before the King. In a startlingly ironic twist on the Joseph story, He will reply, "Truly I say to you, to the extent that you did it to one of these brothers of Mine, even the least of them, you did it to Me." The brothers of Yeshua are the Jewish people. He is the King of the Jews.

How frightening, then, that the Jewish people have been the subject of systematic persecutions in every nation where they have sojourned. And Christians have been the chief among their persecutors. Is it possible that the King has been among us all these years in the guise of His brothers—the Jewish people?

> He was despised and rejected by men, a man of sorrows, and acquainted with grief; and like one from whom men hide their face, he was despised, and we did not esteemed him. (Isaiah 53:3)

The apocryphal book of Enoch brings a parallel passage that may have inspired or been inspired by the lost parables of Matthew 25. From Enoch (62:5–11) we read of the final judgment, when all nations are gathered before the throne of glory on which is seated the Son of Man. They hope for mercy at His hands but are dismayed to find they will be punished for how they oppressed God's children and His chosen.

> When they see that Son of Man sitting on the Throne of His Glory, and the kings and the mighty and all who possess the earth...and all the elect shall stand before Him on that day. And all the kings and the mighty and the exalted and those who rule the earth shall fall down before Him on their faces, and worship and set their hope upon that Son of Man, and petition Him and supplicate for mercy at His hands. Nevertheless that Lord of Spirits will so press them that they shall hastily go forth from His presence, and their faces shall be filled with shame and the darkness

grow deeper on their faces. And He will deliver them to the angels for punishment, to execute vengeance on them because they have oppressed His children and His elect. (Enoch 62:5–11)

BEHIND THE DISGUISE

The King is among us today. We need to learn to see through His disguises. He is among us in the shape of the infirm, the elderly, the sick and the poor. He is in the guise of the famine-faced children placed before us by charitable organizations. He is among us in the faces of our brothers and sisters persecuted by hateful men and satanic regimes around the world. He is among us in the guise of His beloved Jewish people. The Master is among us now. The King is in disguise, and one day, it will be the big Rosh HaShanah—the day of reckoning—and the disguise will come off. He will recognize us; will we recognize Him?

The Master teaches us that our faith must be primarily a faith of doing good deeds. Ours must be a faith of giving. It must be an open-handed faith that results in kindness toward human beings. God is not impressed with us for keeping the Sabbath. He is not indebted to us for keeping the festivals. The Master is not handing out pats on the back for attending worship services or blowing the *shofar*. But He is touched when we meet the needs of the needy. Whatever we do for the least of His brothers, we do for Him.

As we prepare to face the King of the Jews, let's set our hearts and our hands to the tasks that have been laid before us so that when we stand before Him we will not be ashamed. Let's place the things of the kingdom before our own needs and desires. Seek first His kingdom, His righteousness.

Chapter 15

YESHUA THE
~~NAZARENE~~ NAZIRITE

"So they feasted and drank freely with him."
With Joseph they drank, but away from him
they did not drink. For Rabbi Levi said, "During
the whole of the twenty-two years that Joseph
did not see them he tasted no wine, and they
too tasted no wine until they saw him. (Genesis
Rabbah 92:5, quoting Genesis 43:34)

As children we were captivated by the story of Samson, the strongest man in the world. We were in awe of his heroics and mighty feats of strength. We remember how he killed a lion with his bare hands. How he defeated a Philistine contingent with only a donkey's jawbone for a weapon. How he carried the gates of Gaza on his back. But more than any of these episodes, we remember Samson's hair. He was a Nazirite, and Nazirites have long hair.

But Samson wasn't the only Nazirite in the Bible. Did you know that John the Immerser was a Nazirite? Paul was too. And James the brother of Yeshua. Even Yeshua Himself was a Nazirite.

Let's examine the particulars of the Nazirite vow.

THE NAZIR

The Hebrew word for Nazirite is *Nazir* (נזיר). It is from the verb *nazar*, meaning "to separate." From its usage in the Torah, it would seem that *Nazir* means a "separated one." The Nazirites were under a vow of separation.

Samson, Samuel, and John the Immerser were set aside as Nazirites prior to birth. They were all conceived in otherwise barren wombs and were dedicated by their grateful mothers into lives of separation under the Nazirite vow. But according to Torah, the life of a Nazirite was open to any who desired it. The typical Nazirite took a short-term vow, ranging from a month to several years. (The Mishnah specifies a minimum of thirty days.[149])

In the days of the Temple, if a man or woman desired to take a special vow of separation to the Lord, he or she could take a Nazirite vow. The specifications of the vow are found in Numbers chapter 6. While under the term of the vow, the *Nazir* was prohibited from consuming any of the fruit of the vine, whether raisins or grapes, new wine or old wine, or any intoxicating drink. The *Nazir* was also to avoid corpse contamination. In Torah law, contact with a dead body transmits ritual uncleanness. Therefore, the *Nazir* had to avoid contact with a corpse, even close family members. Also, while under the vow, the *Nazir* could not cut his hair.

NAZARENE AND NAZIRITE?

English readers are often confused by the similarity between the terms Nazarene and Nazirite. As we learned in chapter four, Nazarene is from the Hebrew word *netzer* (נצר), which means "branch." It is used to refer to anyone from the city of Nazareth (*Natzeret*), "Branch Town." The name is also applied to the early believers, followers of the Man from *Natzeret*.

Nazirite is from the Hebrew word *Nazir* (נזיר), which means "separated." It refers to those who have taken the special vow described in Numbers chapter 6.

A HAIRCUT FOR SHAUL

Paul took a Nazirite vow (see Acts 18:18). It has not always been recognized as a Nazirite vow because rather than saying, "He let his hair grow long," the text says, "He had his hair cut for he was keeping a vow." We would assume that if he were taking a Nazirite vow, he would not have his hair cut. This mistake may stem from a misunderstanding of the meaning of the Nazirite's hair.

The hair of the Nazirite, both symbolically and literally, represented the amount of time the Nazirite spent under the vow. When the term of the Nazirite's vow was completed, he cut his hair and burned it in the Temple. Burning the hair was a gesture symbolizing that the Nazirite was offering up to God the amount of time he had dedicated to the Lord as a Nazirite. If he had been a Nazirite for only a few months, the length of hair would represent only a few month's growth. If he had been a Nazirite for several years, it would have been several feet of hair. In order for the length of hair to accurately represent the term of the vow, the vow must be begun with a shaved head. Acts 18:18 may be an indication that Paul had his hair cut in order to take a Nazirite vow.

Another possibility is that Paul completed the term of his vow while in the Diaspora. Because a Nazirite vow can only be fulfilled at the Temple, the sages say that one who completes a Nazirite vow outside the land of Israel must repeat the vow within the land of Israel.

> One who made a Nazirite vow and completed his Nazirite term and afterwards came to the Land ... must be a Nazirite all over again. It once happened that Queen Helene, whose son went to war, said, "If my son return safely from the war, I will be a Nazirite for seven years; and at the conclusion of the seven years she came up to the Land, and the School of Hillel instructed her that she had to be a Nazirite again for seven years more. (m.*Nazir* 3:6)

Perhaps in Acts 18 we see Paul completing a personal Nazirite vow before going on to Jerusalem, where he intends to formally undergo the vow again under the auspices of the priesthood.

A third possibility is that Paul became ritually unclean through corpse contamination during the course of the vow, so he shaved his head until he could return to Jerusalem for purification and to offer the sin offering and burnt offering that are required for such an instance. If the vow was inadvertently broken through contamination via a dead body, Numbers 6:9–12 mandates that the defiled Nazirite shave his head and start the vow over from the beginning of the term he had chosen.

Regardless of which situation Paul was in, the terms of the Nazirite vow required him to return to Jerusalem and the Temple to make the necessary sacrifices and to have his hair shaved in the Temple. Once he arrived in Jerusalem (see Acts 21), he joined four more believers who had also taken Nazirite vows, and they all went to the Temple together for haircuts and sacrifices.[150]

PRIESTS AND NAZIRITES

Why would anyone want to be a *Nazir*? What was the allure of the Nazirite life?

The laws of the Nazirite bear a striking resemblance to several of the laws of the priesthood. Just as the priesthood was forbidden to drink wine (*yayin*, יין) or any fermented drink (*shechar*, שכר) when serving in the Tabernacle or Temple, so too the *Nazir* was forbidden any wine or fermented drink.[151] Both the priesthood and the Nazirite were commanded to avoid ritual contamination through a human corpse.[152] In fact, this prohibition extended further for Nazirites than for the priests. The average priest was allowed to become unclean for close relatives. Only the high priest was under purity restrictions as severe as the Nazirites.[153] Finally, the priests were not allowed to shave their heads. So too the Nazirites were not allowed to cut their hair while under the vow.[154]

The Torah states that the high priest has been separated *(nezer)* by virtue of the anointing oil poured on his head:

> The priest who is the highest among his brothers, on whose head the anointing oil has been poured, ... [shall not] approach any dead person, nor defile himself even for his father or his mother ... for the consecration *(nezer)* of the anointing oil of his God is on him. (Leviticus 21:10–12)

The Torah uses almost identical language to explain the Nazirite's high level of purity.

> All the days of his separation *(nezer)* to the LORD he shall not go near to a dead person. He shall not make himself unclean for his father or for his mother, for his brother or for his sister, when they die, because his separation *(nezer)* to God is on his head. All the days of his separation he is holy to the LORD. (Numbers 6:6–8)

Notice the identical construction of the Nazirite passage and the high priest passage. By virtue of their construction and content, the two passages clearly point toward each other. Both high priest and Nazirite receive a ritual marking on their heads. For the high priest, it is the anointing oil that grants him the *nezer* status. For the Nazirite, it is the hair on his head.

The Torah gives us another connection between the *Nazir* and the priesthood regarding things on their heads. The *nezer hakodesh* is the holy crown that the high priest wore as part of the priestly vestments.[155] Inscribed on the *nezer hakodesh* were the words "Holy to the LORD." Numbers 6:8 says the Nazirite is regarded as "holy to the LORD."

A further parallel between Nazirites and the priesthood is obvious in the list of sacrifices both are to present to the Lord. Exodus 29 lists the sacrifices the priests are to bring for their ordination. They include a sin offering, a burnt offering and a peace offering, along with a basket of unleavened bread, cakes mixed with oil and wafers spread with oil. The sacrifices the Nazirite must bring at the termination of his vow are the same.

Three Would-Be Priests

Perhaps the Nazirite vow was the layman's response to the priesthood. To the average Israelite, priesthood was inaccessible. According to Torah law, only the descendents of Aaron qualified for that honor. Perhaps being a Nazirite was a sort of quasi-priestly status that could be attained by anyone who was willing to make the vow.

This may help to explain how Samuel the prophet rose to the position of high priest. Samuel was not from the house of Aaron. He was an Ephraimite (or, according to some texts, a Levite). His formal adoption into the family of Eli granted him the position in Aaron's house to take on the role of priest. But it is also possible that his status of Nazirite since conception allowed him priestly privileges that would otherwise not have been available to him.

John the Immerser was another Nazirite from birth. Unlike Samuel, John was from a priestly family. However, like the Essene sect of his day, he opted not to participate in the Temple services with a politically compromised and morally corrupt priesthood. When John reached the age of priesthood, rather than going to serve as a priest, he went to the Jordan to baptize. Perhaps his Nazirite status from conception was priesthood enough to satisfy the layman.

A third and particularly tantalizing Nazirite account is that of *Yaakov HaTzaddik*, James the Righteous, the brother of the Master.

Eusebius quotes Hegesippus in his ecclesiastical history regarding the martyrdom of James:

> James drank no wine or intoxicating liquor and ate no animal food; no razor came near his head; he did not smear himself with oil, and took no baths.[156] He alone was permitted to enter the Holy Place, for his garments were not of wool but of linen. He used to enter the Sanctuary alone, and was often found on his knees beseeching forgiveness for the people.[157]

This text raises an intriguing problem. We find here a strong and early tradition that places James inside the Temple sanctuary. The sanctuary is forbidden to all except the priesthood. James, a man descended from the house of David and the tribe of Judah, should not have had access to the sanctuary. How is it that James prayed inside the Temple? Is it because he was a Nazirite? We must either accept it as so or reject the tradition of Hegesippus altogether. Regardless of which option we choose, we cannot ignore that again a connection between priest and Nazirite has been drawn.

The Torah ties the priesthood and the Nazirites more tightly together by following the passage about the Nazirites with the priestly benediction of Numbers 6:22–27. It seems to be an awkward juxtaposition unless there is some connection between the Nazirite vow and the priesthood.

YOSEF THE NAZIRITE

The Torah refers to Joseph the son of Jacob as a Nazirite twice; once in Jacob's blessing of the tribe of Joseph (Genesis 49:26) and once in Moses' blessing of the tribe of Joseph (Deuteronomy 33:16). The wording in both instances is "Let all these [blessings] rest on the head of Joseph, on the hairy head of the *nazir* among his brothers."[158] But was Joseph a Nazirite? Surely not. The institution of Levitical priesthood had not yet been introduced, much less the rites of the Nazirite. Most translators understand the reference to Joseph as a *Nazir* simply in the sense of being separated. Just as a *Nazir* lives a life of separation, so too Joseph was separated from his brothers. The Midrash opts for a literal interpretation, claiming that Joseph abstained from wine until he was able to sit and eat and drink with his brothers:

Rabbi Yitzchak of Magdala said in the name of Rabbi Yehudah the Prince, "From the day that Joseph departed from his brethren, … Joseph drank no wine until that day [on which he was reunited with them], but abstained from wine, as it says [in Genesis 49:26], 'On the head of the *nazir* among his brothers.'" (*Genesis Rabbah* 93:7)

The astute reader of the Gospels will notice a parallel between this Joseph midrash and the words of the Master when He says to His disciples, "I will not drink of this fruit of the vine from now on until that day when I drink it new with you in My Father's kingdom" (Matthew 26:29). Like Joseph, the Master knows He is about to be separated from His brothers. But He also knows that, just like Joseph and his brothers, they will one day sit and eat and drink again.

Yeshua the Nazirite

Yeshua makes a Nazirite-like vow when He utters these words to His disciples. According to the Mishnah, two components are necessary for an official Nazirite vow: an oral declaration and a statement of term. The sages regarded the oral declaration as binding even if it was stated in less than explicit language. Thus one who said, "I will abstain from haircuts," or "I will abstain from grape stones and grape skins," or "I will be like Samson," is regarded as having formally taken a Nazirite vow.[159] The Mishnah also states, "If they filled a cup [of wine] for him and he said, 'I will be an abstainer (*nazir*) from it,' then he becomes a Nazirite."[160] The Master's words, "I tell you truth, I will not drink of the fruit of the vine," are formulated as a vow. According to the Mishnah, such a statement should be regarded as a Nazirite vow.

In addition to the oral declaration, a statement of term is necessary. The sages said that one who did not state his term at the outset of the vow is bound for at least thirty days.[161] The Master states the term of His vow at the outset. He will not drink of the fruit of the vine again "until that day when I drink it new with you in My Father's kingdom."

Thus, according to the legal interpretations of His day, Yeshua bound himself to a Nazirite vow at His last *seder*.

The Gospels tell us that during the crucifixion, Yeshua was twice offered vinegar (literally, sour wine). The first time He refused it.[162] However, at the point of death and ultimate ritual defilement through uncleanness, He accepted it.[163] How is it possible that He would break His vow to not drink of the fruit of the vine? If the vow was a Nazirite vow, it would be defunct at the point of death because of His contact with death. Hence He refused the vinegar earlier but received it at the moment of death. Both the vinegar and the death sever the vow. The Master's acceptance of the vinegar symbolizes His acceptance of death.

A vow severed by corpse contact can be reentered only after purification. The Master's resurrection is His purification from death.

The significance of His accepting the vinegar is punctuated by a comment in the *Midrash Rabbah* on Ruth. There it is written, "Dip thy morsel in the vinegar refers to Messiah's sufferings, as it is said [in Isaiah 53:5], 'But he was wounded because of our transgressions'" (*Ruth Rabbah* 5:6).

If we are to regard the Master as entering a Nazirite state as He prepared to go to the cross, we are better equipped to understand how His role and function change after the resurrection. After His resurrection we see the Master in a role similar to the Nazirites. We see Him as a priest and yet not a priest. He has entered an immortal state that, like the Nazirite, cannot be touched or corrupted by death.

Although He is not an Aaronic priest, He has entered into a quasi-priestly status, a status vigorously defended by the writer of the book of Hebrews. He will retain that priestly role until He returns to His disciples as King. At that time He will drink again of the fruit of the vine and usher in the kingdom.

Perhaps there will be a great haircut on that day.

Chapter 16

ONE LONG DAY

> On the eve of Passover they hung [Yeshua] the
> Nazarene. For forty days a herald went before him
> and cried, "[Yeshua] the Nazarene is going forth
> to be stoned because he has practiced sorcery and
> led Israel to heresy. Any one who knows anything
> to speak in his defense, let him come and explain
> for him." And none was found and nothing in his
> defense [was brought forward] and they hung him
> on the eve of the Passover. (b.*Sanhedrin* 43a)

"Early in the morning the chief priests with the elders and scribes and the whole Council, immediately held a consultation; and binding Yeshua, they led Him away and delivered Him to Pilate." So begins Mark 15, probably one of the earliest composed and certainly one of the most solemnly told chapters in the Gospels. It tells the story of one very long day. The chapter begins early in the morning, just before dawn, as the mock Sanhedrin reach a guilty verdict regarding Yeshua. The chapter does not conclude until the sun has begun to set, with the Sabbath coming and Yosef (Joseph) of Arimathea rolling the stone door of the tomb shut. Using Mark 15 as our compass to the Passion narrative, we will draw on material from all four Gospels to tell the story.

THE ARREST, 6:00–8:00 A.M. (MARK 15:1–14)

Mark tells us that it was "early in the morning" when the Sanhedrin delivered Yeshua to Pilate. What was the rush? What motivated Caiaphas and his Sadducean colleagues to convene their kangaroo court[164] before dawn? Why go banging on Pilate's door so early in the morning? If that day was the fourteenth day of *Nisan* (as the gospel of John indicates)—the day the Passover lambs were to be slain—everyone had a busy day ahead.[165] The whole of the priesthood needed to be on duty by afternoon. Thousands of Israelites would soon be converging on the Temple, and with them came the possibility of riot. Soon the streets would be packed with people making preparations for their *seder* meals. Whatever was to be done with Yeshua needed to be done quickly and efficiently. Word of the proceedings would spread rapidly through the city. The crowds loved Yeshua. They had even proclaimed Him their Messiah. In a few short hours, all those hot-headed Galileans would be shouting and demanding the release of Yeshua.

Besides, if they waited until later in the day, the Romans' daily executions would already be carried out. Caiaphas would be forced to leave Yeshua in custody over the Sabbath, probably until the end of the festival. That would allow His followers time to rally support. The Pharisaic side of the Sanhedrin would cry foul. They would appoint a defense attorney. The whole thing could topple. Caiaphas and the Temple authorities knew the execution had to happen quickly and discreetly. The timing was critical.

So they brought Yeshua to Pilate as soon as the sun came up. Pilate was in Jerusalem for the festival. Apparently in an attempt to try to appease the zealots, Pilate had established the custom of releasing a prisoner on the festival. All those who had sons or brothers or husbands who had been arrested for political activism (terrorism) would have gathered at Pilate's Jerusalem residence first thing in the morning to petition for the release of their man. The famous rebel-hero Barabbas[166] (*Yeshua Bar Abba*, ישוע בר אבא) had recently been arrested and sentenced to crucifixion for his crimes against Rome. The Bar Abba crowd had already gathered that morning to shout for the release of their hero.

What strange bedfellows the zealots and Caiaphas' colleagues must have made! The zealots usually stabbed men like Caiaphas in the back for their collusion with Rome. On that morning, however, they heard representatives from the priesthood cheering them on to shout for the release of their hero Bar Abba! The irony was never thicker than when those two sworn enemies were both shouting for the release of Yeshua Bar Abba and demanding the crucifixion of Yeshua from Galilee.

The Talmud records that forty years prior to the destruction of Jerusalem the Sanhedrin withdrew from the Hall of Hewn Stone in the Temple. As a result, capital cases were no longer heard in Israel. The Sanhedrin had ceased to pronounce capital sentences.[167] Roman law had stripped them of the right to pronounce death sentences. In his commentary on John, Beasley-Murray (1999) quotes a passage from the *Jerusalem Talmud* that spells this out specifically.

> Forty years before the destruction of the Temple they took from Israel the right to inflict capital punishment. (y.*Sanhedrin* 1.1; 7.2)[168]

By common reckoning, forty years before the destruction of the Temple would have been the year 30 CE, the very year Yeshua was tried and executed. "We are not permitted to put anyone to death," the high priests complain to Pilate (John 18:31). Thus a change of venue was necessary. Yeshua had to be tried and convicted in a Roman law court if He was to be executed; hence, the trip to Pilate's palace. Furthermore, the overwhelming popularity of Yeshua made it dangerous for Caiaphas and crew to publicly move against Him. They needed the Romans to do their dirty work.

Pontius Pilate

In 1961, in the city of Caesarea, the Roman capital of the province, an inscription was unearthed that mentions both Pilate and Emperor Tiberius Caesar, who appointed him. Pilate ordinarily stayed in Caesarea, but during the festivals, he made the journey to Jerusalem along with an extra detachment of soldiers in order to keep an eye on things.

Pilate was only in his fourth year as procurator of Judea when he condemned Yeshua to die, but he had already established his reputation among the Jews as a villain and a tyrant. As procurator, he had full control of Judea and kept a legion of troops to back him up. His first act upon arriving in Jerusalem each year was to bring the Roman standards bearing the imperial image of the golden eagle and other images into the city. This infuriated the religious Jerusalemites and caused protest and resentment.

Pilate was known for subduing protestors by having them clubbed to death.[169] Though later Christian writings are usually sympathetic toward Pilate (in one tradition he is even dubbed a saint and prayed to as Saint Pilate), he was in fact a ruthless despot with few moral scruples.

When the priestly prosecution arrived at Pilate's palace that morning, the gospel of John tells us, they refused to enter Pilate's palace lest they be rendered unclean. If they were made unclean, they would be unable to enter the Temple that afternoon to participate in the sacrifice of the Passover lambs. They would have no lamb on their *seder* tables that night.[170]

The Caiaphas crew could hardly hope for an execution order from Pilate simply on the basis that they believed Yeshua to be a blasphemer. They needed to present a charge that would be of concern to the Roman government. Hence the accusations they leveled included subverting the nation (treason), opposing payment of taxes to Caesar, and claiming to be a king.[171] Those issues would be of concern to a Roman governor.

Pilate conceded to their request to hear the case.

ARE YOU THE KING OF THE JEWS?

In a semiprivate interrogation, Pilate asked Yeshua, "Are You the King of the Jews?" (John 18:33) It was a natural conclusion to reach. After all, He had been preaching, "The kingdom of heaven is now" while being followed by crowds of messianic enthusiasts. In asking the question, Pilate was looking for a pretense on which to try and convict Yeshua as a criminal against Rome.

"Are you saying this on your own initiative, or did others tell you about Me?" (John 18:34), Yeshua asked.

Pilate answered, "I am not a Jew, am I? Your own nation and the chief priests delivered up You to me; what have You done?" (John 18:35).

Yeshua understood where Pilate was trying to lead the conversation and deflected the line of inquiry. He made it clear to Pilate that He was neither a revolutionary nor a zealot-terrorist, nor was He attempting to start a political kingdom. But He did admit to Pilate, "You say correctly that I am a king. For this I have been born, and for this I have come into the world" (John 18:37).

His Blood Be upon Us

Pilate's apparent reluctance to execute Yeshua was not the result of any moral rectitude; it was because of his wife's urging:

> While he was sitting on the judgment seat, his wife sent him a message, saying, "Have nothing to do with that righteous Man; for last night I suffered greatly in a dream because of Him." (Matthew 27:19)

Though his wife tried to dissuade him, Pilate could not work up the moral fiber to prevent an innocent Jew from being crucified. He had sent many such men to their deaths before, and he would send many more before his term in Judea was over. Instead of pursuing justice he conducted a hypocritical hand-washing ritual in front of the crowd and passed the buck of responsibility to them. They replied, "Let his blood be on us and on our children!" (Matthew 27:25)

Traditional Christianity has typically taken a curious and morbid delight in this passage, deeming it a justification for brutalizing the Jewish people. It should go without saying that a small band of zealots and a few cheerleaders from the ranks of a corrupt priest-politician are hardly able to invoke an eternal curse upon all Jewish people for all time. Nonetheless, both the Jerusalem Zealots and the elite Sadducean priesthood sponsoring the crucifixion were virtually erased from the face of the earth in the Jewish revolt a generation later.

Perhaps thinking, *If I just have him flogged the Jews will be content*, Pilate sent Yeshua to be flogged.

The Scourging, 8:00–9:00 a.m. (Mark 15:15–20)

After His appearance before Pilate, the Master was shuffled off to Herod Antipas[172] for a short interrogation. Herod provided a royal robe for the "King of the Jews" before returning Him to Pilate. Prior to pronouncing His final sentencing, Pilate had Yeshua flogged by Roman soldiers. The Romans used whips embedded with spurs to tear and lacerate the flesh. Many victims of a Roman flogging never survived to make it to their execution.

The flogging was followed by a mock coronation:

Then the soldiers of the governor took Yeshua into the Praetorium and gathered the whole Roman cohort around Him. And they stripped Him and put a scarlet robe on Him. And after twisting together a crown of thorns, they put it on His head, and a reed in His right hand; and they kneeled down before Him and mocked Him, saying, "Hail, King of the Jews!" And they spat on Him, and took the reed and began to beat Him on the head. (Matthew 27:27–30)

The scarlet robe, the crown of thorns, the scepter and the acclamations of "Hail, King of the Jews" are all cruel mockeries of the Messianic coronation. In fact, He is the King of the Jews, and one day He will be crowned, robed and handed a scepter to rule over Jerusalem.

In his book *Judaism and the Origins of Christianity*, David Flusser cites two similar mock coronations in the first- and second-century Roman world. One is recorded by Philo, who tells of an incident that happened when King Agrippa I visited Alexandria. Anti-Jewish sentiment was running high. The Alexandrians accosted a hapless lunatic, "crowned him with reeds, robed him in a coat of straw, and gave him a stalk of papyrus to serve as a scepter." [173] A second incident from the time of Trajan describes a Roman prefect's treatment of what is believed to be a captive leader of the Jewish revolt in Cyrene. Like Yeshua, the failed revolutionary was publicly displayed as a king to be mocked.

Behold the Man

With Yeshua reduced to this piteous state, Pilate declared to the crowd, "Behold, I am bringing him out to you so that you may know that I find no guilt in him." He stood the comic king before them and declared, "Behold the man!" (John 19:5)

David Flusser says that if we think Pilate was trying to generate sympathy for Yeshua by declaring, "Behold the man," we have misunderstood Pilate:

The most widely accepted interpretation of Pilate's words today is the following: the Roman Prefect displays the unfortunate Jesus, humiliated and looking ridiculous, in order to prove to the Jews that such a pathetic figure could

never have been a rebel against Rome. There is no doubt
that this modern interpretation, along with other interpretations which have been proposed, have failed miser-
ably to understand the intentions of Pontius Pilate.[174]

Flusser demonstrates that Pilate's "Behold the man" was an
acclamation similar to "Hail the King!" For Pilate, the charade was
an opportunity to poke fun at the Jewish religious leadership as
well as the entire zealot movement.

The reaction from the Barabbas crowd and the Caiaphas crowd
was immediate. "Crucify Him!"

Pilate responded, "I find no guilt in Him." When the crowd
repeated their demand, Pilate said, "Take Him yourselves and
crucify Him," knowing full well that they could not. Thrown off
balance by this remark, the Caiaphas crowd found themselves
trying to explain the Torah's laws regarding blasphemy to Pilate,
protesting, "He made Himself out to be the Son of God!" (John
19:6–7)

Behold Your King

When Pilate heard that Yeshua might be the son of a god, he was
afraid. Perhaps his wife's dream was more than a dream. In the
Greco-Roman religion, god-men were a real possibility. "Wasn't
there something rather eerie about this Jew?" he must have mused.
He turned to Yeshua and asked, "Where are you from?" Yeshua did
not answer. Pilate turned back to the crowd and tried to reverse
their sentiment, but they shouted, "If you release this man, you
are no friend of Caesar; everyone who makes himself out to be a
king opposes Caesar" (John 19:12).

This was a thinly veiled threat to denounce Pilate as a col-
laborator in an anti-government plot. Many high-ranking Roman
officials had been dismissed, been executed or simply disappeared
on the basis of such unprovable allegations. If Pilate were to let
Yeshua go, the religious leadership would lodge a formal complaint
to Caesar that he had aided and abetted a known revolutionary. It
could be the end of his career.

Pilate's political survival instinct overruled his superstition.
Seated on the tribune, an elevated platform from which he could
make public pronouncements, with Yeshua standing next to him,

Pilate repeated his line, "Behold your king!" They responded again, "Crucify him!"

"Shall I crucify your king?" he asked magnanimously. The crowd responded, "We have no king but Caesar" (John 19:15).

Pilate, however, had the last laugh. He had a placard posted above the cross that read, "Yeshua of Nazareth, King of the Jews." Lest anyone should miss the joke, he had it written in Hebrew, Latin and Greek, and he refused to remove it.

Shimon from Cyrene, 9:00 a.m. (Mark 15:21)

When at last the Master was led off to be crucified, He was so weakened from the scourging that He was unable to carry the heavy crossbeam they laid over His shoulders. In keeping with Roman custom, the convict was to carry his own execution stake. The first-century historian Plutarch wrote, "Every wrongdoer who goes to execution carries out his own cross." [175] After a short distance, He could go no further. The soldiers were not about to carry it themselves, so they conscripted an early-morning Passover pilgrim. "They pressed into service a passer-by coming from the country, Simon of Cyrene (the father of Alexander and Rufus), to bear His cross" (Mark 15:21).

Shimon had probably spent a considerable sum to travel to Judea in order to participate in the Passover that year. Participating in a Roman execution was certainly not part of his original travel plans. He was probably just entering the city on his way to the Temple for the morning sacrifice and prayers when he was accosted and forced to carry the Master's cross. Most likely, he had no clue who Yeshua was or why He had been sentenced.

Though we don't know anything more about the man, we may assume that he became a believer. Otherwise Mark would probably not have known his name, much less the names of his two sons, nor would those names have any relevance to Mark's readership (the believers in Rome).

Mark explains that the man who carried the cross is Shimon the father of Alexander and Rufus, which implies that Alexander and Rufus were contemporaries of Mark's readership at the time he was composing his gospel. We may assume that Alexander and Rufus were well known among the believers and that the mention of their names would have been a point of connection to the events described. It may be pure coincidence that Paul mentions a Rufus among the Roman believers in his epistle to them, or it may be that this Rufus is the same man whose father carried the cross of the Master.

> Greet Rufus, chosen in the Lord, and his mother, who has been a mother to me, too. (Romans 16:13 NIV)

For us, the mention of Shimon and his sons lends a voice of authenticity to the gospel.

No doubt Shimon of Cyrene later made inquiries about the man whose cross he had carried. "Who is this man, the King of the Jews whom they have crucified?" He would have still been in Jerusalem three days later when the rumor spread that the man whose cross he had carried had risen from the dead.

PLACE OF THE SKULL, 9:00 A.M. (MARK 15:22–23)

Shimon of Cyrene was compelled to carry the cross for Yeshua from Jerusalem to the hill of Golgotha. The Hebrew *gulgolet* (גלגלת), or *galgalta* (גלגלתא) in Aramaic (with the definite article) means "the skull." On arriving at Golgotha, the soldiers offered Him a drink before crucifying Him. Matthew tells us it was wine mixed with gall. Mark says it was myrrh. The Talmud says frankincense was used on such occasions. Whatever it was, it was meant as a sedative and painkiller to numb the victim. We read about the custom in tractate *Sanhedrin* of the Talmud:

> Reb Chiya ben Ashi stated in Reb Chisda's name, "When a man is led out to be executed, a chalice of wine containing a small amount of frankincense is given to him in order to anesthetize his nerves, as it is written [in Proverbs 31:6], 'Give strong drink to those who are perishing, wine to those who are in anguish.'" (b.*Sanhedrin* 43a)

Yeshua refused it.

THE CRUCIFIXION, 9:00 A.M. (MARK 15:24–25)

Crucifixion was a Roman mode of execution. The great torment suffered by the crucified was meant to serve as a deterrent to others. Crosses were an all-too-common sight outside the walls of Jerusalem. The Romans probably never took the crosses down; they just changed the bodies hanging on them.

The skeletal remains of a crucified man were discovered in a Jerusalem tomb in 1968.[176] Based upon the remains, it seems that the crucifixion nails were driven through the wrists and ankles instead of through the palms and feet, as Christian artwork usually depicts.

The Master was crucified at the third hour (approximately nine a.m.). Mark, who is not in the habit of giving his readers the time of day, wants us to know that this happened at the third hour. Why? What is the significance of the third hour?

The Torah mandated two daily worship services in the Temple.[177] Every day, a single male lamb was offered up as burnt offering for the morning sacrifice. The morning sacrifice began at dawn and concluded by the third hour (nine a.m.).[178] The second lamb sacrifice was made at the ninth hour (approximately three p.m.).[179] Morning and afternoon prayers corresponded to these times of sacrifice.

At the same time that the Master was being tried by Pilate's court, the lamb of the morning sacrifice was being placed upon the altar. Later that morning, as the smoke of the morning sacrifice ascended from the altar, the full complement of priests on duty in the Temple lifted their hands and sang the priestly blessing.[180] At about the same hour that the Master's hands were lifted and stretched out in the dreadful crucifixion pose, the hands of the priesthood in the Temple were being lifted to pronounce the priestly blessing. He was the morning sacrifice.

NUMBERED WITH TRANSGRESSORS, 9:00 A.M. (MARK 15:26–28)

The placard above His head that declared His crime was called a *titulus*. The Roman authorities attached a *titulus* to serve as a warning to others. The condemned sometimes carried them, hung about their necks, while on their way to execution. Normally the *titulus* would say "Terrorist" or "Murderer" or "Insurrectionist," etc. Yeshua's simply declared, "King of the Jews."

Two zealots were crucified with Him that day, possibly colleagues of Yeshua Bar Abba. One was crucified on His left, the other on His right. Ironically, those are the stations that the sons of Zebedee, Yaakov and Yochanon (James and John), had rashly hoped to occupy.[181]

THE MOCKING, 9:00 A.M.–NOON (MARK 15:29–32)

Passover was Jerusalem's busiest day of the year. The thousands of pilgrims who had come up for the festival began to file into the city. Flocks of lambs were herded toward the Temple. The roads into Jerusalem became choked with worshippers going up to the Temple to slaughter their Passover lambs.

As they approached the gates of the city, they saw a row of execution stakes on a bare hilltop, visible from the road, reminding everyone that Rome was still in charge. "It may be the Festival of Redemption, but you're not redeemed yet," the crosses seemed to say to the Jews. It was a small relief to see that there were only three victims that day.

Those who had sneered at Yeshua's ministry were quick to cast insults when they saw where the young would-be Messiah-King had ended up. Mark records the insults and derision of passersby and the mockery of the Temple authorities. Even the two other convicts joined in the chorus of mocking.

But there were other voices as well. There was the weeping of the women of Jerusalem and Galilee. There was the disciple John, whom He loved, and the innumerable crowds who had been "hoping that it was He who was going to redeem Israel." [182] Those who had hailed Him Messiah during the triumphant entry just a few days before must have felt their stomachs sink and their hands grow limp. Their hoped-for Messiah-King was dying the death of a common insurrectionist. They hurried on into the city, unable to even look.

DARKNESS, NOON–3:00 P.M. (MARK 15:33)

More worshippers with sacrifices squeezed into the Temple on Passover (on the fourteenth day of Nissan) than on any other day:

> One time Agrippa the King wished to [count the hosts of] Israel. He said to the High Priest, "Pay attention to the Passover sacrifices." The High Priest took a kidney from each one, and six-hundred-thousand pairs of kidneys

were found there, twice as many as those who departed from Egypt, excluding those who were unclean and those who were on a distant journey; and there was not a single Pesach lamb for which less than ten people had registered. They called it, "The Passover of the dense throngs." (m.*Pesachim* 64a)

Hundreds of thousands of lambs needed to be sacrificed in just a few hours' time. In order to accommodate the incredible numbers, the whole priesthood was on duty. Thousands of priests filled the inner Temple courts while the outer courts jammed with men and their animals.

The Passover lambs were to be offered at the ninth hour.[183] In order to accommodate the dense throngs, the priests slaughtered the lambs for the evening sacrifice an hour earlier:

> The continual burnt offering was slaughtered at half after the eighth hour [2:30 p.m.] and offered up at half after the ninth hour [3:30 p.m.]. On the eve of Passover it was slaughtered at half after the seventh hour and offered up at half after the eighth hour." (m.*Pesachim* 5.1)

Yet on this Passover, something was amiss. Mark tells us that a strange darkness, beginning at noon, settled on all the land. It might have been heavy clouds, an eclipse, a sudden dust storm, or something akin to the plague of darkness that came upon Egypt just before the first Passover. Darkness shrouded the Temple. In the court of Israel, the altar fires burned hot and bright as the afternoon sacrifice was consumed. The flames cast swirling shadows all around the courtyard. The sky stayed dark for three hours.

THE TRUMPETS, THE GATES, AND THE CURTAIN, 3:00 P.M. (MARK 15:33–37)

At half past the eighth hour (2:30 p.m.) the priesthood blew *shofar*-trumpets in the Temple. A *tekiah, shevarim, tekiah* blast was the signal to open the gates.[184] A short distance away, just outside the city walls, the sound of the *shofar*-trumpets blowing reached the ears of the three men hanging on the execution stakes.

The heavy gates of the Temple courts swung open and the first wave of Israelites with lambs ready for slaughter poured into the courtyard. Row upon row of priests stood at attention in lines, ready to receive the virtual flood of blood. The Mishnah describes the scene as follows:

> The priests stand in rows with basins of silver and gold in their hands. One row had wholly silver ones, another wholly gold ones; they were not mixed up. And the basins did not have [flat bottoms] lest the priests set them down and the blood congeal. An Israelite slaughtered [his Passover lamb] and a priest received the blood. He hands it to his fellow, and his fellow to his fellow, [each one] receiving a full basin and handing back an empty one. The priest nearest the altar splashes [the blood] in a single act of tossing toward the base. (m.*Pesachim* 5.5–6)

Within moments, the white-plastered and polished, two-story altar of the Temple was running red with the blood of lambs. Channels and gutters cut into the stones of the floor carried away rivers of blood. At the same moment, just outside the city walls, the last drops of life bled out of the Master's body. The Master cried out, "My God, My God, why have you forsaken me?" (Mark 15:34)

With a loud cry, Yeshua breathed His last. The sun burst through the darkness and the curtain of the Temple was rent.

THE WOMEN STAND VIGIL, 3:00–5:00 P.M. (MARK 15:40–41)

A group of women from Galilee and Jerusalem had followed the execution party from the city that morning. Six hours later, they were still waiting at the cross when He died. Even then they did not leave Him, but fulfilled the Jewish custom of keeping a watcher (*shomer*, שומר) with a corpse until burial. They stayed at the cross for several more hours.

As they mourned in silent vigil before His body, the sacrifice of the Passover lambs continued in the Temple. The dead lambs were hung on hooks and on wooden poles, their forearms spread in a crucifixion pose as they were skinned and prepared for roasting.[185] While the lambs were being skinned, additional waves of worshippers were slaughtering. All the while the Levites led the people in chanting out the melodies of the Psalms of the *Hallel* (Psalms 113–118). The sound of their voices provided the background music for the death of the King. The glad sounds that came reverberating from inside the city must have seemed out of place to the small group standing vigil with His body. Yeshua and the Twelve had sung those same Psalms just the night before, at the Last *Seder*.[186] How different they sounded today!

As the Psalms of the *Hallel* continued, soldiers came to break the legs of the crucified so they would finish dying before the Sabbath. They were surprised to find Yeshua already dead.

Taking Down the Body, 5:00–6:00 p.m. (Mark 15:46)

Yosef of Arimathea, a Pharisee who is described as a prominent member of the Sanhedrin, a man awaiting the kingdom of heaven and a secret disciple of Yeshua, went to Pilate to negotiate for the body of Yeshua. Time was critically short. Only a few hours remained until sunset and the beginning of the Sabbath. Once the removal of the body was guaranteed, he enlisted the help of a fellow Sanhedrinist (another believer), the wealthy Nakdimon ben Gorion (Nicodemus), to assist him with the burial.[187]

They wrapped Yeshua's body and carried Him to a nearby rock-cut tomb owned by Yosef of Arimathea. It may be that Yosef had purchased it just hours before as part of the arrangements he made for the burial that day. By caring for the body of the Master, Yoseph and Nakdimon rendered themselves Levitically unclean. As a result, both were disqualified from eating the Passover that evening. They were men of prestige and influence. They could have sent servants to take care of the burial of Yeshua so as not to forfeit their Passover *seders*. But these two obscure disciples of the Master showed their love and devotion by attending to His body personally.

In Numbers 9:10–11, the Torah provides for those who find themselves in such a situation, allowing them to keep the Passover a month later. One month later, somewhere in Jerusalem, on the fifteenth day of the second month, Yosef of Arimathea and Nakdimon ben Gorion probably sat down to their *seder*.

Closing the Tomb, 6:00–7:00 p.m. (Mark 15:46–47)

The sun had already touched the western horizon and begun to slip below the hills of Jerusalem as Yosef and Nakdimon rolled the stone across the entrance to the tomb. The air over the city was filled with the smoke from hundreds of outdoor ovens in which the thousands of Passover lambs were being roasted. Luke tells us that the Sabbath was already drawing near as the tomb was sealed. Miriam from Magdala and Miriam the wife of Chalphi were present. As they turned to leave, the fifteenth day of *Nisan* and the Festival of Unleavened Bread was beginning. A full moon was rising over the Mount of Olives. That night was *seder* night.

SEDER NIGHT

Why is this night different from all other nights? All over Jerusalem that night, cups were being lifted while the ancient story of the redemption from Egypt was told and retold.

In haste we went out of Egypt. … This is the bread of affliction which our fathers ate in the land of Egypt. … On all other nights we dip once, tonight we dip twice. … The more one tells of it the more the praiseworthy. …Bitter herbs, what is the reason for them? The Egyptians made our lives bitter. …This year we are slaves, next year may we be free men.

This night is different. It is the anniversary of the night when the blood of the lamb was smeared over the doorways of the houses of Israel. It is the anniversary of one long day.

Chapter 17

THE KING OF ISRAEL LIVES

> "On the third day ..." What does it refer to? It refers
> to the third day of resurrection as it is written [in
> Hosea 6:2], "After two days he will revive us; on the
> third day he will raise us up." (*Genesis Rabbah* 56:1)

The resurrection stories are the most significant narratives of
the Gospels. Critics object, however, that there are glaring
inconsistencies between the four versions. For example, John 20:1
says that Mary Magdalene went to the tomb alone while the day
was yet dark and saw the stone rolled away. Mark shows Mary Magdalene and Mary the mother of James (Yaakov ben Chalphi) and
Salome (the mother of James and John) going to the tomb together.
He implies that the sun had risen, but this might be understood
as "close to dawn." [188] The three women encounter an angel at the
tomb, but they flee and tell no one. In John, Mary Magdalene goes
to the tomb alone and returns to get Shimon Peter and Yochanon,
then returns to the garden, where she encounters the risen Messiah. Matthew tells it still differently. He describes the two Marys
going to the tomb (without Salome) at the end of the Sabbath;
that is, Saturday after sunset. There is an earthquake, the guards
faint and the women encounter the angel at the tomb. (None of
these details are mentioned in Mark or John.) On their way back
to tell the disciples, both Marys encounter the risen Messiah. Luke
says a fourth woman, Joanna, went to the tomb. He also reports a
second angel there.

Such discrepancies are not surprising. No other story from the
life of Yeshua would have been told and retold so many times. Each
person telling the story doubtlessly told all he (or she) remembered. Where was he when he heard the first report of the empty

tomb? What did he think about it? Who brought the second report? What happened next? "Where were you when you first saw Him risen?" Everyone would have had a personal slant, a specific detail to tell from their own recollection. The result of the eyewitness-style testimony is the various narratives we have in the Gospels. As it stands, with its various tensions and difficulties, the story of the resurrection bears the marks of eyewitness accounts relating the incident as they experienced it and remembered it.

They Bought Spices

On the Sabbath the women rested according to the commandment.

Mark tells us that when the Sabbath was over, the two Marys went out and bought spices. They could not have done so early on Sunday morning, for what merchants would be selling their wares before dawn? As is the Jerusalem custom even today, shops opened after the Sabbath on Saturday night. Thus Mary and Mary went to the Jerusalem market Saturday night at about seven.

On arriving there, they probably would have found the post-Sabbath marketplace busy with vendors selling the produce of the barley harvest, which was now deemed fit for sale and consumption.

> After the first barley sheaf (omer) was offered, they would leave the Temple and find the market of Jerusalem full of [barley] flour and roasted [barley] grain. ... After the barley sheaf was offered, new grain was permitted from then on. (m.*Menachot* 10:5)

After the Sabbath

Matthew 28:1 says, "Now after the Sabbath, as it began to dawn toward the first day of the week ..." The Greek text, however, does not say "as it began to dawn." That is a mistranslation. Instead, the word is the Greek *epifoseko*, which means "to draw on." What was beginning to draw on at the time of the resurrection? The first day of the week. Our English translators were thinking in Western terms, with the day starting at dawn, so they translated it as such. But the original text says, "Now after the Sabbath, as it began to *draw on* toward the first day of the week ..."

The end of the Sabbath, as it begins to draw on to the first day of the week, is the twilight dusk of a Saturday night. In Judaism, it is the time for performing the traditional *havdalah* ritual, which ends the Sabbath. [189]

We always imagine the resurrection occurring at dawn on the first day of the week. To be sure, the other three gospels make it clear that the empty tomb was discovered by the women at dawn. When Peter and John ran to investigate, the sun had surely risen. But when did the resurrection of the Messiah happen? According to the tradition Matthew records in his gospel, it happened at *havdalah* time, just after the Sabbath on Saturday night.

Early on in Christian interpretation, a misunderstanding arose among Gentile believers disconnected from Jewish tradition. When they read Matthew 28:1 regarding the dawning of the first, to them, that meant Sunday morning. How ironic that the church fathers lobbied for Sunday as "the Lord's day" because it is the day of the resurrection. In actuality, the resurrection was probably a Saturday event, albeit after the Sabbath, Saturday night.

We cannot be sure when the Master actually rose. Not one of the Gospels explicitly tells us. Indeed, they cannot because there were no eyewitnesses. Only the soldiers were present when it happened, and they fell unconscious. No one saw the Master leave the tomb.

Thus the question is not "When did He rise?" but "When was the resurrection discovered?"

THE WALK TO THE TOMB

Saturday night, when the Sabbath was over, Mary Magdalene, Mary the wife of Alphaeus and Salome the wife of Zebedee bought spices to prepare the body.[190] Very early the next morning, before the sun had risen, they set out for the tomb. Joanna went with them this time. As they neared the tomb, the women asked, "Who will roll away the stone for us from the entrance of the tomb?" (Mark 16:3).

On arriving at the tomb, they were surprised to find the stone had already been rolled away. The women were uncertain what to make of the open tomb. The absence of the soldiers must have been equally alarming. The obvious implication seemed to be that the body had been removed, probably at the orders of Caiaphas or

Pilate or both, and taken to some undisclosed location. Apparently this was Mary Magdalene's initial conclusion, for she did not even enter the tomb. Instead, she turned back and ran into the city to warn Shimon Peter and the rest of the disciples that the tomb was open and the Master's body gone.[191] Thus she did not hear the announcement of the angel that the other women in the group heard.

Entering the Tomb

The remaining women at the tomb did not wait for Mary Magdalene to return with the men. They decided to investigate. In the phantom gray light of dawn the open tomb before them was pitch black. Plucking up their courage, they stooped down and entered that shadowy place of darkness. Undoubtedly they had brought lamps along with them in order to illumine their work. Imagine their shock and surprise when the light of their lamps fell upon a mysterious young man, sitting motionless in the darkness, seated on a funeral bench and dressed in a white robe! The heart leaps into the throat, the hair stands on end and the knees buckle. With the subtle power of understatement, Mark says, "They were alarmed" (Mark 16:5 NIV). The angel says (with a straight face), "Don't be alarmed" (Mark 13:7 NIV). It's a nasty trick to play on someone, even if you are an angel.

The Earthquake and the Soldiers

Matthew 28 implies that this angel was at the tomb prior to the women's arrival. Therefore, we can connect the timing of the resurrection (at the end of the Sabbath, just after sunset Saturday) with the arrival of the angel. Matthew says that at about *havdalah* time, "There was a violent earthquake, for an angel of the Lord came down from heaven and, going to the tomb, rolled back the stone and sat on it. His appearance was like lightning, and his clothes were white as snow. The guards were so afraid of him that they shook and became like dead men" (Matthew 28:2–4). When the guards awoke (whether hours or minutes later, we cannot know) they saw the tomb standing open, but the frightening young man with the lightning-like appearance had vanished. Not until after the women arrive do we realize that the angel has withdrawn to inside the tomb. When the guards awoke, they realized that the tomb was empty and fled to report the incident to their superiors "while the women were on their way" (Matthew 28:11).

MARY MAGDALENE AT THE TOMB

By the time Mary Magdalene, Peter and John returned to investigate the empty tomb, the other women (and the angels) were gone. Peter and John saw the empty tomb and returned to the city, leaving Mary alone to weep in the garden.

In her mind, the Master's enemies have dealt one more indignity to Him by stealing the body. The possibility of a resurrection has not occurred to her. Alone with her grief, Mary finally looks into the tomb herself. She sees what the other women saw: two angels, clothed in white, seated where Yeshua's body had been. One stands at the foot of the bench, the other at the head. How is it that Peter and John, who had looked into the tomb only a moment before, had not noticed the angels? That's the way it is with men and women.

The angels ask, "Woman, why are you weeping?" (John 20:13).

She explains her theory that the body of Yeshua has been stolen. In her grief, shock, and surprise, she apparently does not think it odd to be speaking with angels, or perhaps she does not realize they are angels. Mary turns around to leave, and as she wheels about, she finds herself face to face with a stranger.

The stranger repeats the question of the angels: "Woman, why are you weeping? Whom are you seeking?" (John 20:15). Mary mistakes Him for the caretaker of the cemetery. Who else would be in the garden at such an early hour? She assumes the caretaker has moved the body to a less expensive tomb. In her disorientation, she begins to ask Him if He knows where the body has been lain, but He gently interrupts her, speaking her name: "Miriam."

Suddenly, her eyes are opened and she recognizes Yeshua. "*Rabboni*," [192] she declares as she falls at the feet of the King.

Chapter 18

HANDMAIDEN OF THE KING

Jesus as a married man makes infinitely more
sense than our standard biblical view of
Jesus as a bachelor. (*The Da Vinci Code*)[193]

Ever since Mary Magdalene mistook the Master's identity at the tomb, people have been mistaking her identity. Mary Magdalene has everyone confused. Some say she was a prostitute. Others say she worked as a hairdresser. Still others say she was the Master's wife. In the Talmud, she is confused with Mary the mother of Yeshua.[194] Pope Gregory I confused her with Mary the sister of Martha and with the sinful woman who anointed the Master's feet. According to the Talmud, even the angel of death got it wrong when it came to Mary Magdalene. She may be the most frequently mistaken identity in the Gospels.

Part of the confusion results simply from her name. Mary is the Anglicized version of the Hebrew *Miriam* (מרים). First-century Jews loved to name their baby girls Miriam in honor of the sister of Moses, just as Catholics love to name their daughters Mary in honor of the mother of the Master. In the Gospels, we can identify at least six different women with the first name of Miriam:

1. the mother of the Master
2. the wife of Alphaeus (and of James and Joses)[195]
3. the sister of Martha and Lazarus[196]
4. the mother of John Mark[197]
5. Miriam of Rome[198]
6. Miriam Magdalene[199]

The mother of the Master, of course, is the most famous of all Marys. Miriam Magdalene runs a close second. She is one of the central characters in the resurrection narratives. Her reputation as a reformed prostitute has inspired countless artists to paint portraits of sensual-looking women with long, flowing hair suitable for foot-wiping. But who is this long-haired, foot-wiping hairdresser/prostitute and how did she get involved with the Master and His disciples?

In order to find out, we need to go back to the early days of the Master's ministry along the western shores of the Sea of Galilee.

The Women among the Disciples

In addition to the Twelve and other men who followed Him, Yeshua also took women as disciples. Luke says, "The twelve were with Him, and also some women who had been healed of evil spirits and sicknesses" (Luke 8:1–2). In first-century Judaism, women were accorded a higher status than the rest of the ancient world afforded them. Torah guaranteed women certain rights and a sense of dignity. For that reason, many women of the first century converted to Judaism.

Yeshua's attitude toward women was progressive even in Judaism. He violated cultural norms, freely talking with women[200] and receiving them as disciples.[201] When He was arrested and executed, all of Yeshua's male disciples abandoned Him (except John). Only the women stayed with Him at the cross, even following His body to the grave.

Some of the women who followed Yeshua were women of significant financial means. They funded the ministry of the Master out of their purses. Luke singles out three women for special mention. All were apparently recipients of healing or deliverance and had subsequently shown their gratitude by committing themselves and their financial resources to discipleship:

> The twelve were with Him, and also some women who had been healed of evil spirits and sicknesses: Mary who was called Magdalene, from whom seven demons had gone out, and Joanna the wife of Chuza, Herod's steward, and Susanna, and many others who were contributing to their support out of their private means. (Luke 8:1–3)

Luke mentions Susanna (*Shoshanna*, שושנה), a woman named after the famous Israelitess in the apocryphal book by the same name. Unfortunately, we know nothing more about her than what Luke tells us here. She was a woman of some means who had been cured of evil spirits and diseases and committed herself to a life of discipleship to Yeshua.

Luke describes Joanna (*Yochanna*, יוחנה) as the wife of Chuza, the manager of Herod's household. Translators are uncertain if the Greek should be understood to mean that Chuza was an official in Herod Antipas' government or the manager of his palace. In either case, Chuza was a man of wealth and prestige. Given the political connections, Yochanna almost certainly made her home in Tiberias, not far from where the Master ministered along the shore of the Galilee.

Yochanna left her expensive home and influential position behind in Tiberias in order to strap on the sandals of a disciple. She and Miriam from Magdala seem to have been acquainted. Luke pairs the two women again in Luke 24:10. Yochanna is one of the women who discovered the empty tomb.

MAGDALA

Yochanna came from Tiberias, but the Master never set foot in Tiberias. Herod Antipas built the city of Tiberias on an old cemetery. Observant Jews in the days of the Master would not enter the city because of uncleanness of the graves.

Before Antipas built Tiberias, the regional administrative center was the nearby Jewish town of Magdala. *Magdala* means "the tower." The seaside city may have been so named for a large stone and masonry tower structure, which the archaeology of the site has revealed. Magdala sat on the western shore of the Sea of Galilee, about a mile north of Tiberias, beneath the towering slopes of the Arbel cliff. It had a stadium and was probably one of the cities out of which Antipas governed Galilee prior to building Tiberias.

In the Talmud, we meet several sages who come from Magdala, including Yitzchak of Magdala and Yudin of Magdala. The Talmud refers to Magdala as Migdol Nunnaya, which means "the tower of the fish."[202] The Greek name of the city, often mentioned in the works of Josephus,[203] is Tarecheie, which could be loosely translated as "sardines." Magdala was famous for its pickled and smoked fish industry. The fish of Magdala were exported all over the Roman world. The fish the Master divided when He fed the multitudes probably came from Magdala. One of the feedings of those multitudes may have happened a short distance up the shore from Magdala.

In the days of the Master, Magdala boasted the largest harbor and docks on the Sea of Galilee. The disciples must have often tied their boats at the docks there to bring their fish to market. The archaeology of the site has revealed a first-century synagogue similar to the one discovered at Korazin.

Miriam from Magdala

Mary Magdalene means Miriam from Magdala. From the clues Luke gives us (8:1–3), we can piece her story together. Miriam from Magdala was a woman of some wealth and means. She apparently had friends in high places, including Yochanna the wife of Chuza, and may have been married to someone in Antipas' administration. However, she suffered from some debilitating affliction caused by seven evil spirits that vexed her.

She might have first encountered Yeshua when He and the disciples were in town selling a load of fish. She must have heard of His reputation as a healer and sought Him out for help. She was one of hundreds of people who came to the Master seeking His healing touch. When Yeshua saw her, He recognized that her affliction was caused by seven demons. He drove them out of her with a word, releasing her from satan's grip.

The healed and restored woman demonstrated her gratitude by giving her life and finances to discipleship. She followed the Master and seems to have become the first among His female disciples.

Miriam the Prostitute

In Christian tradition, Mary Magdalene is known as a former prostitute. How did the first among the Master's *talmidot* (female disciples) come to be identified as a prostitute? Miriam's traditional identification results from a tangled net of intertextual coincidence. At the end of Luke 7, a few verses before introducing us to Miriam Magdalene, Luke tells the story of the sinful woman who washed the Master's feet with her tears, anointed His feet with perfume, wiped His feet with her hair and kissed His feet with her lips. Simon the Pharisee, at whose table this embarrassing scene occurs, notes that the woman is a sinner. The implication is that she is a woman of ill repute—a prostitute. The Master points out that her gratuitous display of affection is the result of her repentance.[204] However, Luke never implies that the sinful woman of Luke 7 is the Miriam from Magdala mentioned in Luke 8.

The traditional reading of Luke's sinful woman story is confused by its similarity to the story of Yeshua's anointing in Bethany as told in Mark 14:1–11 and John 12:1–8. The differences between the anointing in Bethany and the incident reported in Luke 7 leave little doubt that the two stories arose from separate but similar events. The parallels between the anointing in Bethany and the anointing in Galilee suggest that there has been some amalgamation of the details. The alabaster jar appears in both accounts (but there certainly could have been two such jars), and a woman wipes His feet with her hair in both (as well as in John 12:3). The confusion is heightened by the fact that John tells us Miriam the sister of Martha performed the anointing, while in Luke the story of the anonymous anointing woman is immediately followed by a list of women that begins with Miriam from Magdala.

These cross-textual coincidences have led some readers to collapse the stories and the women into a single narrative. Church tradition has erroneously identified the sinful woman of Luke 7 as Miriam from Magdala and made her into the same Miriam as the sister of Martha. The sixth-century Pope Gregory I sealed this interpretation by delivering a homily in 591 CE:

> She whom Luke calls the sinful woman, whom John calls Mary, we believe to be Mary from whom seven devils were ejected according to Mark. And what did these seven devils signify, if not all the vices? … It is clear, brothers, that the woman previously used the unguent to perfume her flesh in forbidden acts. [205]

Pope Gregory's interpretation is mistaken. A careful reader of the Gospels will see that these are actually three different women.

THREE DIFFERENT WOMEN:

◊   Miriam of Bethany (Mark 14; John 12)

◊   The sinful woman/anointer (Luke 7)

◊   Miriam of Magdala (Luke 8)

Neither Miriam the sister of Martha nor Miriam from Magdala deserve the ill repute of the woman in Luke 7 that has been traditionally associated with them.

MIRIAM THE HAIRDRESSER

Miriam from Magdala suffers just as much an identity crisis in Jewish tradition as she does in church tradition. In two passages of the Talmud long ago censored by the church,[206] Miriam from Magdala is mistakenly identified as Miriam the mother of the Master. The passage is confused and convoluted as different sages offer their opinions on who she was married to and who was the father of her so-called illegitimate child. The sages who proffered their professional opinions on the matter were obviously not familiar with the gospel narratives. Miriam the mother of the Master and Miriam from Magdala were completely different women.

In their wrangling over the subject, the Talmud identified Miriam from Magdala as "Miriam the hairdresser." "[Yeshua's] mother was Miriam the hairdresser," the Talmud insists. (b.*Shabbat* 104b). A hairdresser? Where does that come from?

The notion that Miriam was a hairdresser comes from a similarity between the word *Magdalene* (*Magdalete*,מגדלית), meaning "from Magdala," and the word *Megadelet* (מגדלת). In the Aramaic and Hebrew of the sages, the word *Megadelet* could mean a hairdresser, a child's nurse or a household maidservant.[207] As a result, the Sages thought that Miriam from Magdala meant Miriam the hairdresser. Calling her a hairdresser is kinder than mistaking her for a prostitute guilty of all seven cardinal sins, but it is still far from reality.

The church incorporated this tradition as well, and Mary Magdalene has been regarded as a patron saint of hairdressers at least since the Middle Ages.

HOW MIRIAM FROM MAGDALA ESCAPED DEATH

Sometimes being mistaken for someone else can be to your advantage. According to the Talmud, the identity crisis regarding Miriam from Magdala even confused the angel of death and his minions.[208] The *Babylonian Talmud* says that Bibi ben Abaye was often visited by the angel of death, meaning he survived several close brushes with death. He once told a story he had apparently learned from that unwelcome visitor about Miriam from Magdala.

Every day, he said, the angel of death comes to collect the souls that are destined to die on that day. There are so many souls to round up that he needs help. On the day that Miriam from Magdala was supposed to die, he told his helper, "Go and bring me the soul of Miriam Magdala the hairdresser."

The assistant went out and returned with the soul of a woman named Miriam who was a children's nurse. The angel of death was flabbergasted when he saw that his assistant had brought the wrong person. "I told you to bring me Miriam Magdala the hairdresser!" His assistant replied, "If that's who you meant, I will put this one back."

"No, never mind," said the angel of death. "Since you have already brought her, let her be included in today's quota instead."

MIRIAM THE WIFE OF THE MASTER

Even stranger than any of the above misunderstandings about Miriam from Magdala is the notion that she was the secret lover and/or wife of Yeshua. And yet this rumor has been circulating for a long time, and has recently been popularized by Dan Brown's best-selling novel *The Da Vinci Code.*

According to Brown's fictional story, Mary Magdalene is the real "holy grail" of Jesus because she was His wife and bore His child, His own blood. Thus the cup with the blood of Christ in it is Miriam Magdalene's baby. In the story, the Catholic Church knows about this and has been trying to hide the evidence for centuries.

While it is often said that "truth is stranger than fiction," the strangest thing about this work of fiction is that author Dan Brown claims it is true. Not the actual characters and situations, but he does claim that all of his sources and research into the Magdalene conspiracy are based on fact. He points to lost Gnostic gospels from the Nag Hammadi library as evidence, such as the gospel of Philip and the gospel of Mary Magdalene. He claims that Constantine and the Council of Nicea suppressed the truth by doctoring our current gospel texts. He claims that the church is part of a massive conspiracy to hide the truth about Jesus' identity.

He points to Jewish culture to reinforce his argument. In first-century Judaism, celibacy was never practiced; therefore, he says, Jesus must have had a wife.

THE MAGDALENE IN GNOSTICISM

Dan Brown's *The Da Vinci Code* purports that the Gnostic gospels discovered in the Nag Hammadi library are earlier and more authentic than the canonized gospels.

In the early second century, many Christians rejected a literal reading of the Bible and began to pursue mystical interpretations of the Gospels. They believed that Jesus taught some of his disciples secret knowledge (*gnosis*)—hidden esoteric truths about the soul, physical matter, spiritual emanations, angelic beings and cosmology in general. These secret teachings of Jesus, they claimed, were only hinted at in veiled allusions in the canonical Gospels. The Gnostics believed that only those who properly understood their secret teachings could be saved. One common component of their cosmology was a demonization of the God of the Jews who in His foolish conceit imagined Himself to be the only god.

The greatest problem with the Gnostic belief system was that it had no textual justification. That is to say, they were teaching a version of Christianity that had no basis whatsoever in the gospels. In fact, the writings of the Apostles contradicted the Gnostic Christian worldview at every turn. Traditional Christianity continually pointed this out, forcing the Gnostics to fabricate apostolic tradition and text. To explain why the Apostolic Scriptures did not transmit the secret knowledge of Gnosticism, many Gnostics claimed that most of the disciples of Jesus had utterly misunderstood Him. Therefore Jesus chose to conceal His true teaching from them and revealed it only to a select few such as Philip, Thomas, Judas and Mary Magdalene.

Recently, for example, a Coptic version of the Gnostic gospel of Judas was discovered and translated. Its release in April of 2006 created a media sensation because, in that gospel, Judas is portrayed as a savant rather than a traitor. He is the only disciple who understands the true (secret) teachings of Jesus. The other disciples are portrayed as immoral men, serving an immoral god (the God of the Jews) and destined to be damned with their generation. That explains why they defame Judas as a traitor in their gospels.

In addition to Judas, the Gnostics also looked to Mary Magdalene as a source for justifying their existence. They chose Mary Magdalene as one of their founders and imagined that she must have had a secret relationship with the Master. This secret relationship explains why none of her teachings (Gnostic teachings) appear in the other gospels. The "Gnostic Jesus" did not give the same teachings to the other disciples.

Dan Brown cites passages from the Gnostic gospels to textually support the idea that Miriam from Magdala was the lover and/or wife of the Master. For example, in the gospel of Phillip, the following passage appears, depicting Christ kissing Mary Magdalene:

> Wisdom (Sophia), whom they call barren, is the mother of the angels, and the consort of Christ is Mary Magdalene. The [Lord loved her] more than all the other disciples, and he kissed her on the [mouth many times]. The other [women/disciples saw] him. They said to him, "Why do you [love her] more than all of us?" The Savior answered and said to them, "Why do not I love you as I do her?" (Gospel of Philip, 55)[209]

The gospel of Philip gives Mary Magdalene the epitaph, "whom they call His lover." In the gospel of Mary Magdalene, Mary relates the secret knowledge (*gnosis*) that Christ imparted to her. After Christ's ascension, Peter says to Mary, "Sister, we know that the Savior loved you more than the rest of women. Tell us the words of the Savior which you remember." She responds with a long treatise on how the human soul can escape the mortal cage of the body and the physical world by ascending past the intermediate ruling powers and the usual flights of escoterism. At the conclusion of the gospel, Peter and Andrew express their disbelief, but Levi rebukes Peter and points out that Mary was Jesus' favorite:

> Now I see you contending against the woman like the adversaries. If the Savior made her worthy, who are you indeed to reject her? Surely the Savior knows her very well. This is why he loved her more than us.[210]

Obviously, if these gospels are reliable, Yeshua had less than a purely platonic relationship with Miriam from Magdala. Of course, they are not reliable. No credible scholar in the world has suggested they are. They are the products of Gnostic Christianity and were written generations after the canonical Gospels. In the predominant Gnostic worldview, all physical matter is evil and all that really counts is the life of the soul. Torah, because it relates to the illusory physical world, is irrelevant and even evil. Therefore, we read in the gospel of Mary Magdalene that "Gnostic Jesus" tells Peter, "There is no sin, but it is you who make sin why you do the things that are like the nature of adultery, which is called 'sin.'" [211] In other words, there is no such thing as sin unless you think something is sinful. Adultery is not sin unless you make it sinful.

In another passage, the last words of instruction the Gnostic Jesus gives His disciples before ascending to heaven is a warning against Torah. He says, "Do not lay down any rules beyond what I appointed for you, and do not give a Law (Torah) like the lawgiver (Moses) lest you be constrained by it."

The Gnostic gospels all purport to transmit the secret teachings of Yeshua that were not recorded in the canonized Gospels. According to the canonized Gospels, though, Yeshua had no secret teachings.

Contrary to the Gnostic heresies, Yeshua declared, "I have spoken openly to the world." There are no private teachings, no secret knowledge and no hidden riddles. He said, "I have spoken openly to the world; I always taught in synagogues, and in the temple, where all the Jews come together; and I spoke nothing in secret" (John 18:20–21).

Gnostic texts like the gospel of Judas and the gospel of Mary Magdalene do not stand up under the scrutiny of a Jewish reading. The canonical Gospels all possess genuine Jewish character and complete consistency with the Torah and the Prophets. The Gnostic gospels do not. Anyone who entertains the notion that the Gnostic gospels might contain historical truth needs to read them and compare them with the canonized Gospels. Then compare both with ancient rabbinical literature. The complete disconnect from Judaism is obvious: The Gnostic Jesus has almost nothing in common with the historical Yeshua. It would be absurd to ascribe any historical validity to the narratives and teachings in the Gnostic gospels.

THE CELIBACY OF THE MASTER

In *The Da Vinci Code*, Dan Brown writes, "Jesus as a married man makes infinitely more sense than our standard biblical view of Jesus as a bachelor."[212] He is right about that. First-century Judaism placed a high priority on early marriage and reproduction. According to the Gospels, Yeshua chose a path of celibacy. In one passage, He even seems to encourage others to choose the same path.

When Yeshua warned His disciples against divorce on grounds other then immorality, they replied, "If the relationship of the man with his wife is like this, it is better not to marry" (Matthew 19:10).

Their objection must be understood in the context of the discussion. It refers to the very real danger of an unsuccessful marriage. If the only legitimate reason for divorce is infidelity, the disciples are saying, maybe it's better not to take the risk of getting married at all. For what if you marry and end up being unhappy with your wife?

As far as we know, all the disciples (with the possible exception of Yochanon ben Zavdai) were married. It was unusual in Jewish culture not to be married by the age of eighteen.

> Our Rabbis taught, "A man who loves his wife as himself, who treats her with more respect than himself, who guides his children in the right path and arranges for them to be married near the their time of puberty, concerning such a man the scripture says [in Job 5:2], 'You will know that your tent is *at peace.*'" (b.*Yevamoth* 62b)

> Raba said to Rabbi Nathan ben Ammi, "While your hand is still on the back of your son's neck, [marry him off]." That is while he is between sixteen and twenty-two. Others state, while he is between eighteen and twenty-four. (b.*Kiddushin* 30a)

The disciples were probably all married men with children and (in some cases grandchildren) of their own. It would not be unusual in first-century Jewish culture to be a grandparent by the age of thirty. Marrying and begetting children was a *mitzvah* derived from the command given to Adam and Eve to "be fruitful and multiply" (Genesis 1:22). The schools of Hillel and Shammai differed on the number of children required to fulfill this commandment, but two progeny was generally accepted as the very minimum.

That marriage was highly regarded is well demonstrated with the following quotation:

> Reb Tanhum said in the name of Rabbi Hanilai, "A man who has no wife lives without joy, without blessing, and without goodness. ... It is not good for man to be alone." (b. *Yevamoth* 62b)

In light of the commandment to be fruitful and multiply and the high value Judaism places on marriage and family, Yeshua's response to His disciples seems troubling. Torah Judaism celebrates marriage and human sexuality by raising them to the level of holy commandment. Yet here in Matthew 19:11–12 Yeshua seems to shrug off marriage as a necessary evil, allowable only for those who cannot receive the higher call of celibacy for the sake of the kingdom:

> But He said to them, "Not all men can accept this statement, but only those to whom it has been given. For there are eunuchs who were born that way from their mother's womb; and there are eunuchs who were made eunuchs by men; and there are also eunuchs who made themselves eunuchs for the sake of the kingdom of heaven. He who is able to accept this, let him accept it." (Matthew 19:11–12)

The early church took His statement regarding becoming "eunuchs for the kingdom of heaven" as a justification for the extreme ascetic celibacy movement that had been imported from ascetic and stoic branches of Gnosticism. In the literature of the church fathers, marriage is deemed at best a necessary evil and at worst "filthy intercourse."[213]

Did Yeshua really mean to encourage His disciples to forsake marital relations in favor of a celibate lifestyle? No. The context of Matthew 18–19 makes that clear. In His teaching in Matthew 18:5–6, Yeshua demonstrates the high value He assigned to marriage. Matthew 18:3–11 and 19:13–14 show us the high value He assigned to children.

What, then, do His comments on the celibate life imply? The answer is not to be found by looking outside Judaism to the cultures of the monasteries, convents and seminaries that were spawned by a mishandling of this passage. Rather, we find the impetus for celibacy within traditional Jewish thought.

MOSES SEPARATES FROM HIS WIFE

Yeshua's words regarding "eunuchs for the kingdom" are likely a response to criticism of His own marital status. He, a thirty-three-year-old Israelite, never married. What possible justification could He have for not fulfilling the commandment to "be fruitful and multiply"? The Talmud records how the sages similarly criticized Ben Azzai for remaining single:

> They said to Ben Azzai, "Some preach well and live well, others live well but do not preach well; you, however, preach well but do not live well [since you are unmarried]!" Ben Azzai replied, "But what shall I do, seeing that my soul is in love with the Torah; the world can be carried on by others." (b. *Yevamot* 63b)

Ben Azzai justified his choice of a celibate life on the basis that his soul was in love with the Torah. The same could be said of the Master.

Besides, celibacy and asceticism were not unknown in the Judaism of Yeshua's day. Yeshua was so fully occupied with His Father's work that there was really no time to also serve a wife and family. Or perhaps, knowing that He was to die in His early thirties, He regarded it an injustice to leave behind a young widow and orphans.

One need not look outside Judaism to find the practice of celibacy. In the days of the Master, the Essene movement practiced a severe asceticism that separated men and woman and frowned on marriage.[214]

Yeshua's choice of celibacy may also have been influenced by traditional teachings about Moses.

MOSES CHOOSES CELIBACY

In the Torah we learn that Moses sent his wife away.[215] In Numbers 12, his brother and sister criticize his marriage. Jewish tradition explains Moses' marital troubles as the result of his decision to be celibate. According to these traditions, Moses withdrew from sexual relations because he needed to maintain a constant state of ritual purity. Moses heard directly from God and was required to enter the presence of God in the Tabernacle every day. Therefore he needed to remain perpetually ritually pure. Sexual relations would have made that an impossibility.[216]

God commanded Israel to remain celibate for three days prior to the revelation at Mount Sinai (Exodus 19). Moses reasoned that if Israel was commanded to keep celibate in preparation for hearing the voice of God only once, how much more so should he remain celibate in preparation for hearing the voice of God every day:

> Moses separated himself from his wife. On what basis did he do so? He said, "If the Torah said 'let no man approach a woman' to the Israelites with whom the Dwelling Presence spoke only for a short time and at a designated appointment, how much more should I abstain! God speaks to me at any moment and without warning." (b.*Yevamot* 62a; cf. b.*Shabbat* 87a, b.*Shemot Rabbah* 19:3)

Yeshua is the prophet like unto Moses.[217] Like Moses, He was in the unique position of receiving direct divine communication on a daily basis. Perhaps for Yeshua, as with Moses, marriage was not an option because of the demands of His prophetic ministry. Though He never flinched from contracting ritual impurity if it meant alleviating human suffering, He might have avoided marriage for the sake of maintaining a state of purity. If so, Yeshua was a "eunuch for the sake of the kingdom of heaven."

For most of the rest of us, who are not Moses or Yeshua (or Paul), a spouse is probably a good thing. Regarding purity issues, short terms of abstinence are sufficient. Paul understood the tension between ritual purity for the sake of revelation and the obligations of marriage. He warned husbands and wives, "Do not deprive each other [of sexual relations] except by mutual consent and for a time, so that you may devote yourselves to prayer" (1 Corinthians 7:5 NIV).

CHILDREN OF THE MASTER

If we were in doubt over the Master's love for children and family or had any questions regarding His obligation to beget children, Matthew supplies us with a short episode in which Yeshua lays His hands on the children of Jericho to bless them.[218]

Yeshua regarded His disciples as His children. He once told them, "I will not leave you as orphans; I will come to you" (John 14:18). On another occasion He said, "Whoever does the will of My Father who is in heaven, he is [My family]" (Matthew 12:50).

Isaiah prophesies regarding the Master's marital status in the passage of the suffering servant. He says, "And who can speak of his descendants? For he was cut off from the land of the living."[219] But he goes on to say, "He will see his offspring and prolong his days."[220] Regarding natural children born into this world Isaiah says, "Who can speak of his descendants?" Regarding spiritual children who have been born into the world to come Isaiah says, "He will see his offspring."

Obviously, Miriam from Magdala was not the secret wife of the Master, nor His paramour. The texts that imply a physical or exclusive relationship between them are without credibility. Yeshua's choice of a celibate life was not unprecedented in Judaism of His day, and was actually practiced by Moses himself. However, she did have a special relationship with Yeshua. He was her healer, who had exorcised seven demons from her. He was her teacher, for whom she had committed her life to a path of discipleship. "Rabboni!" she cried out in the garden. He was her Savior, her Messiah and her King. And to her was entrusted the glad news. The resurrected Yeshua told her, "Stop clinging to Me, for I have not yet ascended to the Father; but go to My brethren and say to them, 'I ascend to My Father and your Father, and My God and your God'" (John 20:17).

Chapter 19

HE LIFTED HIS HANDS

YESHUA AND THE PRIESTLY BLESSING

> Rabbi Yehoshua ben Levi said, "How do we
> know that the Holy One, blessed be He, desires
> to hear the priestly blessing?" As it is written [in
> Numbers 6:27], "They shall invoke My name on
> the sons of Israel, and I then will bless them."
> Rabbi Yehoshua ben Levi also said, "Every
> priest who pronounces the blessing is himself
> blessed, but if he does not pronounce it he is
> not blessed; as it is said [in Genesis 12:3], 'I will
> bless those who bless you.'" (b.*Sotah* 37b–38a)

All the priests wanted to have the opportunity to offer the incense. They so coveted the incense detail that each member of the priesthood was only allowed to perform it once in his entire lifetime. They cast lots to determine who would get the privilege. The lucky priest chosen to offer the incense came as close to the Holy of Holies as a common priest could.

That morning, they had already sacrificed the lamb. The smoke was rising from the altar, and the Levites were singing the morning psalms. The standing men, representing all of Israel, took their places in the Temple court to witness the morning sacrifice and to pray the daily prayers.[221] The time for offering the morning incense had come.

Zechariah had been serving as a priest his entire life, and now he was very old, but he had never won the lot to offer the incense. That day, when they cast the lots for the incense, Zechariah won. Trembling with joy, he took the golden shovel and the covered golden dish heaped with incense. He climbed the steps to the sanctuary and passed through the great gates. Priests, Levites and worshippers all fell silent as the old man disappeared inside the Temple to perform the daily incense service.

THE PRIESTLY BLESSING

The rest of the priesthood ascended the platform in front of the sanctuary doors and prepared to conclude the morning prayers and sacrifice with the priestly blessing. They called it the "priestly blessing" (*birkat cohanim,* ברכת כהנים) because God commanded the priesthood to bless Israel with it:

> Then the LORD spoke to Moses, saying, "Speak to Aaron and to his sons, saying, 'Thus you shall bless the sons of Israel. You shall say to them:
>
> "The LORD bless you, and keep you;
>
> The LORD make His face shine on you, and be gracious to you;
>
> The LORD lift up His countenance on you, and give you peace."
>
> So they shall invoke My name on the sons of Israel, and I then will bless them.'" (Numbers 6:22–27)

In the Temple, the priests recited this blessing every day at the conclusion of the morning sacrifice. The custom is remembered even in modern times in the morning prayers of the synagogue service. In synagogues in the land of Israel (and in Sephardic synagogues everywhere) the descendants of the priesthood go up to the front of the synagogue to offer this blessing to the congregation during the morning prayers. In Ashkenazi Diaspora congregations, the priests perform the blessing only on holidays. On all other mornings, the cantor recites the blessing on behalf of the priests.

"Our God and God of our fathers," the cantor prays, "bless us with the three-verse blessing that was written in the Torah by the hand of Moses and that was pronounced by the sons of Aaron, the holy priests, as it is written, 'The LORD bless you and keep you.'" The congregation then responds, "Yes, may it be His will." The cantor says, "The LORD make His face shine on you, and be gracious to you". The congregation responds, "Yes, may it be His will." The cantor says, "The Lord lift up His countenance on you, and give you peace." The congregation responds, "Yes, may it be His will."

Lifting the Hands

The recitation of the priestly blessing is sometimes called *duchaning* (going up to the platform) because in Temple times, the priests ascended the Temple steps to a platform (*duchan,* דוכן) before conferring the blessing on the assembled worshippers.

Another ancient name for the blessing is the "Lifting of the Hands." [222] In Temple times, the priests lifted their hands over the people while pronouncing the blessing. Their basis for doing so is in the Torah. In its description of the first Tabernacle worship service, the Torah says, "Then Aaron lifted up his hands toward the people and blessed them" (Leviticus 9:22).

When they lifted their hands over the people, the priests made the sign of the priesthood. To make the sign of the priesthood, the priest spreads the thumb and index finger of each of his hands. Turning his palms outward, he brings the thumb and index finger to touch the thumb and index finger of the opposite hand. The third and fourth fingers of his hands are also spread apart. This creates a "W" shape with the fingers. Science fiction fans are familiar with Mr. Spock's Vulcan sign of peace—a hand sign actor Leonard Nimoy borrowed from his own synagogue upbringing. The Vulcan hand sign is one half of the sign of the priesthood. "Live long and prosper" is apparently the Vulcan equivalent of the priestly blessing.

The holy sign of the priesthood represents the shape of the ancient letter *shin* ש. In ancient Hebrew (before the introduction of square Aramaic characters) the letter ש looked more like a W. That the sign of the priesthood is modeled after the ancient form of the letter proves the great antiquity of the ritual lifting of the hands.

The Glory of God's Name

In Judaism, the letter *shin* is an accepted Jewish abbreviation for the name of God. In Temple times, the priesthood lifted their hands, making the sign of the letter *shin* while pronouncing the blessing in order to fulfill the commandment, "So they will put my name on the Israelites, and I will bless them" (Numbers 6:27 NIV). Even though the holy name of God (Y/H/V/H) was never pronounced in the days of the Master, the priesthood pronounced it aloud during the priestly blessing with the morning sacrifice.

According to the Talmud, when the priests lifted their hands in the Temple and blessed the people, the glory of God's name rested upon their hands. This was the interpretation of Numbers 6:27, which says, "So they will put my name on the Israelites" (NIV).

Out of respect for the glory of God, the custom arose to avert one's eyes from the hands of the priest. Medieval Torah commentator Rashi explains that the radiance of the divine presence emanated from the priest's fingers as they pronounced the blessing in the Temple.[223] If staring at the sun blinds a man, how much more does staring at God's glory! The Talmud explains that one who stared at the priest's hands risked losing his eyesight.

> Rabbi Yehudah Berabbi Nachmani, the interpreter of Resh Lakish explained, "Anyone who looks at three things, his eyes become dim; at the rainbow, and at the Prince, and at the priests [while they bestow the blessing]. At the rainbow, because it is written [in Ezekiel 1:28], 'Like the appearance of a rainbow in the clouds on a rainy day … was the appearance of the likeness of the glory of the LORD.' At the Prince, for it is written [in Numbers 27:20] 'And you shall put your glory upon him.' One who looks at the priests—at the time when the Temple still stood, when they stood upon their platform [pronouncing the priestly blessing] and blessed Israel with the Unspeakable Name [of God]." (b.*Chagigah* 16a)

Did people really lose their eyesight from looking at the priest's hands? Probably not, but it is a tradition of the rabbis that carried over into early synagogue practice. Even today, when the descendants of the priesthood pronounce the blessing in the synagogue, they drape their lifted hands in a prayer shawl to protect the congregation from inadvertently looking at their hands. It is also customary for the congregants to look at the floor, or perhaps to look upon the priest's feet as he blesses.

Zechariah's Hand Signs

Everyone within the Temple waited in silent anticipation for Zechariah, the chosen priest for the day, to emerge and lead the priesthood in the priestly blessing. As he tarried inside the sanctuary, they began to worry. The Mishnah notes that the high priest on the Day of Atonement was not allowed to make a long prayer inside the sanctuary lest he frighten those waiting for him to reemerge. If he stayed in too long, they might suspect that God had struck him dead. "He uttered a short prayer. He did not make the prayer too long lest he frighten Israel," Scripture says.[224] Zechariah's long delay began to frighten Israel. When at last he emerged into the midst of the assembled priests, they expected him to lift his hands, spread his fingers toward the worshippers with the sign of the priesthood and pronounce the priestly blessing. Instead, when Zechariah emerged, he lifted his hands in frantic gestures and signs. He was unable to speak, much less deliver the blessing:

> The people were waiting for Zacharias, and were wondering at his delay in the temple. But when he came out, he was unable to speak to them; and they realized that he had seen a vision in the temple; and he kept making signs to them, and remained mute. (Luke 1:21–22)

He Lifted His Hands

At the end of the book of Luke, the resurrected Messiah is depicted walking and talking with the disciples on the Mount of Olives near the village of Bethany. He stops, turns to the disciples, lifts His scarred hands and blesses them. "And He led them out as far as Bethany, and He lifted up His hands and blessed them" (Luke 24:50).

According to what we have learned from the Talmud, to say "He lifted up His hands and blessed them" is idiomatic for the pronouncement of the priestly blessing. How many times had the disciples heard the priests in the Temple make this blessing? Every day the priests finished the sacrifices by lifting their hands, spreading their fingers and making the blessing over Israel. What a shock it must have been for them to see Yeshua do the same. After all, Yeshua was not a priest.

According to the Torah, only the descendants of Aaron could serve as priests. Aaron was a Levite. Yeshua was from the tribe of Judah, and as the writer of the book of Hebrews says, "It is evident that our Lord was descended from Judah, a tribe with reference to which Moses spoke nothing concerning priests" (Hebrews 7:14). Yeshua was legally incapable of serving as an Aaronic priest. But if He was not a priest, why did He bless His disciples with the ancient sign of the priesthood?

According to the Talmud, if a non-priest raises his hands, makes the sign of the priesthood, and pronounces the blessing, he is transgressing a commandment. Even the kings of Israel were not allowed to usurp priestly privileges. King Saul lost the kingdom for making a sacrifice without a priest. King Uzziah was struck with leprosy for attempting to offer incense. By lifting His hands and making the priestly blessing, Yeshua was apparently transgressing the positive commandment for the priests to do those things.

The Talmud says that "if a person was not a priest, he would not have the *chutzpah* [to lift up his hands and make the priestly blessing]." [225] Yeshua was never short on *chutzpah*, but would He have violated the purview of the priesthood by taking it upon Himself to lift His hands and pronounce the priestly blessing?

The writer of the book of Hebrews solves the dilemma. He teaches that after His resurrection, Yeshua did become a priest. He did not become an Aaronic priest, nor did He topple or replace the Aaronic priesthood. According to the writer of Hebrews, He entered into a different priesthood, a higher priesthood, that serves in the eternal Temple of God in heaven rather than in the Temple on earth. By virtue of His resurrection, Yeshua entered into the priesthood of Melchizedek:

> [He has become a priest] not on the basis of a law of physical requirement, but according to the power of an indestructible life. For it is witnessed of Him [in Psalm 110:4], "You are a priest forever according to the order of Melchizedek." (Hebrews 7:16–17)

By lifting His hands and blessing His disciples with the priestly blessing, Yeshua was taking upon Himself the office of priest. The Talmud maintains that a person who pronounces the priestly blessing with the lifting of the hands declares himself to be a priest.[226] Yeshua was declaring His priesthood to the disciples.

THE PRIEST WITH SCARRED HANDS

The Talmud contains an interesting discussion on the lifting of the hands.[227] As mentioned above, the etiquette of the Temple required the congregation to avert their eyes out of respect for the name of God and to avoid being blinded by the glory of God resting upon the priest's hands. The sages prohibited a priest with deformities on his hands from performing the priestly benediction, lest the deformities distract the people receiving the blessing. Even a priest with discolored hands was discouraged from offering the priestly benediction.

However, when the Master lifted His hands to bless the disciples with the priestly benediction, the scars left by the nails were clearly visible. The scars of Messiah are testimony to the glory of God. They reminded the disciples that this was not the first time He had lifted those hands to bless them. He had lifted them on the cross.

The disciples would have been familiar with the custom of lowering one's eyes when the priests lifted their hands. Upon seeing the Master raise His nail-scarred hands and hearing Him begin to chant the priestly blessing over them, they would have been quick to avert their eyes and look at the ground. As their eyes fell upon Yeshua's nail-scarred feet, they would have been amazed to realize that those feet were no longer touching the ground. As Yeshua blessed them, He ascended into the sky, rising to take His place as priest in the heavenly sanctuary. The gospel of Luke says, "While He was blessing them, He parted from them and was carried up into heaven" (Luke 24:51 NIV).

The disciples dropped to the ground and prostrated themselves before Him.

THE INTERRUPTED BLESSING

In presenting us with this final scene of the Master pronouncing the priestly blessing as He ascends, Luke alludes back to the beginning of his gospel, which opened with Zechariah the priest unable to join the priesthood in pronouncing the priestly blessing after the angel Gabriel had struck him dumb. At the end of the book of Luke, that interrupted blessing is finally resumed, with the Master Himself stepping into the role of priest, lifting His hands and pronouncing the final blessing.

Luke tells us that after He ascended, the disciples returned to Jerusalem with great joy. They stayed at the Temple, praising God. The gospel of Luke ends where it began—in the Temple of God in Jerusalem.

Epilogue

RESTORING THE KINGDOM TO ISRAEL

The Messiah you are expecting will never
come, the Messiah that is coming you
never expected. (Old Yiddish Proverb)

After His resurrection, Yeshua appeared often to the disciples over a period of forty days and taught them things concerning the kingdom of heaven.

On one occasion, when they were all eating together with the Master, the disciples asked Him the question that was pressing on all their minds. "Master, is it at this time you are going to restore the kingdom to Israel?"[228] After all, that's what being the anointed Messiah-King was all about.

Theologians often fault the disciples for having misunderstood the message of the kingdom. They point out that the disciples, in their thick-headedness, were still anticipating a literal kingdom on earth. "Even after all they had seen, those foolish disciples still did not understand that the kingdom of heaven is a spiritual kingdom," many clergymen remark.

On the contrary, the disciples had finally come to understand the kingdom of heaven. They now understood that the kingdom could only come as the result of the suffering of Messiah. That suffering having been completed, they asked, "Master, are You at this time going to restore the kingdom to Israel?"

Throughout the apostolic age, believers confidently asserted that Yeshua would return and establish His kingdom on earth in a real and tangible manner. They believed that He would sit on the throne of His father David in Jerusalem, administering justice and righteousness for the kingdom of Israel and ruling over the nations with a scepter of iron.

The apostolic community often quoted Psalm 2, which speaks of that coming day when God installs His King upon Zion, the holy mountain, and shatters the nations with a rod of iron. In that day, the kingdom of heaven and the kingdom of Israel will merge into one. In fulfillment of all the promises of the prophets, the scion of David will conquer the nations and reign over all the kingdoms of the earth.

Numerous passages from the ancient prophets testify to the restoration of the kingdom of Israel. One passage typifies the rest. In Ezekiel 37:24–28, the prophet says, "My servant David will be king over them." In Ezekiel, the name *David* is a title for the promised Davidic king. The passage goes on to say that in those days, "they will walk in My ordinances and keep My statutes and observe them," which is to say that in the days of Messiah, Israel will keep the Torah. The prophet also says that they will live in the land of Israel, the land in which their fathers Abraham, Isaac and Jacob lived. "They will live on it, they, and their sons and their sons' sons, forever; and David My servant will be their prince forever" (Ezekiel 37:25). Ezekiel says that in that day God will make an everlasting covenant of peace with Israel, He will greatly multiply their numbers and He will rebuild the Temple, setting it in their midst, never to be destroyed again. "And the nations will know that I am the LORD who sanctifies Israel, when My sanctuary is in their midst forever" (Ezekiel 37:28).

By and large, the church has misunderstood the meaning of the kingdom. Rather than take the prophets at their word, the anti-chiliast sentiments in Christian theology reinterpreted those prophecies to apply to the church. Rather than a literal kingdom being restored to Israel, the church understood the prophets to be speaking metaphorically of the church age during which the church takes over the world. This theology lent itself well to the political aspirations of the Roman church. More importantly, it justified the pervasive theology of supersessionism and the practice of anti-Semitism. To the traditional Christian church, a literal future kingdom of the Jews seemed ludicrous. Yet that was the hope of the disciples when they asked the Master, "Is it at this time You are going to restore the kingdom to Israel?"

Yeshua did not deny that the time will come when He will restore the kingdom to Israel, just as the disciples anticipated. On the contrary, He spoke of that day frequently. The kingdom of heaven fully revealed will mean the restoration of Israel. The disciples looked forward to the day when the risen Messiah will sit enthroned in Jerusalem as the recognized and crowned King of Israel and all the earth.

As they ate together, perhaps for the last time before His ascension, He answered them, saying, "It is not for you to know times or epochs which the Father has fixed by His own authority" (Acts 1:7). In other words, "None of your business." However, His answer makes it clear that there is a set time for the restoration of the kingdom to Israel. It is a date that "the Father has fixed by His own authority." As for the exact hour of that day when Messiah will come and Israel will be restored, even Yeshua did not know. "But of that day or hour no one knows, not even the angels in heaven, nor the Son, but the Father alone" (Mark 13:32). But be sure of this. When that hour does come and Messiah returns in glory, He will rule over the world as king of the Jews. And another thing—when He comes, He will still be Jewish.

May He come speedily, soon and in our lifetimes.

Selected Bibliography

Beasely-Murray, George R., *Word Biblical Commentary: John,* second edition (Dallas, Texas: Word Books Publisher, 1999).

Bivin, David, "Jesus' Education," *Jerusalem Perspective,* 14-15, 1988.

Bivin, David and Blizzard, Roy Jr., *Understanding the Difficult Words of Jesus* (Dayton, Ohio: Center for Judaic Christian Studies, 1994).

Bruce, F. F., *Hard Sayings of Jesus* (Downers Grove, Illinois: InterVarsity Press, 1983).

Bruce, F. F., *The Book of Acts* (Grand Rapids, MI: Wm. B. Eerdmans Publishing Co., 1988).

Culpepper, R. Alan, *John, the Son of Zebedee* (Columbia, SC: University of South Carolina Press, 1994).

Cohen, Abraham, *Everyman's Talmud* (New York: Schocken Books, 1975).

Daube, David, *The New Testament and Rabbinic Judaism* (Great Britain: University of London, The Athlone Press, 1956).

De Vaux, Roland, *Ancient Israel* (London: Darton, Longman and Todd, 1964).

Donin, Hayim, *To Pray as A Jew: A Guide to the Prayer Book and the Synagogue Service* (USA: BasicBooks, Harper Collins, 1980).

Douglas, J.D., ed., *The Illustrated Bible Dictionary,* three volumes (Wheaton, IL: Tyndale House Publishers, 1980).

Edersheim, Alfred, *Sketches of Jewish Social Life in the Days of Christ* (Grand Rapids, MI: Wm. B. Eerdmans Publishing Co., 1990).

Edersheim, Alfred, *The Temple, Its Ministry and Services* (Grand Rapids, MI: Wm. B. Eerdmans Publishing Co., 1992).

Edersheim, Alfred, *Jesus the Messia.*(Peabody, MA: Hendrickson Publishers, 1993).

Ehrman, Bart D, *Lost Scriptures: Books that Did Not Make It into the New Testamen.*(Oxford University Press, 2005).

Evans, Craig A, *Word Biblical Commentary. Mark 8:27-16:20* (Dallas, Texas: Word Books Publisher, 2001).

Falk, Harvey, *Jesus the Pharisee: A New Look at the Jewishness of Jesus* (New York/Mahwah: Paulist Press, 1985).

Feur, Avrohom Chaim, *Tehillim: A New Translation with a Commentary Anthologized from Talmudic, Midrashic and Rabbinic Sources* (Brooklyn, New York: Mesorah Publications, 1985).

Fitzmeyer, Joseph A., *The Semitic Background of the New Testament* (Grand Rapid, MI: William B. Eerdmans Publishing Co., 1997).

Flusser, David, "Do You Prefer New Wine?" *Immanuel* 9:26–31, 1979.

Flusser, David, *Judaism and the Origins of Christianity* (Jerusalem: The Magnes Press, The Hebrew University, 1988).

Ginzberg, Louis, *Legends of the Jews,* vols. 1-7 (Baltimore and London: The Jewish Publication Society of America, John Hopkins University Press, 1998).

Guelich, .Robert A., *Word Biblical Commentary: Mark 1-6:26* (Dallas, Texas: Word Books Publisher, 1989).

Good, R. S., "Yeshua, Protagonist of the Old, in Luke 5:33–39), *Novum Testamentum* 25(1):19–36, 1983.

Goodman, Phillip, *The Rosh Hashanah Anthology* (Philadelphia/Jerusalem: The Jewish Publication Society, 1992).

Hagner, Donald A., *Word Biblical Commentary: Matthew,* two vols. (Dallas, Texas: Word Books Publisher, 1995).

Hammer, Reuven, translator, *Sifre: A Tannaitic Commentary on the Book of Deuteronomy* (New Haven and London: Yale University Press, 1986).

Kee, Alistair, "The Old Coat and the New Wine: A Parable of Repentance," *Novum Testementum,* 1970.

Kitov, Eliyahu, *The Book of Our Heritage,* three vols. (Jerusalem, New York: Feldheim Publishers, 1997).

Lachs, Samuel Tobias, *A Rabbinic Commentary on the New Testament* (Hoboken, NJ: Ktav Publishing House, Inc., 1987).

Lehreman, S. M., translator, *The Soncino Midrash Rabbah,* ten vols. (London, New York: The Soncino Press, 1983).

Levine, Moshe, ed., *The Soncino Talmud,* thirty vols. (London, New York: The Soncino Press, 1965).

Lightfoot, Jonathan, *Commentary on the New Testament from Talmud and Hebraica,* four vols. (Hendrickson Publishers, 1997).

Lindsey, Robert L., *Jesus, Rabbi and Lord* (Oak Creek, WI: Cornerstone Publishing, 1990).

Lindsey, Robert, *A Hebrew Translation of the Gospel of Mark* (Jerusalem: Dugith Publishers Baptist House, 1969).

Mead, A. H., "Old and New Wine: St. Luke 5:39," *Expository Times* 99(8):234–235, 1988.

Neusner, Jacob, *The Mishnah: A New Translation* (New Haven and London: Yale University Press, 1988).

Nolland, John, *Word Biblical Commentary: Luke,* two vols. (Dallas, Texas: Word Books Publisher, 1989).

Notely, Steven, "John's Baptism of Repentance," *Jerusalem Digest Vol. 2, No. 3,* 1998, 6–8.

Nun, Mendel, "Cast Your Net upon the Waters," *BAR* vol. 19, No. 6, 1993.

Patai, Raphael, *The Messiah Texts* (Detroit, MI: Wayne State University Press, 1988).

Pixner, Bargil, *With Jesus through Galilee according to the Fifth Gospel* (Israel: Corazin Publishing, 1992).

Roberts, Alexander and Donaldson, James, eds., *The Ante-Nicene Fathers* (Grand Rapids, MI: Wm. B. Eerdmans Publishing Co., 1978).

Robertson, A. T., *A Harmony of the Gospels for Students of the Life of Christ* (San Francisco, CA: HarperSanFrancisco, 1922).

Santala, Risto, *The Messiah in the New Testament* (Kukkila, Finland: Bible and Gospel Service, 1992).

Scherman, Nosson, *The Complete ArtScroll Machzor: Rosh Hashanah* (Brooklyn, NY: Mesorah Publications Ltd., 1985).

Scherman, Nosson, *The Complete ArtScroll Machzor: Pesach* (Brooklyn, NY: Mesorah Publications Ltd., 1994).

Scherman, Nosson, *The Complete ArtScroll Machzor: Succot* (Brooklyn, NY: Mesorah Publications Ltd., 1994).

Stern, David H., *Jewish New Testament Commentary* (Jerusalem: Jewish New Testament Publications, 1992).

Stern, Robert H., *The New American Commentary*, vol., 24, Luke (Nashville, TN: Broadman Press, 1992).

Steinsaltz, Adin, *The Talmud: A Reference Guide* (New York: Random House, 1989).

Synge, F. C., "The Parable of the Patch," *Expository Times* 56:26–27, 1989.

Weissman, Rabbi Moshe, *The Midrash Says: Five Volumes,* (Brooklyn: Bnay Yakov Publications, 1995).

Whiston, William, *The New Complete Works of Josephus* (Grand Rapids, MI: Kregel Publications, 1999).

Williamson, G. A., *Eusebius: The History of the Church* (Minneapolis, MN: Augsburg Publishing, 1965).

Young, Brad, *Jesus the Jewish Theologian* (Peabody, MA: Hendrickson Publishers, 1995).

Young, Brad, *The Parables: Jewish Tradition and Christian Interpretation* (Peabody, MA: Hendrickson Publishers, 1998).

Scripture Index

Subject Index

repentance, 30, 31, 32, 33, 77, 91, 128
  a parable about, 129
  definition of, 34
Replacement Theology, 65, 141, 146
resurrection, 123, 124, 220
  and the Sadducees, 70
  of the Shunamite's son, 107
  of Yeshua, 150, 176, 193–197, 223
Rosh HaShanah, 159, 160, 168
  and the final judgment, 166–167
rosh pinah. *See* capstone

S

Sabbath, 43, 46, 53, 70, 73–75, 130, 190, 193–195
Sadducees, 70, 126, 146
Salome, 98, 100
  the mother of James and John, 193, 195
Samuel, 31, 32, 169, 173
Sanhedrin, 26, 70, 72, 139, 164, 179
Shammai. *See* Hillel and Shammai
Shema, 35
shofar, 134, 160
  and Passover, 188
  and Rosh Hashanah, 166
Simon of Cyrene, 184
Sons of Thunder, 117
Son of Man, 91, 113, 147, 162, 166, 167
stonecutting, 151
sukkah, 114, 116, 119, 132
Sukkot, xvii, 113, 116, 118–120, 131–133, 136
  and Hoshana Rabbah, 136
  and the coming Kingdom, 114
  and the Transfiguration, 113
  the water libation, 137–138

T

talmidim, 51. *See also* disciples, discipleship
Talmud, xiii
teffilin, 73
Temple, 25, 73, 74, 131, 133, 134, 139, 153, 170, 174, 178, 179, 188, 189
  and the golden eagle, 27
  service, 173, 186, 215, 216, 217, 219
  the eternal, in heaven, 220
titulus, 186
transfiguration, 113, 118
tzitzit, 73

Y

Yehudah the Prince, 124, 160
Yeshua
  birth, 21
  carpenter, 62
  cornerstone, 149
  declaration of Messiahship, 138
  education, 62
  family, 67
  genealogy, 23
  name, 22
Yom Kippur.
    See Day of Atonement
Yosef
  of Arimathea, 177, 190

Z

Zechariah, 215, 219

Endnotes

INTRODUCTION

[1] Bart D. Ehrman, *Lost Scriptures: Books that Did Not Make It into the New Testament* (Oxford University Press, 2005).

PROLOGUE

[2] m.*Ketubot* 5:2 states that twelve months was the normal betrothal for a virgin.

[3] However, there is no truth to the allegation that the name "Jesus" is derived from a pagan god like Zeus. Neither is there any credibility to the curious belief that His name was originally pronounced "YAH-shua," thereby superimposing half of the Divine Name. Both of these theories arise from an ignorance of the simple mechanics of language.

[4] Not to mention the strange omission of a generation in the third list of fourteen generations.

[5] 2 Samuel 7:16.

[6] Sixth century BCE.

[7] 168 BCE.

[8] Deuteronomy 17:15. The story of Herod and the Sanhedrin is told in b.*Bava Batra 3b.*

[9] Macrob. Sat. 2.4.11.

[10] Josephus, *Antiquities,* 17.11.2.

[11] *Exodus Rabbah 1:18.*

CHAPTER 1

[12] Cited by Patai, *The Messiah Texts* (Detroit, MI: Wayne State University Press, 1988).

[13] Roland De Vaux, *Ancient Israel: Its Life and Institution* (Dartman, Longman and Todd, 1994), 104.

[14] 1 Samuel 10:10.

[15] Mark 1:2.

[16] Matthew 4:17.

[17] Matthew 10:7.

[18] 1 John 3:4.

[19] David Bivin and Roy Blizzard, *Understanding the Difficult Words of Jesus: New Insights from a Hebraic Perspective* (Center for Judaic-Christian Studies, 1994), 63.

[20] Acts 19:9, 23; 24:14, 22. "The Way" was also a title for the Messiah, as in John 14:6.

[21] Acts 1:22–23.

CHAPTER 2

[22] We should not assume that the two groups are mutually exclusive.

[23] Also Matthew 9:14–17; Mark 2:18–22.

[24] The unanimity of this interpretation of Yeshua's words has been so normative to Christian thinking that the term "old wine" is figuratively used to refer to Judaism in Christian writings.

[25] Alistair Kee, "The Old Coat and the New Wine: A Parable of Repentance," (*Novum Testamentum* 12(1): (13–21), 1970). Kee is not alone in his observation of the difficulty with the incompatibility interpretation. Several other notable scholars make the same observation, including Nolland (1989), Mead (1988), and Stern (1992). Kee also notes that the double parable has nothing to do with fasting. His own explanation, however, is less than satisfying and it necessitates a cut and paste that completely removes the parable from the narrative context.

[26] Or, "the old is better."

[27] A. H. Mead, "Old and New Wine (St. Luke 5:39), *Expository Times* 99(8): 234–235, 1988.

[28] David Flusser, *Do You Prefer New Wine?* (*Immanuel* 9:26–31, 1979).

[29] George Rice says that by removing the statement that the old is good (or even better), the gospel editor felt that he had removed "any suggestion that the Jews would reject the teachings of Christianity because they were well satisfied with Judaism." If Rice is correct, the double parable was being read according to the incompatibility interpretation at a very early stage. George E. Rice, "Some Further Examples of Anti-Judaic Bias in the Western Text of the Gospel of Luke," (*Andrews University Seminary Studies*, 1980), 18 (2):149–156.

[30] Flusser, however, contends that Luke preserves the original form.

[31] Luke 5:30.

[32] Luke 5:33.

[33] It could certainly be argued that the two sages quoted are *Tannaim* (teachers) from a century after the time of Yeshua, but the metaphors and analogies that these *Tannaim* employed, that constitute the proverbs of *Pirkei Avot*, belonged to a body of oral tradition, much of which predates the day of Yeshua. For example, see the passage from *Nedarim* 50b quoted at the beginning of the article, which uses the same symbolic values for wine and containers.

[34] Flusser cites other related rabbinical and Talmudic passages in which wine is symbolic for Torah and the interpretation of Scripture.

[35] David Bivin, "Jesus' Education," (*Jerusalem Perspective*, 1988), 14–15.

CHAPTER 3

[36] See b.*Bava Metzia* 33a and other places where a teacher takes precedence over a father, because one's father brings one into this world, but one's teaching brings one into the world to come.

[37] E.g., Matthew 10:24.

[38] A *mezuzah* is a small scroll that traditional Jews affix to their doorposts in fulfillment of the commandment of Deuteronomy 6:9.

[39] m.*Avot* 1:1.

[40] Matthew 19:28.

[41] Revelation 12:14.

[42] Matthew 10:25.

[43] Matthew 10:2–4; Mark 3:16–19; Luke 6:12–16; Acts 1:13.

[44] For those who are genuinely interested, it might be worth noting that among those commands is the command to keep the Torah: every jot and tittle of it, as He commands in Matthew 5:19. The laws of Torah are components of imitation and obedience in that regard.

CHAPTER 4

[45] b.*Shabbat* 23b.

[46] Luke 2:52.

[47] He wrote, "If we might venture on a general characterization, we would infer from the Epistle of St. James, that his religious views had originally been cast in the mould of Shammai. Certainly, there is nothing of the Hillelite direction about it, but all to remind us of the earnestness, directness, vigour, and rigour of Shammai." (Alfred Edersheim, *Jesus the Messiah* (Peabody, MA: Hendrickson Publishers, 1993), 174.

[48] For example, see b.*Pesachim* 115a or Targum on Psalm 118. See also Jonathan Lightfoot, *Commentary on the New Testament from Talmud and Hebraica*, Vol. 2 (Hendrickson Publishers, 1997), 435.

[49] *Genesis Rabbah* 23:4

[50] John 2:12.

[51] 1 Corinthians 15:7.

[52] Acts 24:5.

Chapter 5

53   In actual practice, the Karaites embrace a whole host of Jewish traditional interpretations.   •

54   For examples of apostolic incorporation of oral law in the Gospels and Acts, see Tim Hegg's paper "Can We Speak of Law in the New Testament in Monolithic Terms?" at www.torahresource. com. See also David Bivin's article "Jesus and the Oral Torah" at www.jerusalemperspective.com.

55   Acts 5:34–39; 9:1–2.

56   But see Harvey Falks's *Jesus the Pharisee*, (Wipf and Stock Publishers, 1985).

57   For example, Luke 20:29; Mark 12:32.

58   Luke 13:31.

59   The exact nature of the covering—whether length of hair or an actual head covering—is disputed.

60   Deuteronomy 8:10.

61   Luke 4:16.

62   Matthew 23:5.

63   Matthew 23:23.

64   See *Torah Club Volume Four*, comments on Mark 5:18–20.

65   In the Greek of Acts 1:14, the word *prayer* is definite and plural, indicating traditional liturgy.

66   According to what may be ascertained in the LXX Leviticus 23:11, Josephus, *Antiquities*, 3.10.5–6 and Philo, Special Laws 2.29.150, *Shavuot* (Pentecost) was celebrated in the Temple according to the reckoning of the Pharisees during the first century. The presence of other Jews from all over the world in the Temple celebrating the festival makes it clear that the believers kept the festival according to the Pharisaic reckoning, not the Sadducean.

67   Luke 15:1–2.

68   David Stern, *Jewish New Testament Commentary*, quoting y.*Berakot* 14b, y.*Sotah* 20c; b.*Sotah* 22b (1992), 69–70.

Chapter 6

69   Mark 6:20.

70   Josepus, *Antiquities*, 18.5.2.

71   For an extensive treatment of the two-Messiah theory and the various legends about the Suffering Servant Messiah, see Raphiel Patai's work on the subject: *The Messiah Texts* (Detroit, MI: Wayne State University Press, 1988).

72   Flusser's explanation appears in Brad Young's *The Parables: Jewish Tradition and Christian Interpretation*, (Peabody, MA: Hendrickson Publishers, 1998), 20.

73   Matthew 18:4.

74   John Nolland, *Word Biblical Commentary, Luke*, 2 vols. (Dallas, Texas: Word Books Publisher, 1989), 338.

75   Robert L. Lindsey, *Jesus, Rabbi & Lord: The Hebrew Story of Jesus behind Our Gospels* (Oak Creek, WI: Cornerstone Publishing, 1990), 62; David Bivin and Roy Blizzard Jr., *Understanding the Difficult Words of Jesus*, (Dayton, Ohio: Center for Judaic Christian Studies, 1994), 123ff.

76   For example, see *Genesis Rabbah* 85:14.

77   Tim Hegg, comment on text in personal communication.

78   Brad Young, *The Parables: Jewish Tradition and Christian Interpretation* (Peabody, MA: Hendrickson Publishers, 1998), citing Gleichnisse Flusser), 20.

79   Bivin and Blizzard, 59–60.

CHAPTER 7

80   Matthew 4:12.

81   Ironically, after the fall of Jerusalem Tiberias became a center of Jewish learning. The *Talmud Yerushalami* was largely compiled there. However, before Jews would enter the city the locations of the tombs needed to be ascertained. Shimon bar Yochai is reputed to have accomplished this on behalf of the city. See b.*Shabbat* 33b-34a.

82   Mark 6:16.

83   Mark 6:20.

84   The *vav* conjunction *and* can carry this sense.

85   *Esther Rabbah* 1:12.

86   Mark 6:27-29.

87   b.*Megillah* 16b.

88   b.*Chullin* 53a. See also b.*Berachot* 61b, where Rabbi Akiva compares the Roman government to a fox.

CHAPTER 8

89   Alfred Edersheim, *Sketches of Jewish Social Life in the Days of Christ* (Eerdmans Publishing Co., 1990), 167–171.

90   b.*Ketubot* 17a.

91   Mark 7:10-11.

CHAPTER 9

92   Leviticus 23:42–43.

93   See Zechariah 14:16 and *Torah Club Volume Two*, 438–439.

94   Deuteronomy 19:15.

95   For example, see Luke 24:27.

[96] This midrash adds to the common theory that Moses and Elijah are the two witnesses of Revelation 11.

[97] Mark 3:17.

CHAPTER 10

[98] John D. Sinclair, translator, *The Divine Comedy* (New York: Oxford University Press, 1961).

[99] In the ancient world, only wool could be dyed.

[100] Lightfoot, *Commentary on the New Testament from Talmud and Hebraica*, Vol. 3, 1997), pp.168–169.

[101] I call this the broad view because, although contradicting opinions can be found in rabbinic literature (e.g., "soul sleep"), the standard of Pharisaic belief is that the soul leaves the body at death and will be returned to the body in the resurrection.

[102] b.*Chagigah* 12b.

[103] 2 Corinthians 12:2–5.

[104] היום יושב בחיקו של אברהם. For an explanation of who is being described as dead in that passage, see Jonathan Lightfoot, *Commentary on the New Testament from Talmud and Hebraica*, Vol. 3, 1997), pp. 169–170.

[105] *Deuteronomy Rabbah* 11:10.

[106] 2 Corinthians 5:8.

[107] And in several instances, for the Hebrew *sheol*, as in Matthew 16 and Revelation 1.

[108] Various derivations are suggested. The word is related to the same root from which we derive the word "hall."

[109] Ephesians 2:2.

[110] Revelation 20:10.

[111] In 2 Kings 23 it is the Valley of the Sons of Hinnom, so we should understand Hinnom as a proper name.

[112] 2 Kings 23:10.

[113] Quoted by Lachs, *Rabbinic Commentary on the New Testament*, (Hoboken, NJ: Ktav Publishing House, Inc., 1987), p. 315.

[114] Mark 9:48.

[115] Matthew 8:12; 13:42, 50; 22:13; 24:51; 25:30; Luke 13:28.

CHAPTER 11

[116] Deuteronomy 16:15–16.

[117] Matthew 26:18 NIV.

[118] John 8:1.

[119] See Leviticus 23:42–43 regarding the Torah instructions that command the Israelites to construct and live in these booths.

[120] m.*Sukkot* 4:9.

[121] m.*Sukkot* 5:2–3.

[122] Leviticus 23:40.

[123] For example, see Isaiah 44:3–4; 55:1; Ezekiel 47:1–11.

[124] See John 7:40–41.

CHAPTER 12

[125] Jeremiah 25:4, NIV.

[126] Quoted by Jonathan Lightfoot, *Commentary on the New Testament from Talmud and Hebraica*, vol. 2 (Hendrickson Publishers, 1979), 433.

[127] *Song of Songs Rabbah* 8:14. But see VIII:15, where the vineyard represents the Sanhedrin.

[128] Quoting Craig A. Evans, *Word Biblical Commentary*, Mark 8:27–16:20 (Dallas, Texas: Word Books Publisher, 2001), 221.

[129] However, it is not completely verbatim. Evans (2001) points out that Mark's allusions to the Isaiah passage share just as many, if not more, affinities with the Masoretic text and Targum versions, 223–226.

[130] The Brenton English Translation reads, "My Beloved had a vineyard."

[131] See *Torah Club Volume Four*'s comments on Matthew 26:3–5; 14–16 for an introduction to Caiaphas.

CHAPTER 13

[132] Mark 14:26.

[133] Avrohom Chaim Feur, *Tehillim* (Brooklyn, New York: Mesorah Publications, 1985), citing Radak on Psalm 118.

[134] b.*Pesachim* 119a.

[135] Eliyahu Kitov, *The Book of Our Heritage*, vol. 3 (New York: Feldheim Publishers), 647–862.

[136] The *Targums* are the early Aramaic translations of the Hebrew Scriptures.

[137] Jonathan Lightfoot, *Commentary on the New Testament from Talmud and Hebraica*, vol. 2 (Peabody, MA: Hendrickson Publishers, 1995), 435.

[138] *Pesachim* 119a. See also Brad Young, *Jesus the Jewish Theologian* (Peabody, MA: Hendrickson Publishers, 1995), quoting the *Midrash HaGadol* on Deuteronomy 1:17, 218.

[139] b.*Shabbat* 114a; *Berachot* 64a.

[140] Risto Santala, *The Messiah in the Old Testament* (Kukkila, Finland: Bible and Gospel Service, 1992), 138–139.

CHAPTER 14

141 The Feast of Trumpets is known in Scripture as *Yom Teruah*, or the "Day of Blowing." It is also commonly called *Rosh HaShanah*, which literally means "head of the year" and represents the traditional Jewish New Year.

142 See Matthew 25:31–46 for the complete parable.

143 Matthew 13:37–43.

144 See m.*Sanhedrin* 2:6, b.*Gittin* 68b, *Ruth Rabbah* 5:6.

145 In some sources, "an angel."

146 For example, b.*Sukkah* 49b.

147 b.*Shabbat* 127a.

148 Genesis 45:3.

CHAPTER 15

149 m.*Nazir* 1:3.

150 Those who argue that his vow was not a Nazirite vow do so out of reluctance to see Paul bringing a lamb, a ewe and a ram as burnt offerings, sin offerings and peace offerings. New Testament commentators typically indicate that Paul is exercising his principle of "being all things to all men" (1 Corinthians 9:22) by participating in the vow. Those who propound that the apostle would make such a disingenuous and hypocritical pretense are ignoring the fact that Paul took the vow in Acts 18 long before coming under the pressure of James and the Jerusalem believers.

151 Leviticus 10:9; Numbers 6:3.

152 Leviticus 21:1–4.

153 Leviticus 21:11; Numbers 6:7.

154 Numbers 6:5.

155 Exodus 29:36.

156 These two basic forms of first-century hygiene are not part of the Nazirite restrictions, nor is there a prohibition from meat. These seem to be self-imposed restrictions. Although Scripture says James took no baths, we are to understand this as trips to the Roman bathhouses, a luxury enjoyed by many of the pious sages of his day. It goes without saying that James passed through the *mikvah* regularly.

157 G. A. Williamson, translator, *Eusebius: The History of the Church, Ecclesiastical History* 23.4 (Minneapolis, MN: Augsburg Publishing, 1965).

158 Genesis 49:26; Deuteronomy 33:16, my translation.

159 m.*Nazir* 1:1–2.

160 m.*Nazir* 2:2.

[161] m.*Nazir* 1:3–7.

[162] Mark 15:23; Matthew 27:34; Luke 37.

[163] Only in John 19:29.

CHAPTER 16

[164] It is well established that the court that condemned Yeshua was not the Sanhedrin, but an ad-hoc assemblage of Yeshua's enemies among the Sadducean side of the court. See Alfred Edersheim's *Jesus the Messiah*, p. 556. See also *Torah Club Volume Four*'s comments on Matthew 26:57–72 and Mark 14:53–62.

[165] *Torah Club Volume Four* offers several theories of chronology that attempt to ascertain which day all this happened. See the comments on Mark 15 for the argumentation to support the Thursday, *Nisan* 14 theory.

[166] We know his first name from a textual variant in the manuscripts of Matthew.

[167] *Avodah Zarah* 8b. Also, Alfred Edersheim's *Jesus the Messiah*.

[168] Beasley-Murray, *Word Biblical Commentary: John*, second edition (Dallas, Texas: Word Books Publisher, 1999), p. 309.

[169] Luke 13:1–4; Josephus, *Antiquities*, 18.3.2.

[170] In order to rectify the Johanine chronology with the synoptic accounts, several commentators have posited the dubious theory that John 18:28's "they wanted to be able to eat the Passover" referred not to the Pesach lamb but the *Chagigah* sacrifices that accompanied the lamb. The text of John, however, mentions only the Pesach.

[171] Luke 23:13–23.

[172] Luke 23:6–12.

[173] David Flusser, *Judaism and the Origins of Christianity* (Jerusalem: Magnes Press, the Hebrew University, 1988), 596.

[174] Flusser, *Judaism and the Origins of Christianity*, 596.

[175] Craig A. Evans, *Word Biblical Commentary*, Mark 8:27-16:20 (Dallas, Texas: Word Books Publisher, 2001), 497.

[176] See Tzaferis's article "Crucifixion: The Archaeological Evidence," *Biblical Archaeological Review*, vol. XI. No.1.

[177] Exodus 29:38–42; Leviticus 6:9–13; Numbers 28:3–8.

[178] Alfred Edersheim, *The Temple, Its Ministry and Services* (Grand Rapids, MI: Wm. B. Eerdmans Publishing Co, 1992), 143.

[179] Josephus, who served as a priest, fixes the afternoon sacrifice at "about the ninth hour" (Josephus, *Antiquities*, 14.4.3). See also m.*Pesachim* 5:1.

[180] Numbers 6:24–26. See chapter 19.

[181] Matthew 20:20–27.

182　Luke 24:21.

183　Literally, "between the evenings" (Exodus 12:6).

184　m.*Pesachim* 5.5.

185　m.*Pesachim* 5.9.

186　See *Torah Club Volume Four*'s comments on Mark 14:26.

187　John 19:39. See *Torah Club Volume Four*'s comments on John 3:1 for more on Nicodemus.

CHAPTER 17

188　Mark 16:2. Evans, *Word Biblical Commentary: Mark 8:27–16:20*, makes a good case for reading it, "The sun was not yet risen."

189　See Lachs, *A Rabbinic Commentary on the New Testament*, 439.

190　Mark 16:1.

191　John 20:1–2.

192　One of the various extended versions of the word *rabbi*.

CHAPTER 18

193　Dan Brown, *The Da Vinci Code* (Random House, 2003), 245.

194　b.*Sanhedrin* 67a, uncensored version.

195　John 19:25; Mark 15:40.

196　Luke 10:39.

197　Acts 12:12.

198　Romans 16:6.

199　Luke 8:2.

200　John 4:27; m.*Avot* 1:5; b.*Eiruvin* 53b.

201　Note that Miriam of Bethany "was seated at the Lord's feet, listening to His word" (Luke 10:39), an idiom for discipleship (as in Acts 22:3).

202　b.*Pesachim* 46a.

203　Magdala played an important role in the Jewish revolt and features prominently in Josephus's *Jewish War* as the scene of the disastrous naval battle of that confrontation.

204　See *Torah Club Volume Four*'s comments on Luke 37:37–38.

205　Mary Magdalene, online article at *http://en.wikipedia.org/wiki/Mary_Magdalene*, (accessed March 31, 2006).

206　b.*Shabbat* 104b; b.*Sanhedrin* 67a.

207　*Megadelet* (מגדלת) comes from the word *gadol* (גדול), which means "big." The maidservant or nurse in a household was responsible for raising the children (making them big) and tending to their grooming.

208　b.*Chagiga* 4b.

209 Bart D. Ehrman, *Lost Scriptures: Books that Did Not Make It into the New Testament* (Oxford University Press, 2005), 42.

210 Ehrman, *Lost Scriptures*, 42.

211 Ehrman, *Lost Scriptures*, 36.

212 Dan Brown, *The Da Vinci Code*, 245.

213 As in the *Acts of the Apostle Thomas*.

214 They may have been an influence on Paul in 1 Corinthians 7.

215 Exodus 18:2.

216 Leviticus 15:15–18.

217 Acts 3:22; 7:37.

218 Matthew 19:13.

219 Isaiah 53:8 NIV.

220 Isaiah 53:10 NIV.

CHAPTER 19

221 They prayed the proto-*Amidah*; that is, the Eighteen Benedictions, though in what form we know not. The standing men were the *maamidot* spoken of in b.*Taanit* 27a and Luke 1:10.

222 For examples, see b.*Taanit* 26a–b and b.*Megillah* 23b–24b.

223 Hayim Donin, *To Pray as a Jew* (Basic Books, a division of Harper Collins, 1980), 135.

224 m.*Yoma* 52b.

225 b.*Ketubot* 24b.

226 b.*Chullin* 133a; b.*Ketubot* 24b.

227 b.*Megillah* 24b.

EPILOGUE

228 Acts 1:6.

Additional Resources

First Fruits of Zion publishes many resources that will help you learn more about God's Word.

BIBLE STUDY PROGRAMS, BOOKS AND TEACHING MATERIALS

Do you want to understand God's Word in its historical, cultural and linguistic context? First Fruits of Zion resources will help you better understand the Bible.

◊ Messiah magazine

Published five times a year, each full-color issue provides fresh articles and perspectives about our Torah-observant Messiah, the grace we have in Him, and the truth He taught. For more information or to subscribe, visit *www.messiahmagazine.org*.

◊ Restoration

Returning the Torah of God to the Disciples of Jesus

Biblical Christianity was originally a sect of Judaism that believed in Yeshua and revered the Torah. In this riveting book, author D. Thomas Lancaster calls Christians back to the Torah and that original, biblical expression of faith in Yeshua. This best-seller is a thought provoking and inspiring journey into the world of the Bible.

◊ It is Often Said (4 Volumes)

Comments and Comparisons of Traditional Christian Theology and Hebraic Thought

Author Tim Hegg addresses and answers some of the most common misconstrued theologies and statements of our time. He reconciles the teachings of Yeshua and Paul in a way that supports the belief that the Bible, and God Himself, is unchanging, consistent and authoritative.

◊ The Letter Writer

Paul's Background and Torah Perspective

This book by Tim Hegg challenges traditional Christian viewpoints of Paul, his message, and the foundation of his theological approach. Through this book, Hegg re-establishes a biblical, historical and cultural understanding of Paul—the Torah observant Apostle.

◊ Fellowheirs

Jews & Gentiles Together in the Family of God.

A masterful piece of scholarship! This book seeks the biblical perspective on identity within the family of God. Is the Torah for all of God's children, or is it only for Jews? The powerful results of Tim Hegg's research demonstrate from the biblical text that Jews and Gentiles are both beholden to the same covenant norms and responsibilities.

◊ The Mystery of the Gospel

Jew and Gentile and the Eternal Purpose of God

Addressing the question of Jewish/Gentile relationships within the body of Messiah, D. Thomas Lancaster works through the Apostle Paul's rabbinic scholarship to piece together the deep mystery of the Messiah, about the identity of Gentile believers and their relationship to Israel through the Messiah. Long-sought answers for everyone who is confused about where they fit in the House of Israel and the Torah of God.

◊ Holy Cow!

Does God Care About what We Eat?

Join best-selling author Hope Egan on her personal journey through what the Bible says about eating meat. See how science and Scripture brilliantly intertwine. Promoting neither legalism nor vegetarianism, Holy Cow! gently challenges you to take a fresh look at how you live out your faith!

◊ HaYesod

This 14-week video Bible study delves into the Hebraic roots of Christianity and is ideal for group teaching or personal study. For more information visit *www.hayesod.org* or call 800-775-4807 and request a HaYesod info pack.

◊ Torah Club

Study the Torah, the Gospels and Acts passage-by-passage from within the context of Torah and classical Judaism. It is FFOZ's most comprehensive resource for providing biblical context. Visit *www.torahclub.org* or call toll free 800-775-4807 to request a brochure.

WWW.FFOZ.ORG

For more information about these and other FFOZ books, magazines and multi-media products, or to download free samples, please visit *www.ffoz.org* or call toll free 800-775-4807.

◊ FREE Online Resources

FFOZ provides numerous free online resources, including a weekly e-mail teaching that focuses on Messiah and Torah, and hundreds of articles from previous FFOZ magazines. For more information, visit *www.ffoz.org*

◊ Online Store

Visit the FFOZ's online webstore to securely purchase any of these and other resources. Go to *www.ffoz.org/store.*